D1606318

Russian Journalism and Politics
1861–1881

The Career of Aleksei S. Suvorin

Russian Journalism and Politics

1861–1881

by EFFIE AMBLER

Wayne State University

Wayne State University Press, Detroit, 1972

Library of Congress Cataloging in Publication Data

Ambler, Effie, 1936–
    Russian journalism and politics, 1861–1881.

    "Writings and publications of A. S. Suvorin": p. 222.
    Includes bibliographical references.
    1. Suvorin, Aleksei Sergeevich, 1834–1912.
2. Journalism—Russia—History.   3. Russia
—Politics and government—19th century   I. Title
PN5276.S8A8   070.5'0924   72–173671
ISBN 0–8143–1461–9

this book is dedicated to my parents

contents

preface

If Aleksei Sergeevich Suvorin is remembered at all today, it is for his timely assistance to the young writer Chekhov. Yet at the turn of the century he was admired and hated as a leading nationalist columnist and the press king of the Russian Empire. Starting with a single mortgaged newspaper, he constructed a cultural latifundium (the phrase of opponents) that ranged from a historical journal to a type foundry, with a theater on the side. His several jubilee celebrations constituted, in the words of one radical publicist, "a semi-official apotheosis both in character and in extent unequaled in the annals of Russian journalism."[1] On the twenty-fifth anniversary of his newspaper ownership in 1901, a grand duke and five ministers of state called to offer congratulations. Prince Nikolai of Montenegro sent a decoration of the Order of Saint Daniil, Second Class. The police protected arriving guests from youthful demonstrators outside the newspaper building. On the fiftieth anniversary of his literary activity in 1909, conservative periodicals and rightist Duma fractions delivered formal addresses of greeting, but not a single well-known name from the world of Russian literature offered good wishes. When he died in 1912, the emperor sent a wreath to his grave; tens of thousands rejoiced in his death.

The whole anti-autocratic intelligentsia loathed Suvorin for his chauvinism and his reactionary political pronouncements. They feared him as well for his command of the printed word and undoubted ability to gain readers—if only, as his enemies said, among "certain circles." Gorkii concluded during the revolution of 1905 that he was "much more harmful than Meshcherskii, Gringmut, and company, since more intelligent than all of them together."[2]

Most odious of all, Suvorin was a renegade. As a young man in the rebellious sixties he had been, in the now classic characterization of Lenin, "a poor man, a liberal, and even a democrat."[3] One of his sketches of peasant life appeared in the journal *Contemporary*, the oracle of progressive youth. His first book was burned by the censor while its author sat briefly in jail.

In the late sixties and early seventies, when Suvorin was a popular liberal feuilletonist, the radical press denounced him for "principle-less" and "idea-less" writing. Yet reactionaries and nihilist hunters identified him as one of the enemy. Katkov linked his name with those of leading populist publicists of the time. Prince Meshcherskii claimed he founded his infamous newspaper *Citizen* in 1872 to combat the "crazy nihilistic policy" of Suvorin and a few others.[4]

In 1876 Suvorin acquired his own newspaper, *New Times* (*Novoe vremia*). From the reputation of the new publisher and his staff, literate society supposed that *New Times* would carry on the liberal tradition of another paper—recently closed by government order —with which Suvorin had been associated. But these expectations were disappointed. Within two years it had become a target of student protests, and as its circulation skyrocketed, a nightmare for the intelligentsia. In the course of time, to cite again from the classics, "new-timism" (*novovremenstvo*) became a synonym for "apostasy, desertion, sycophancy."[5]

Opinion differs on the precise moment of Suvorin's transformation from "progressive" to "sycophant" and "obscurantist." He himself apparently regarded his views as unchanged in essence: he had always stood for the good of Russia and Russians. In old age he insisted that he would not amend a word of his most radical youthful writings. Some of his opponents agreed that he had remained true to himself, although they interpreted this phenomenon negatively. Mikhailovskii advanced the arresting paradox that Suvorin's essence could not change, for his essence was constant change. "A weathervane is not a traitor, though it constantly changes its position."[6] But most hostile contemporaries, as well as modern reference works, agree that Suvorin moved perceptibly from left to right and that the most rapid movement took place soon after 1876 in the pages of *New Times*. By 1880 his name was often linked with that of Katkov. The Society of the Lovers of Russian Letters placed him on its blacklist of *literati non grati*. On the other hand Dostoevskii and Ivan Aksakov, along with thousands of lesser folk, acknowledged his paper their favorite.[7] If future fame were based on accumulation of readers and wealth in one's own lifetime, Suvorin in the twentieth century would be celebrated rather than forgotten.

Suvorin was hardly a systematic philosopher or even a notably original publicist. Although specific issues concerned him deeply over a period of years—for example, the lengthy controversy over classical education—yet he made no attempt to elaborate alternate programs. His own chosen genre, the feuilleton, is necessarily superficial and ephemeral. He boasted that his newspaper avoided the long and boring lead articles of rival publications.

Precisely because he was unoriginal and highly impressionable, Suvorin's career may be more instructive to the student of the Russian social movement than would be that of a more thoughtfully independent or consistent writer. Examination of his work reveals the day to day concerns of the serious press in a country where journalism constituted the closest legal approximation to the prohibited activities associated in the west with political parties. The stages of his spiritual odyssey from left to right define the boundaries and positions of Russian "literary parties" during a period of great social changes.

Suvorin's most prolific years as a journalist, the years of his much remarked transformation, coincide with what Russians once called the Era of Great Reforms. In 1861, when Suvorin first came from beyond the Don to live by his pen in Moscow, the Emperor Alexander II inaugurated the era with the emancipation of more than twenty million serfs. The end of peasant bondage was followed by other reforms, most notably in the army, judiciary, educational system, and local government. A wave of railroad construction produced Russia's first authentic industrial-financial boom. It was against such a background of turbulent and often reluctant modernization, within the peculiar context of a censored press, that Suvorin and his fellows fought out their battles of words. (Since little information is available in English on the pre-revolutionary Russian press, I have introduced my protagonist with a short survey of the conditions within which he worked and wrote.)

The era came to an end with the assassination of Alexander II in 1881. His son and successor determined to maintain autocracy by police power rather than by social experimentation. By that year Suvorin's political metamorphosis had been completed; he willingly lent his newspaper as an organ of apologia for the policies of the new regime. The rest of his long and prosperous life is no more than epilogue.[8]

Dates throughout have been given according to the Julian calendar, current in the Russian Empire until 1917; add twelve days to determine the corresponding date in the west during the nineteenth century. A modified version of the Library of Congress system has been followed for the transliteration of Russian words.

I should like to thank Professors John M. Thompson and Boris I. Esin, who gave so many hours of their time to me, and the Inter-University Committee on Travel Grants, which made possible much of the research for this book.

E.A.

introduction

*T*he first printed Russian newspaper appeared by edict of Peter I in December 1702, less than a century after similar journalistic beginnings in western Europe. Peter's newspaper, which came out with remarkable irregularity and in issues varying from 30 to 4,000 copies, bore the forthright name *Notices* (*Vedomosti*). Like all Russian newspapers for over a hundred years, it was initiated by the government to provide officially sanctioned information, chiefly announcements of governmental actions, for those members of educated society who ought to be informed; it also supplied accounts of selected events abroad.

Notices scarcely outlived its founder and was replaced in 1728 by the semi-weekly *Saint Petersburg Notices,* entrusted for publication to the newly established Academy of Sciences. This was supplemented in 1756 by *Moscow Notices,* founded by Moscow University. These two publications proved to be the longest lived in Russia; they were closed only after October 1917. M. V. Lomonosov and N. I. Novikov, writing in them, did much to develop the modern Russian literary language and to establish certain enduring characteristics of Russian journalism: its strongly literary nature; its comparatively great importance to national cultural life; its strong sense of mission to enlighten and elevate; its preference for analysis and interpretation rather than for "news" properly speaking; and its close, informed attention to political, social, and cultural developments in western European countries.[1]

The literary-critical journal, like the informational newspaper, lagged in development behind western Europe. Although the Academy of Sciences produced several collections of scientific articles and translations during the first half of the eighteenth century, the journal as an instrument of intellectual contention assumed importance only after the accession of Catherine II in 1762.[2] Governmental permissiveness gave rise to a flurry of journalistic excitement in the new capital. Following the example set by the empress herself, who covertly launched a small satiric weekly in January 1769, private persons established seven similar publications within a few months. Polemic briefly raged on the correct nature and range of satire, a question of practical importance to an enlightened nobility in a backward and autocratic state. Even Catherine employed obscure allegories to make politically tinged statements. At the height of interest, the reading public was small. Most journals printed about 600 copies, while the imperial organ and the best of the private publications, Novikov's *Drone* (*Truten*), managed to double that figure.[3] Only these two persevered into the following year (1770). Although new would-be satirical journals were established, their total number and circulation were smaller with each passing year until, with the Pugachev uprising of 1773–1775, the permitted bounds of satire became so narrow as to discourage that genre altogether.

The rapid rise and fall of the satiric journal illustrates in embryo a phenomenon typical of the entire growth of the Russian periodical press to about 1930. This process lends itself to periodization by moments of widespread and turbulent journalistic activity. Such episodes often were distinguished by development of a specific periodical genre and were dominated by one or two outstanding publicists and journals, ever after to be recalled by the genealogically conscious intelligentsia as significant stages of social and moral development: Novikov and socio-political satire in the late 1760s; N. M. Karamzin and *Herald of Europe* (*Vestnik Evropy*), the first literary journal seriously and consistently to discuss socio-political questions of current interest (early 1800s); V. G. Belinskii and the evolution of the literary critic and guru (early 1840s)—to name a few important examples.

Again and again, official permissiveness or even example, unleashing public interest, led in a short time to numbers of publications and an enthusiasm on the part of readers for ideas and controversy, typically hailed by publicists as proof at last of Russia's intellectual maturity. Previously unmentionable political or moral problems became open to discussion. Whether the issue was the right of the nobility to criticize governmental policy (as in 1769) or the manner of the emancipation of the serfs (as in 1858), the customary mode of argument was by literary polemic. After a time, however, the initial excitement aroused by daring public expression of hitherto unprintable thoughts would pass, and most of the new publications would find themselves with too few subscribers to continue (bringing into question the recently announced attainment of maturity). Of the recent combatants, other than subsidized official and semi-official publications, only the liveliest and most audaciously oppositional could survive for very long.[4] And it was precisely these which were soon closed or rendered toothless by a government that invariably took fright at the results of its own incautious relaxation of control over public expression of opinion.

Despite a spasmodic pattern of development, the number of periodicals rose throughout the nineteenth century. In 1806 there were only 30 periodicals in Russia, while by the end of the century, despite the untimely demise of 1,561, still 804 remained. Publication was highly centralized. Over half the survivors (including two-fifths of daily newspapers) came out in either Saint Petersburg or Moscow. While the general and literary press grew by spurts and almost entirely during the second half of the century, the technical-scientific press grew steadily throughout the period. By the end of the century, half of all periodicals were devoted to some field of specialized knowledge. Of the remaining publications, slightly less than half were official governmental issues. Thus only 26 percent were private publications of general character; the famous thick journals of Russian political and cultural life constituted less than 4 percent.[5]

The imperial government issued a wide variety of periodicals for informational and educational purposes. While some of these were of a type that might be encountered in any European country, for example, the weekly *Senate Notices* (*Senatskie vedomosti*) and numerous supplements which recorded laws and administrative arrangements, others would be more likely to be published elsewhere by independent or semi-official occupational organizations. Almost every ministry and some important departments of ministries undertook a periodical organ for the interested public. Subject matter ranged from the *Journal of Horse Breeding* (*Zhurnal konnozavodstva*), official organ of the Central Administration of State Stud Farms, to the *Journal of the Ministry of Public Education* (*Zhurnal Ministerstva narodnogo prosveshcheniia*), with its erudite articles on German pedagogy and classical philology. Certain publications might serve as instruments of intra-governmental policy struggles, as when D. A. Miliutin used the *Military Journal* (*Voennyi zhurnal*) and *Russian War Veteran* (*Russkii invalid*) to propagate his ideas on army reform.

Government periodicals typically contained official and unofficial sections, which were sometimes bound and sold separately. The official section consisted of ministerial decisions, relevant imperial decrees, and other announcements within the area of competence of the publishing ministry. The unofficial portion might contain scholarly historical studies, technical advice to correspondents, short stories, or even social, that is, political, commentary. The precise proportions depended upon the political aims of the minister, the daring of the editor, and the temper of the times. Although in theory even belles lettres reflected the publisher's special area of concern, this was not in fact always true. For example, *Naval Collection* (*Morskoi sbornik*), the organ of the Ministry of Marine, did not limit itself to accounts of interesting sea voyages and the reasons for the defeat of the Russian fleet in the Black Sea; in the late 1850s it achieved great popularity and numerous subscribers for its articles bearing on serfdom, the court system, and other non-naval areas in which reforms were then being considered. Apart from such moments of radicalism, however, commercial success was rare. Except for a handful that carried advertisements, most official publications required financial assistance from the imperial treasury.[6]

In addition to the more-or-less specialized ministerial publications, government agencies provided a variety of newspapers of general information content. *Saint Petersburg Notices* and several lesser papers had subscribers throughout the empire. Beginning in 1838, a newspaper for purely local consumption was established in each of the provinces, published by local civil servants under the supervision of the provincial governor. These *Provincial Notices* (*Gubernskie vedomosti*) usually appeared weekly and were divided, like their city cousins, into official and unofficial sections. The former carried official documents and decrees plus news items copied from more important official newspapers; the latter, which often became the center of provincial intellectual life, published some valuable studies on local history, ethnography, and statistics. In the stormy sixties many of these provincial papers introduced lead articles, book reviews, foreign chronicles, and other features adapted from private journals and newspapers. However, this dangerous tendency was nipped in the bud by censorship authorities, who soon returned them to their former positions as local spokesmen for the central government.[7] Especially in the second half of the century, so-called police newspapers were established by the town commandants of many large cities. These papers, modeled on *Notices of the Saint Petersburg City Police* (*Vedomosti Sankt-Peterburgskoi gorodskoi politsii*), carried local decrees, advertising, and news bulletins, as well as the police chronicle and court announcements.

The official press of the civil authorities was complemented by numerous publications issued under the jurisdiction of the Holy Governing Synod of the Russian Orthodox Church, in essence an imperial ministry. Most of these arose only after 1855. In addition to the organs of the Holy Synod itself and of theological academies, biweekly *Diocesan Notices* (*Eparkhialnye vedomosti*) appeared in many of the Church's sixty-two episcopal dioceses, which corresponded in Russian-inhabited areas to the provinces of the secular administration.[8]

Parallel to the development of the Russian periodical press was the growth of the non-Russian press in the empire. The majority of foreign language periodicals appeared in the borderlands, published for and sometimes by the literate minority peoples. Most important to the empire as a whole, however, was the handful of newspapers printed in Saint Petersburg in western European languages. The oldest of these, *Sankt-Petersburger Zeitung,* the leading German daily, was established at the Academy of Sciences in 1729. The important French-language paper, *Journal de St. Pétérsbourg,* was the organ of the Ministry of Foreign Affairs. These two publications, with a few lesser German papers, were carefully read in Saint Petersburg and abroad for clues to the foreign and fiscal policies of the Russian government, as well as for general political, economic, and financial information on the mysterious northernmost investment possibility of nineteenth century Europe.

Much of the non-Russian press was justly suspected of fostering nationalistic separatist tendencies and therefore was supervised with special care by the censorship. Nonetheless, even government publications could become weapons in a nationalist struggle. In the 1870s *Sankt-Petersburger Zeitung* upheld the special privileges of the German ruling class in the Baltic provinces and in fact managed to print articles that the provincial censors would never have allowed.[9] The government employed its publications in its own linguistic battles too. For example, the Baltic *Provincial Notices,* published in German from mid-century, became bilingual in 1886 and from 1900 appeared in Russian only.[10] In view of the Russifying tendencies of the central government and the suspicion with which it viewed all sources of nationalist infection among minority peoples, it is not surprising that the non-Russian press developed even more slowly than that which used the official language.

As noted, at the end of the nineteenth century, despite phenomenal growth by the private sector of Russian journalism, a fourth of all periodicals were issued by ministries or local administrative officers. To the governmental sector must be added also most scholarly and specialized literature, since publications of this type generally served as organs of state institutions of higher education or government sponsored learned societies. Hence it is apparent that well over two-thirds of Russia's periodical press was initiated and sustained by the state. Yet, between the dawn of the nineteenth century and the second quarter of the twentieth, no law prohibited private ownership of printing equipment or private publication of books and periodicals. In the sphere of book publishing, a field of endeavor which the state from the late eighteenth century had mainly been willing to leave to commercial entrepreneurs and free (unofficial) societies, private activity clearly prevailed throughout the nineteenth and early twentieth centuries. The imperial government originally undertook the publication of periodicals to provide informational and educational services that otherwise would not have existed. The failure of the unofficial periodical press to overcome the initial preponderance of the official press had two chief reasons: (1) the poverty and illiteracy of the Russian people; and (2) the oppressive and often capricious censorship. Both these circumstances were, of course, aspects of the same economically backward and tyrannical bureaucratic state system.

The relative poverty of educated society may have inhibited further growth of the private press. Even a subscription to one of the cheap literary papers of the early sixties, such as the unsuccessful *Russian Speech* (*Russkaia rech*) to which A. S. Suvorin contributed in 1861, cost from six to ten rubles a year without mailing charges. Under conditions in which periodicals found few subscribers, publishers were forced to set high prices, narrowing still more the circle of potential subscribers. On the other hand, the initial success of so many publications during periods of censorship relaxation and intellectual excitement suggests that as early as the late fifties the literate public was sufficiently numerous and wealthy to support far more periodicals than in reality it did. Its failure to do so indicates the political and intellectual immaturity of the educated public—another product of the state system.

Meaningful statistical information on literacy and educational levels in the Russian Empire did not become available until the late nineteenth century. According to the census of 1897, 20 percent of the population was literate; at mid century the rate was probably about 5 percent, in a much smaller total population, and in the early part of the century still lower.[11] By no means all those who achieved literacy enjoyed an educational level and mode of life that disposed them to do much voluntary secular reading. The tortuous development of the private periodical press, together with the low numbers of subscribers to even the best official periodicals, make clear the minute size of that educated minority of Russians who constituted the social movement (*obshchestvennoe dvizhenie*) and who were both willing and able to provide sustained support for the printed word. At the height of its literary and radical glory *Naval Collection* found only 5,000 subscribers, many of them no doubt functionaries of the Ministry of Marine who subscribed automatically with government funds. In the early sixties when *Contemporary* (*Sovremennik*) and *Russian Word* (*Russkoe slovo*) commanded the devotion of a whole generation of radical youth, their combined circulation was slightly more than 10,000. In the same era the politically moderate popular weekly magazine *Son of the Fatherland* (*Syn otechestva*, 1856–1861, not to be confused with earlier and later publications of the same name) reached an edition of 16,000.[12] Given the small reading public, private periodicals that had to depend upon subscriptions for their existence could hardly compete with subsidized publications unless they offered their readers something new and different—unofficial, livelier, even more truthful. Thanks to censorship, this they were not often able to do.

It is difficult to assess the importance of advertising as a second source of revenue for periodicals. Until 1863 only a small number of general official publications had the right to print non-bibliographic advertisements. Even after this date, serious journals rarely carried any other type of paid announcement. In contrast, advertising revenue gradually assumed a position of great importance to the newspaper press. Suvorin estimated that in the mid-seventies it paid for about a fourth or a third of the total expenses of a large daily newspaper.[13] One must bear in mind, however, that most papers failed to achieve large size or long life; advertisers ordinarily prefer to place notices only in publications that have already gained wide circulation.

The Russian press has never been free from official supervision. The imperial government did not, however, find it necessary to organize a general censorship system until the early nineteenth century, at a time when in western Europe the struggle was well under way to abolish such systems. In the seventeenth and eighteenth centuries the Russian public was protected from dangerous reading matter by frontier guards, ecclesiastical censors, and the fact that the government owned the printing machinery. The first independent printing press was not permitted in Saint Petersburg until 1771, and in the provinces until

1783. Attempts to control their output led to numerous inadequately formulated and constantly changing decrees on press surveillance. Not until 1804 was the first general censorship statute published.[14]

From 1804 until 1865 censorship of material prior to publication existed everywhere for all printed works. According to the statute of 1804 and subsequent elaborations, "not one book or composition" might be printed or placed on sale without prior examination by the censor. Works in any way contrary to the Orthodox Christian faith, to the bases of monarchical autocratic power, to morality, or to the honor of individual persons were strictly forbidden. Permanent censorship committees were established, at first by appointing university professors. Compositions of religious content, as always, came under special examination by ecclesiastical censors subordinate to the Holy Synod. During the reign of Nicholas I censorial practice became yet more restrictive. Official interference prevented not only all political and most philosophical discussion, but even the use of an incorrect literary style. Censors with unlimited discretionary powers swarmed like locusts over all the land; they were united by a complex chain of command which culminated in theory in the Ministry of Public Education but in fact in the person of Count A. Kh. Benkendorf, creator and long-time director of the Third Section (political police). At the same time special military, medical, diplomatic, and other censors ensured particular purity of thought within their own spheres of interest.

Nicholas I and Benkendorf considered the periodical press especially dangerous. The police closed many well-known journals. The inauguration of a new publication by a private person required the personal approval of the emperor. Between 1836 and 1855 only a few specialized journals gained approval, a situation which furthered the vogue for literary yearbooks and miscellanies. It also gave rise to the common Russian practice of purchasing from their former publishers the titles that already possessed imperial assent.

At the same time the government undertook to provide a wide range of socially healthy official material for would-be readers. The *Provincial Notices* and many of the specialized ministerial journals were founded in this period. Every periodical published according to a specific program; even official journals generally lacked permission for a political department (foreign political chronicle) or a social chronicle (domestic political comment). Certain official newspapers enjoyed monopolies on foreign, military, and other types of news— although even here information was sparse, truncated, and without discussion.

From this same era also date the first significant attempts to foster press organs of the type called *ofitsioz,* ostensibly independent but secretly backed by the government to unofficially present an official point of view. Prime examples of the *ofitsioz* were the numerous periodicals of F. V. Bulgarin and N. I. Grech, who alone experienced no difficulty in establishing new journals under Nicholas I. Their most successful venture, the first important private newspaper in Russia, was the only non-official publication permitted to print political news. This paper, *Northern Bee (Severnaia pchela* 1825–1864), at various times enjoyed other special privileges, such as the right to print theatrical reviews, all of which assisted it to become one of Russia's first financially profitable periodicals.[15]

Despite harsh repression of independent thought, journalism under Nicholas I found an ever widening reading public. Russian letters enjoyed several brilliant periods of advance. The famous monthly thick journals of encyclopedic content set the tone of the intellectual movement, while Belinskii demonstrated the infinite capacities of the literary review as a vehicle for every sort of declaration. If censorship was oppressive, it was also capricious; what one could and could not say depended as much upon timing and persons as upon the vague letter of the law. The most terrible period (for censors as well as journalists) followed the European revolutionary year of 1848. This "seven-year darkness" ended only with the death of Nicholas in 1855.

The ensuing decade was one of full censorial anarchy as the new emperor himself seemed to blow now liberal, now conservative, and always unpredictable. Deprived of self-confidence and of clear guiding principles, the censors themselves (like the members of other administrative bodies) were divided into separate hostile groupings. New publications gained imperial approval almost every day. The causes and cures of serfdom, the inadequacies of the legal system, the reasons for Russia's defeat in the Crimea, and other hitherto forbidden subjects flaunted themselves openly on the printed page, while permission for any given article seemed to depend less on content than on blind, erratic chance. It was at this time that Suvorin, like many other hopeful young provincials in the "springtime of liberalism," began to submit mildly daring stories, articles, and poems to the burgeoning periodicals of the two capitals.

After the statute for the emancipation of the serfs was made public in 1861, the government hastened to reassert control over the limits of political discussion; the system of emancipation, in particular, was no longer within allowable bounds. The Ministry of Internal Affairs replaced the Ministry of Education as ultimate supervisor of the printed word. In the spirit of the so-called Era of Great Reforms, an effort was briefly made to place the press under conditions of clarity, reason, and strict legality. To further unity of organization and purpose, the old committees of censorship were regrouped under a newly constituted Chief Administration of Press Affairs. In 1865 "Temporary Regulations on Censorship and the Press" were issued to alleviate the position of certain classes of publications until more comprehensive legislation could be prepared. Since the latter never appeared, the Temporary Regulations of 6 April 1865 remained in effect until the Revolution of 1905. During the intervening forty years numerous amendments limited the role of the court system and censorship by law in favor of administrative action and censorship by special decree, thus restoring many of the most stifling features of the system of Nicholas I.

The Temporary Regulations freed from preliminary censorship the following types of printed material: most official publications except the *Provincial Notices;* all publications of academies, universities, and learned societies; works in ancient classical languages and translations from those languages; diagrams, plans, and maps; most periodicals issued in Saint Petersburg and Moscow; and books of not less than a certain rather large size, also if printed in Saint Petersburg or Moscow.[16] Thin books, all satirical and most illustrated periodicals, and the entire output of provincial presses (subject to extraordinary ministerial benevolence in special cases) remained subject to preliminary censorship. Publications freed from preliminary censorship might be destroyed only upon sentence of a court and only if the author or publisher violated a specific article of the law on the press. Several court sentences of accused books—including one by Suvorin— proving unsatisfactory, the state removed literary trials first to a higher court and then in 1872 to the privacy and dependability of the Council of Ministers. The Chief Administration of Press Affairs and the minister of internal affairs, however, increasingly relieved the Council of Ministers of the burden of censorship cases. From 1874 books and periodicals issued less than once a week had to be presented to the censors some days before release to the public, and only after completion of printing and dispersal of the type. All this in effect restored the secret and arbitrary features of the earlier censorship system, but with greater financial hazards to author and publisher.

Special procedures for control of periodicals were similarly supplemented after a short time by extra-judicial action. According to the Temporary Regulations a periodical freed from preliminary censorship, upon publication of material contrary to a specific article of the censorship code, should receive an official warning. At the third warning, it might be suspended for not more than six months, or by decision of the Senate only, it might be closed forever. Participation of the Senate was only the first feature of this system to be eliminated as the minister of internal affairs gradually assumed responsibility for making all decisions, and on an administrative rather than judicial basis. From 1873 the ministry exercised the right to forbid secretly and for any length of time all discussion of some particular question deemed inconvenient for the government. Inconveniences ranged from a rumor (already current in foreign newspapers) that the minister of foreign affairs might go to London, through reports of famine and cholera, to news about military preparations and intentions.[17] A range of lesser punishments was elaborated for mildly errant periodicals: suspension of retail sales, suspension of publication of advertisements, special close censorship supervision, and so forth. The regime of the Temporary Regulations often could weigh as heavily on periodicals as had preliminary censorship. Where previously the official censor had been held to account for the appearance of unacceptable phrases and words, under the new system author and editor were directly liable for every slip and so were forced to become their own censors—a situation which reinforced the timidity and apprehensiveness characteristic of so many Russian editors.[18] As Suvorin pointed out, "one's own censorship became harsher than the state's, and was a great torment."[19]

The rhythm of alternating permissiveness and restraint which characterized the reign of Alexander II gave way after 1881 to two decades of undisguised repression. Censorship penalties forced the two leading political journals of the seventies, *Notes of the Fatherland* (*Otechestvennye zapiski*) and *Cause* (*Delo*), and a number of lesser organs to cease publication in the eighties. Yet the editors and writers of these publications invariably regrouped themselves around other, admittedly even more cautious, periodicals which had managed to avoid suppression. Even during the oppressive last years of the century, censorship was by no means uniform; as at other times, personality and political position meant more than the letter of the law. For example, the liberal *Russian Notices* (*Russkie vedomosti*) and many others found themselves subjected to an entirely extra-legal regime of preliminary censorship. At the same time Suvorin's *New Times* (*Novoe vremia*), usually but not always supporting the government, escaped a temporary suspension to which, according to the Temporary Regulations, it should have been subjected.[20] Moreover, thanks to the increasing size and wealth of educated society, an informational and special interest press gradually grew up during the second half of the century and contributed to the numbers, if not to the political ranks, of Russian journalism. *Field* (*Niva*), an illustrated popular weekly of mildly liberal complexion, became the most widely circulated publication of the period. Devoting most of its pages to fiction, *Field* attempted to provide entertaining material "for family reading," and from an original edition of only 9,000 in 1870, it had reached 235,000 by 1900.[21] Thus by the end of the century, despite great restrictions, the periodical press had developed more fully and was speaking more freely about a wider variety of topics than anyone could have thought possible in the reign of Nicholas I.

The Revolution of 1905 led to the general abolition of preliminary censorship. The dense jungle undergrowth of a century's accumulated censorship decrees all but vanished. Thanks to the restrictive bureaucratic spirit which quickly reasserted itself, however, the new freedom of the press became in some important areas little more than an extension of the essence of the Temporary Regulations.

Such characteristic actions as seizure or suspension of publications, subject to the arbitrary discretionary power of administrative officials, continued without pause. Broad and ill-defined areas of discussion were declared entirely closed to the press. Nevertheless, far greater freedom of publication existed during the period just before World War I than at any time before or since. Thanks to this freedom, to rising literacy, and to the increasing wealth and widespread politicization of Russian society, the number and range of periodicals in circulation grew very rapidly. In 1913 more than 2,500 newspapers and journals were issued, in Russian and almost thirty other languages, representing with varying degrees of openness political views from autocracy to red revolution.[22] Circulation figures for individual publications, while often significantly higher than a generation before, remained low compared to such statistics for western and central Europe. *Russian Word,* the most widely distributed newspaper of the pre-war era, reached an edition of 500,000 just before 1914, but the average for all newspapers was just over 3,000. In 1909 *New Times* reported 36,900 subscribers, high for a serious political daily.[23]

The outbreak of World War I, with the resultant public hunger for information from the front, enabled some daily newspapers briefly to raise their editions to the million mark. But the net effect of even the first years of war was a decrease in the number of books and periodicals and, owing to the special war censorship common to all the combatants, a sharp decline in the liberty of the press. During 1917, despite economic and organizational difficulties, publishing experienced a period of optimistic effervescence. The dislocations of the civil war period, however, caused publishing activity to fall abruptly to very low levels—from which it recovered only under the supervision of the Soviet power.

*   *   *

Between the time of the Crimean defeat and the end of the century, the number of periodicals in the Russian Empire increased six-fold. The daily newspaper, whose existence before 1863 was severely limited by legal restrictions and social backwardness, played an important role in this development. The rise of the newspaper in Russia thus coincided with a similar tendency in more economically advanced areas. In western and central Europe the period from about 1870 to 1914 was truly the golden age of the newspaper press; by the last decades of the century, thanks to technological and mechanical advances, freedom of the press, and general literacy, the popular mass-circulation daily had become an important facet of public life. Although Russian journalism lacked the fertile soil of widespread literacy, publishers such as Suvorin could use imported technique and comparative relaxation of censorship to make their newspapers an accepted part of the daily routine of educated society. Yet without popular education, circulation figures remained low. As noted above, only in the decade before 1914 did a single mass-circulation daily comparable to those flourishing in the West at last make its appearance in the empire. Perhaps this restricted circulation, as well as the Russian intellectual tradition, operated to produce the "journalism of opinion" which characterized important Russian newspapers in the last third of the century, as it had important western newspapers before the rise of the mass "journalism of information."

Contemporaneity, the essential characteristic of a daily newspaper, had been unobtainable under Nicholas I, when all printed material had to be submitted for censorship approval well in advance of publication and certain official periodicals enjoyed a monopoly on foreign and military news. In the decade after the Crimean defeat the imperial government abolished numerous monopolies and loosened censorship regulations. Following issuance of the Temporary Regulations of 1865, serious daily newspapers in the two capitals had to deliver copies to the censor no earlier than the hour at which the paper was placed in the mails for subscribers. (Books and less frequent periodicals had to be left with the censor some days before release to the public.) Elimination of former monopolies on private advertising and permission to sell papers individually on the street made possible increased revenues and created conditions for a sharp competition in news and circulation.

At the same time, each relaxation of press regulations gave the censorship another arrow in its bristling quiver of "disciplinary measures." By suspending individual sales or the publication of advertisements, the state could quickly bring to heel an errant newspaper or even force it, through financial loss, to close its doors—all without a possibly awkward trial or the external appearance of undue harshness. The harshest punishment, short of officially withdrawing license to publish, was the system of temporarily suspending publication, after two warnings, for a period of up to six months. From 1882 a newspaper which suffered suspension had thereafter to present each issue to the censor on the eve of release to the public, a burden preventing effective competition with newspapers not so afflicted.[24]

When the Temporary Regulations went into effect in September 1865, all but the most radical periodicals joyously hailed the moment as the beginning of freedom and progress. The new regulations were similar to those adopted in France after the accession of Napoleon III; while regarded as restrictive in France, if administered in the same way in Russia, they would indeed have introduced a new era of freedom of expression. Such expectations were doomed to rapid disappointment. To the liberal *Saint Petersburg Notices* fell the honor of receiving the first warning, after only two weeks of "uncensored" publication, for criticizing a proposed state bond issue—a measure on which no official decision had yet been taken. Within a few months the radical *Contemporary* was warned for, among other things, a satiric poem on censorship, and its radical rival *Russian Word,* for an article on Kant. The arch-aristocratic *News* (*Vest*) was reprimanded for advocating a central zemstvo assembly. Altogether, in the first fifteen months of the new era, six publications received twelve warnings. Five were suspended, including *Saint Petersburg Notices* in 1866.[25] Thus the Chief Administration of Press Affairs made clear that neither criticism of government measures, nor independent opinions, nor unsolicited suggestions would be any more welcome in the future than in the past. Every Russian journalist, no matter what his political tendency, worked under the threat of possibly fatal punishments—from which there was no appeal.

Contemporaries generally divided the non-official daily newspapers of nineteenth century Russia into three categories: the serious political paper ("large press"), the purely informational newspaper or bulletin, and the so-called boulevard press. The serious political papers were the first to develop in number and the only ones to command intellectual prestige, precisely because of their discursive, inter-pretive content. The large press gave far more space to analytical essays, editorials of various sorts, literary features, and surveys of cultural life, than to raw, unexplained information. In fact, to the intelligentsia the phrase "purely informational" implied disapproval. The growth of newspaper reading in general was widely regarded as a step downward culturally and the herald of a new type of half-educated philistine. Since the serious papers drew their editorial staffs and reporters from various elements of the intelligentsia (widely de-fined), it is not surprising that they would strive to adapt as closely as possible the ideal model of the literary-political thick journal. In the evidence consulted for this study, no trace was found of a journal-istic ethos of "getting the news to the people" or publishing "all the news that's fit to print."[26]

Informational bulletins on stock market and financial exchange transactions came into being in the late fifties, in connection with the appearance in Russia of those standard appurtenances of capitalism. However, "economic" papers could not avoid the temptation to sup-port measures conducive to industrial development and often found themselves moving closer to the format and character of the large press. For example, the most important of these papers in the seventies, *Stock Market Notices* (*Birzhevye vedomosti*), took part in polemical exchanges on the liberation of the South Slavs and other political questions—and not only during the period when it became a "colony" of one of the radical journals. Genuine primarily informational news-papers did not develop until the last quarter of the century and with a few exceptions never enjoyed circulations as high as those of the political papers.

A third type of daily or near daily paper, regarded by the intelli-gentsia with utmost loathing, was the boulevard press. These papers, which developed especially after about 1880, were far more numerous than the purely informational ones. By the turn of the century the leading specimens of the boulevard press circulated in larger editions than any other newspapers. They aimed to entertain rather than uplift the reader. In the pursuit of that aim they gave great space to jokes, riddles, and adventure stories. They also specialized in city news, especially of criminal trials and scandals, and city gossip. They were of no intellectual importance. For the intelligentsia, the term boulevard was interchangeable with petty-bourgeois and philistine.[27]

While journalistic tradition and the value system of the intelligentsia account in part for the comparative lack of news in Russian newspapers, one must also take into account the physical difficulties of obtaining rapid dispatches, as well as the social and institutional character of Russian society. This applies especially to the problem of internal news gathering. One might argue the contrary, that lack of interest in news per se impeded development of news gathering activities; however, most of the impediments in fact derived from the backward nature of Russian life. A small educated public, concentrated in a few cities, was attempting to conduct an activity modeled on the forms of western and central Europe—without the social development which supported those forms. Admittedly, continental newspapers have tended to be more analytical and overtly partisan than those in Britain and the United States, but not, it seems, so much to the detriment of information as in the Russian case.

A large proportion of serious news in western journalism concerns itself with the constant hubbub of local and national politics: measures proposed and adopted by government, debates, rumors, statements by parties and leaders, and so forth. Such publicized turmoil was impossible in Russia. The imperial administration preferred to make its decisions in dignified and secretive seclusion. Except during the years of anarchy around 1860, censors interpreted their instructions to forbid press discussion of measures pending. Final decisions of any importance could legally be greeted only by praise—or by silence, as when the radical journals ignored the Emancipation Edict of 1861.[28] Although many Russian publicists (including Suvorin) referred to their periodicals as the organs of "parties," this was little more than wishful thinking; few periodicals had any party activities and none could legally have reported on them.[29] After 1864 news of zemstvo activities became a pallid substitute for politics in the pages of newspapers not so far to the right as utterly to disdain mention of those "autonomous" local institutions. (There were no daily newspapers representative of the far left until the twentieth century.)

Despite the founding of private newspapers, which ended the government's monopoly of the news press, journalists necessarily continued to depend upon the government newspaper and other official publications for much information of national importance. From 1862 to 1918 the major vehicle for official announcements of a general nature was the daily paper of the Ministry of Internal Affairs, called *Northern Post* (*Severnaia pochta*) to 1868, then reorganized as *Government Herald* (*Pravitelstvennyi vestnik*).[30] The press agency Agence Russe Presse, which claimed non-official status, reported the statements and actions of the Ministry of Foreign Affairs to subscribing journalists and foreign diplomats. The lesser status of the agency is perhaps confirmed by the fact that Suvorin's *New Times* complained frequently of the low quality of its services, a criticism the paper never dared to make of the often equally unenlightening *Government Herald*. Nonetheless, Agence Russe Presse spoke with some authority. For example, when rumors arose in late 1877 that Russia might conclude an early peace with Turkey, it was the "nonofficial" press agency which hastened to assure its foreign clients that such rumors were false; *New Times* complained that the agency neglected to let its Russian subscribers in on this information.[31] Neither news source bothered about the piquant details so important to the reader of daily newspapers. A typical result of this neglect was *New Times'* coverage of the emperor's ultimatum to the Porte in October 1876, when Russia threatened severance of diplomatic relations if Turkey did not conclude a favorable armistice with Serbia at once. Thanks to a bulletin from Agence Russe Presse, *New Times* was able to give its readers the contents of the ultimatum on the day after its presentation in Constantinople. Not until almost a week later, however, could the paper report the time and manner of presentation, or even that the Russian ambassador had indeed given the ultimatum to the Turkish government. All such details were copied from Vienna newspapers, received by mail in Saint Petersburg several days after publication.[32]

For news bulletins from abroad, Russian papers were able to rely upon the foreign press, copying articles directly from the leading newspapers of Budapest, Vienna, Berlin, Paris, and London. In the second half of the century the development of the electric telegraph made it possible to use the dispatches of foreign telegraph agencies. The first Russian agency was organized in 1866 but only in order to receive dispatches of foreign agencies; evidently, it had not a single correspondent of its own.[33] Needless to say, full control over incoming foreign dispatches by non-Russian news agencies, some of them even unannounced instruments of their governments, raised the possibility of distortion in the aid of foreign purposes.[34] Such a danger was balanced, however, by the other major source for the external section, the long analytical articles written by Russians resident abroad or by foreign publicists of an agreeable political cast who, over a period of weeks or months, discussed such subjects as the French political scene or the German credit union movement. The second agency, the International Telegraph Agency, was organized in 1872 by A. A. Kraevskii and suffered from its close relationship to his newspaper, *Voice* (*Golos*). *New Times* was not the only subscriber to complain that *Voice* published full accounts of events while rival newspapers, relying upon the International Telegraph Agency, received only minimal information, presumably from the same correspondents. At any rate, Kraevskii rarely sent his own men; most of his foreign telegrams evidently originated in European news agencies. Despite customer dissatisfaction, the agency's practical monopoly remained unchallenged by effective competition. A few large papers, such as Suvorin's, might send correspondents to the wars in the Balkans or to the international exposition in distant Philadelphia, but most papers, especially in the provinces, could not afford this luxury.[35]

Domestic reports of a non-official nature, especially of events taking place in the provinces, had a haphazard character in the sixties and, for most daily newspapers, in subsequent decades as well.[36] City reporters were very often impecunious university students paid by the line, while out-of-town news frequently came from self-appointed writers of letters to the editor. Comparable American newspapers of the same era obtained their provincial news by dispatching reporters to the scene of a curiosity or calamity, through telegraphic dispatches of their own agents or local market reporters, and by copying articles on local events from papers of other towns. In Russia of the sixties little of this was possible. A newspaper's own full-time reporters were few and except for truly extraordinary events stayed in the city. For related reasons, telegraphic dispatches generally traveled from the center to the provinces rather than in the opposite direction. A provincial newspaper press with local reports worth reproducing did not even begin to develop in Russia until the seventies, and then only in the few southern cities of increasing commercial and industrial importance. Not the least reason for the extraordinary preponderance of foreign to domestic news in a Russian paper was the fact that news from abroad lay about, ready at hand and ready-made, while local news had to be sought.

Thus, a serious and intellectually significant Russian daily might carefully develop its external section (foreign coverage) according to a rational program and specific direction, and yet exhibit an internal section that was frivolous, disjointed, and lacking in direction. Throughout the period under study, the liberal and radical thick journals criticized the daily news press for inadequately "studying internal life" or "acquainting Russia with herself," by which they presumably meant that the papers failed to fill their columns with detailed analyses of provincial poverty, ignorance, and bureaucratic tyranny.[37] In the late seventies the spread of domestic telegraphic communications facilitated the gathering of news from outside the two capitals. Subscribers of the International Telegraphic Agency could receive prompt dispatches from the most important provincial centers, although the news thus received of fires, great robberies, and other calamities also proved not to the taste of the thick journals.[38] After the Russo-Turkish War of 1877, Suvorin sent one of his former war correspondents, A. N. Molchanov, on an extended reportorial tour of the country. The resulting articles were incontestably detailed and free from sensationalism, yet they also drew heavy fire from the left. Presumably Molchanov dwelt too much on the financial-industrial prospects for the future and too little on the desperate situation of the peasant in the present. Yet genuinely "exposing" correspondence held real hazards. *Russian Notices,* one of the few newspapers which as early as the late sixties attempted to build up a permanent, ideologically sympathetic staff of regular contributors from the provinces, had to take great precautions lest the names of its writers become known to the police.[39] Clearly, foreign affairs provided a simpler and safer ground for journalistic self-expression and political identification.

*   *   *

In 1863 when Suvorin went to Saint Petersburg to work, there were fourteen Russian-language daily newspapers in the empire—five of which closed within the next two years. As late as 1860, however, there had been only six daily papers, five official and one *ofitsioz*. Of the fourteen, ten appeared in Saint Petersburg: four governmental (one was leased to a private person), one *ofitsioz*, one stock market bulletin, and four privately published papers of general content (among which the death toll was the highest).[40] The realm of the daily newspaper was dominated in the sixties by V. F. Korsh's liberal *Saint Petersburg Notices* and by *Moscow Notices*, guided by M. N. Katkov in a direction which, if not precisely conservative in the strict sense of the word, was certainly increasingly reactionary. These two were constantly denouncing each other for political-ideological sins, while the only editorially important private newspaper, Kraevskii's *Voice*, engaged in incessant polemic with everyone.[41]

Another daily newspaper, which enjoyed great popularity in the provinces, was the military organ *Russian War Veteran*, which had a monopoly on military news and even military belles lettres until 1855.[42] Its political complexion in the early sixties had a faint blush of "democratic tendency." The high point of its liberalism was the publication of a special extra-official supplement in 1862–1863, for which Suvorin wrote a light weekly column. This supplement, whose program called for "equality of citizens before the law" and "decentralization of the system of government administration and development of the elective principle," was closed by order of the emperor himself in June 1863. After several reorganizations, *Russian War Veteran* became a more specialized, specifically military publication which attracted the general reader only in time of war.[43]

After the stormy days of the early sixties, the Russian "social movement" experienced a lull during the decade centering on 1870. The newspaper press grew only slowly. By 1879 the number of daily papers in Saint Petersburg had increased to seventeen.[44] The Slavic uprisings of 1875–1876, followed immediately by the Russo-Turkish War of 1877, created a widespread public demand for news from the Balkans; daily papers were the principal beneficiaries of the intense journalistic activity which resulted. While Suvorin's *New Times* was the only paper to rise to prominence on the basis of the Eastern question, other publications increased their circulation significantly and several new periodicals appeared to quench the general thirst for information.

The enlivenment of the mid-seventies was followed by another, domestically oriented, in 1879–1881. The governmental administrative crisis of the end of the decade brought another relaxation of censorship and quickening of political discussion, as in the era after the Crimean defeat. And once again, as twenty years earlier, journalists became more outspoken and proposals for periodicals which would have been unthinkable several years earlier now suddenly received official assent. By the late seventies, however, truly radical journalists fulfilled their publicistic goals in a variety of underground and émigré publications; hence the new, highly political, short-lived legal periodicals of the era were largely in the hands of liberals and participants in the zemstvo movement. Most outstanding was *Order* (*Poriadok*), published daily throughout 1881 by the editors of *Herald of Europe*. Originally they had intended to name their paper *Legal Order*, but the first word was too much even for a relaxed censorship.[45] In 1880 Saint Petersburg boasted twenty-two daily and forty-three weekly and semi-weekly papers, while figures for Moscow and the provinces showed similar growth.

The assassination of Alexander II on 1 March 1881 put an end to the second great political upsurge of Russian journalism, although the repression of the eighties and nineties gathered force only slowly during the course of the year. By 1891 the number of daily papers in the capital had fallen to the level of 1870. Although the number and circulation of all periodicals continued to increase, most new ones were of a specialized or entertaining rather than overtly political character.[46]

chapter one

Culture in Voronezh

*There were nine of us children ... We
ate with wooden spoons from a
common bowl. We drank tea only
on holidays.*

—*Suvorin*

*A*leksei Sergeevich Suvorin was born in 1834 in the
cattle-breeding village of Korshevo, a large settle-
ment of state peasants in the steppe province of Voronezh.[1] In later
life he took great pride in his village childhood and in the simple
rural poverty of his family, whose material existence was in no way
distinguished from that of the surrounding peasants. In fact, however,
he owed his excellent free education and unrestricted opportunity for
personal advancement precisely to the fact that he was not of peasant
birth.

Although young Aleksei had no shoes and ate with a wooden
spoon from the common bowl, he enjoyed the perquisites and personal freedom of the hereditary gentry. About 0.25 percent of the
population of his native province belonged to this chief and tax-free
estate. His father, once an illiterate villager, won privileged status
for his descendants by one of the sudden turns of personal fortune
possible in the service state. Taken into the army by conscription, the
elder Suvorin distinguished himself in the Napoleonic wars; he was

raised to officer and eventually achieved a rank which brought hereditary nobility. Retiring on a minute pension of fluctuating paper rubles,
he returned to his native village, married the daughter of the local
priest, and raised a large family on the small proceeds from a mill and
other projects of his own construction.

Korshevo had no school. After several years of readings in
Church Slavonic with his mother's clerical relatives, young Suvorin at
the age of eleven had the great good fortune to obtain a state appointment to the newly founded cadet corps in Voronezh city. The Mikhailovskii Voronezh Corps was one of a series of military academies
established in provincial centers by direction of Nicholas I; it accepted
a hundred boys a year from five provinces and the army of the Don
Cossacks. The six-year course of the corps, the best education in the
region, was open only to the sons of the nobility.[2]

As Suvorin later reminisced, the Voronezh corps was for him an
entirely new environment. The other cadets were well prepared and
many already knew French, while he spoke like a peasant.[3] But he
learned much quickly, finished with the first class, and was sent for
two final years of military and general study in the Regiment of
Nobility in Saint Petersburg.

It was in the capital, during the "seven-year darkness," that
Suvorin first became acquainted with thick journals and with that
peculiar Russian literary criticism which then constituted the only
vehicle for expression of notions foreign to the official state ideology.
Although Belinskii was anathema to the autocratic regime, his writings
were somehow to be found in the dark corners of the Regiment of
Nobility. In fact Suvorin compiled a "Dictionary of Outstanding
People," drawing upon the wisdom of Belinskii and including articles
on such personae non gratae as Byron and Voltaire. In an attempt to
gain appointment to the university, he submitted this manuscript to
the commandant of the school—thereby illustrating that dense incomprehension of the seriousness of ideological battlelines which he often
displayed in later life as well. The dictionary earned him a severe
reprimand and an appointment to the field engineers.[4]

In 1853 at the age of nineteen, Suvorin retired from service. Lacking financial means to enter the university, he returned to his native
province and became a teacher in a county elementary school.[5] Despite

his distance from Saint Petersburg, Suvorin did not entirely lose touch with the currents of the time. He had access to publications from the capitals and read copies of A. I. Herzen's émigré journals. For a time he served as secretary to the marshal of nobility in the latter's capacity as chairman of a compulsory local council on "improvement of the living conditions of the peasants" (a euphemism for the committees of provincial nobility ordered by Alexander II to prepare proposals for emancipation of the serfs). Nonetheless, Suvorin missed far more than the experience of university student circles. During the entire period of intellectual awakening and excitement that characterized the late fifties in Saint Petersburg and certain other cities, he was essentially on ice, preserved in the countryside from the direct influence of political ferment as well as from participation in publicistic development and controversy.

*   *   *

In 1859 Suvorin obtained a position in the provincial capital of Voronezh, an administrative and commercial center of 35,000 people, of whom almost a tenth were pupils in one or another of the civil, military, and religious schools which made the city a sort of low-level educational center.[6] The city enjoyed a male literacy rate of 32 percent and a cultural tradition derived largely from the verses and one-time "circle" activity of two local poets of humble origin and quasi-folk inspiration.[7] In the late fifties Voronezh discovered in its midst yet another bard, the civic and nature poet I. S. Nikitin (1824–1861). It was around Nikitin and his newly established bookstore-lending library of current publications that the leading local intelligentsia had gathered when Suvorin arrived and quickly attached himself to the Nikitinites.

The heady intellectual ferment that stirred Russian society in the capitals at this time, after the Crimean defeat, spread quickly into such "regional cultural nests." As a local historian exulted, "Voronezh amazed the passing traveler with its intelligentsia ... If Voronezh lagged behind the capital, it was only by one week, while the mail was still on the road." Two well-stocked bookstores and a public library came into being. Literary discussions and public readings flourished.[8] As elsewhere in Russia, a society for the dissemination of literacy was organized and Sunday schools established for workers. Nor did intellectual Voronezh depend entirely on the capitals for cultural inspiration. Four printing presses issued ethnographic researches, poetic collections, and local periodicals.[9] Enthusiasm reached a peak early in 1861 with the publication of two literary almanacs by rival groups of literateurs; by the following year the imperial autocracy had become less tolerant toward non-official initiative in public life, the Sunday schools were suppressed, Nikitin was dead, and various lesser figures, including Suvorin, had already left Voronezh for the wider opportunities of Moscow or Saint Petersburg.[10]

The challenge by the plebeian "sons" against the patrician "fathers" for leadership of the intellectual movement in Saint Petersburg had its more amiable counterpart in the small society of Voronezh. The youthful circle of Nikitin, composed mainly of men like Suvorin of low service rank and little means, vitally concerned with contemporary civic literature and "current questions," was supplanting the older, higher-ranking "Vtorov circle" which had conducted many archival and ethnographic studies in the early fifties. It was the latter group that first discovered and encouraged Nikitin as a poet. As Suvorin later wrote, these idealists of the forties nurtured Nikitin on the milk of their beautiful thoughts, then reacted with horror when the poet opened a bookstore and energetically tried to make a practical success of it. And yet, concluded Suvorin as a true activist of the sixties, only such "realistic" ideals bear fruit in accomplishment. If Nikitin had lived longer, his bookstore would have exercised that influence of which the idealists dreamed in vain—idealists "full of high aspirations, but . . . wretched in practical matters . . . in whose hands every cause was spoiled."[11]

In the battle of the almanacs, the realists won.[12] Thanks to inclusion of several works by Nikitin which corresponded to the demands then being made of literature by the radical intelligentsia, the almanac of the Nikitinites was praised twice in the space of three months in the pages of the popular radical journal *Contemporary* and

attracted the attention of the reading public.[13] Although unmentioned
by the critics, Suvorin's first serious fiction appeared here, "Chernichka"
and "Garibaldi," socio-ethnographically realistic short stories of peasant life.[14] The first, heavily larded with local color from the region of
his native village, is an unrelievedly depressing tale of peasant
ignorance, superstition, and cruelty. The second consists mostly of a
discussion by a group of peasants about the exploits of *'alibardi* the
'talian. Its humor derives from their ignorant mispronunciations and
the confused, naively domesticated account of recent events in Italy.
This little story brought Suvorin a certain recognition when it was
taken up as a comic recitation by the most famous actor of the time,
A. N. Ostrovskii's friend Prov Sadovskii; even the empress heard it
with pleasure.[15]

This was not Suvorin's first appearance in print; even before
coming to Voronezh, he had published in a variety of periodicals
issued in Moscow and Saint Petersburg. After 1855, when it ceased
to be almost impossible to gain permission for a new periodical, newspapers and journals sprang up like mushrooms after warm rain (and
often vanished again as quickly). During the first decade of Alexander II's reign, 66 papers and 156 journals were established, more than
nine times the number of new titles approved during the preceding
decade.[16] Moreover the earlier publications were usually narrowly
specialized, from medicine to women's fashions but not beyond, while
those of the new dispensation often might treat (however obscurely)
a wide variety of politically delicate subjects. Many of the older periodicals also managed to gain governmental approval for a widened program of content. The great increase in output of printed words and
the quickened growth and interest of a reading public opened the
possibility of publication, and even of a life in journalism, to far more
would-be participants in the so-called social movement than ever before. But by no means all the new undertakings were of a serious
character and even such a journal as *Contemporary* sometimes had to
resort to minor frivolities in order to maintain its subscription lists at
needed strength.[17] Thus Suvorin, like many other aspiring young men
and women of the late fifties, began his journalistic career not with
literary criticism or political analysis but with lyric translations and
humorous sketches.

In the spring of 1858 an epidemic of comic papers suddenly spread through Saint Petersburg.[18] Following the successful example of the first of these purely entertaining publications, the weekly *Jolly Fellow* (*Veselchak*), dozens of entrepeneurs of the printed word appeared on the streets to sell cartoon broadsides, little newspapers of caricatures and anecdotes, and so forth. Although a few were intended for the intelligentsia, most aimed to attract the urban lower classes; some even employed the illustrative manner and sarcastic rhymed text of Russian popular woodcuts (*lubochnye kartinki*), by mid-century largely an art of the past. At the height of the epidemic in April and May, at least thirty-four comic papers appeared. The minister of education and certain other officials—unaccustomed to such popular literary excitement and alarmed by the prospect of secular reading, however apolitical, among the lower classes—acted quickly to restore Russian society to peaceful health. Forbidden to make street sales (a manner of distribution not permitted serious papers and journals), most of the comic publications vanished immediately. *Jolly Fellow,* which was more solidly organized and depended upon subscriptions rather than street sales, lasted out the year. Despite Suvorin's occasional participation and an edition that reached 8,000 at its highest point, lack of subscribers forced the magazine to close early in the following year.[19] Purely comic, idea-less periodicals did not become economically viable until the late 1870s, when numbers of them again appeared and in some cases proved very successful.

Suvorin's contributions to *Jolly Fellow* were of the same insignificant and idea-less nature as the rest of its contents: little dialogues ringing the changes on such well-worn subjects as hysterical poetic ladies, hen-pecked husbands, social-climbing merchants, and the tedious boredom of smalltown life.[20] But at the same time he was also publishing his translations from the poetry of André Chénier and Pierre Jean de Béranger, widely popular among the Russian intelligentsia as poets of the French revolutionary spirit. These were placed not only in various short-lived literary and informational newspapers typical of the period, but also in at least one very durable fashion magazine— illustrating the widespread acceptance of literary fashions originally current among the small group of radical publicists and their followers. Indeed, at that time translations from such poets as Béranger,

Byron, and Heine were if anything more popular with the reading
public than any of the Russian poets (always of course excepting
Nekrasov).

But Suvorin's offerings to the world of Russian journalism
passed unnoted by that world until 1860 when he began to publish
contributions to the "provincial chronicle" which formed a regular
section in almost every serious literary-political periodical of the era.
At that time the social movement and the notion of intellectual activity and public initiative in Russia were so new and fragile that residents
of the capitals read of signs of dawning enlightenment in the provinces
with almost as much eagerness as provincials read the varied messages
coming to them from the capitals—or so at least editors seem to have
assumed. Probably more to the point, the provincial chronicle was a
vehicle to castigate the stubborn immobility of provincial society, the
inadequacies of education, the banality and sloth of gentry life, the
hypocrisy and darkness of the merchant class, and so forth. Against
all of these (in their Voronezh manifestations) Suvorin fulminated
with progressive vigor and westernizing liberal conviction. His faith
in education was boundless. Ignorant, swinish merchants cheat and
abuse the peasants; therefore one must open to them free access to
educational institutions. The same backward merchants control manufacturing and trade, the "great conductors of social development";
thus by their education we can "remove all those factors which retard
the development of our life." Although the gentry have received some
sort of education, they prefer gambling to reading and a bearded lady
to genuine theater; the local noblemen's club is nothing but a tavern.
The greatest insufficiency in their education is their total lack of
scientific information. In fact, public lectures should be organized on
the natural sciences, and also on modern European history. There have
been enough lectures on female education, however; the time has
come for practical experience on the subject. Good translations of
Walter Scott, George Sand, and Charles Dickens should be provided
as healthy light reading for those provincials not yet accustomed to
serious reading. And so forth. The worst feature of life in Voronezh,
however, was the general indifference to the human being, to the
individual. But in 1860 Suvorin was confident that soon "real people"
would appear at last on the scene.[21]

The publication most receptive to Suvorin's correspondence was the semi-weekly Moscow paper *Russian Speech,* "a review of literature, history, art, and public life in the West and in Russia." In the summer of 1861, in response to the invitation of the publisher, Suvorin abandoned pedagogy forever and went to Moscow as a secretary to the editorial council of *Russian Speech.*[22] He spent well over a year in the journalistic milieu of Moscow—the entire period of disillusionment and radicalization that for many young intellectuals followed immediately upon the Edict of Emancipation, the period that came to be known as the "era of proclamations."

chapter two

Moscow Liberalism

I can't recall without laughter how people were asking each other seriously:

Are you a constitutionalist, or a republican?
—I am a constitutionalist.
Do you favor two chambers, or one?
—I favor only one.
Excuse me, why one? and so forth.
                    —Suvorin (1870)

*R*ussian Speech was one of a whole school of weekly and semi-weekly serious private papers which swam the turbulent and wreck-strewn journalistic seas of the decade of awakening. Like most of its fellows, it possessed the coveted license to include the word *political* in its program of publication. Those who lacked this once unobtainable franchise were the first to be wrecked.

In genres and style of contents there was no essential difference between a new semi-weekly paper of a few pages and the monthly thick journals, whose well-established pattern offered a long, wide-ranging essay in each of half a dozen definite and invariable departments. The long awaited political survey section consisted entirely of information and comment on the political scene in foreign countries. The Russian reader delimited and described his political views by reference to issues fought out abroad. Periodicals revealed their "tendencies" by favoring or denouncing this or that foreign state or party.

Domestic news was divided into two categories: official announcements, usually carried by private periodicals of weekly or greater frequency and constituting their closest regular approach to news reports; and the ubiquitous chronicles, whether Saint Petersburg, Moscow, or provincial. A chronicle might contain much or little comment on national policies, but always cautiously expressed. At certain times circumscribed areas of proposed reform, such as educational curricula or military conscription, or specific problems of foreign policy, formed the subject of heated debate between the internal chroniclers of contending periodicals. Announcement of a final official decision customarily ended open controversy.

The remaining two usual departments, belles lettres and criticism, carried a heavier freight of general thoughts on Russian conditions, especially officially unacceptable thoughts. The most furious polemics appeared under the rubric criticism, which sheltered discussion of books on all subjects and in any language. Skillful critics exercised careful choice of review books to provide a maximum of springboards to desired themes. The developing and already strong tradition of ideological seriousness and purposefulness in fiction made it possible for an editor to fill the section of belles lettres with stories and novels which disseminated the political views of his periodical. Thanks to the widespread use of western European fiction in translation, the political survey and the department of belles lettres might be almost indistinguishable except in style of exposition. A periodical whose fiction tended in no political direction was held by the true intelligentsia thereby to have revealed its obscurantist tendency as surely as if it filled its pages with historical romances of monarchical glories or with the novels of the anti-nihilist school.

When Suvorin came to Moscow in 1860 the ideological battle lines were already being drawn among different periodicals. In the years immediately after 1855 a euphoric sense of intellectual fraternity had prevailed in most journalistic circles. In the early sixties, and especially after the Edict of Emancipation, specific publications became the recognized organs of exclusive "parties." There were, of course, no legal political parties or even non-official pressure groups in nineteenth century Russia. The unorganized parties of contributors and readers of leading periodicals were no less real for the absence of platform conventions and membership cards. (The chief group ritual of a journal cult seems to have been silent mass participation in the funeral procession of an editor or writer.) Journalistic parties polarized educated society and shattered whatever incomplete harmony had ever existed between the more and less radical elements of the intelligentsia.

All the political journalism of the early sixties might be roughly divided (as contemporaries did) into four groups. On the far left were the radicals (democrats, plebeians, nihilists) as represented mainly by *Contemporary* and *Russian Word*. Radicals rejected both the old order and the half-way reforms of Alexander II; they hinted in guarded tones of European theories on equality and socialism. On the far right were the conservatives (loyalists, reactionaries, obscurantists, *krepostniki*), whose numbers were few then but swelled by the end of the decade. Conservatives displayed the outlook of unrepentant noblemen, feared all social change, and attempted to preserve as much of the essence of serfdom as possible. They generally distinguished themselves by Great Russian chauvinism and a fondness for censorship (of others).

Between the poles lay a vast throng of periodicals which wished neither to pull up society by the roots nor conserve unchanged the autocratic order. These were usually called liberals (or constitutionalists, parliamentarians, professors, doctrinaires).[1] Even after the terms of emancipation were made public, liberals believed in the possibility of reform from above. They devoted much energy to defending each new reform from bureaucratic depredations, all the while publicizing the most libertarian possible interpretation of the original statute. Although they differed considerably in some areas, liberals of the sixties could be easily recognized by certain common preoccupations. A liberal publication opposed serfdom, juridical inequalities, and the excessively classical secondary school curriculum introduced by Count D. A. Tolstoi; it supported free hired labor, popular literacy, and female emancipation. Like its western European namesake, Russian liberalism devoutly believed in Progress—a blessed state achieved rarely by revolution and least of all by the blind, chaotic, purely destructive uprisings of Russian peasant tradition, but rather by peaceful reform and education. In the sixties its favorite word was publicity (*glasnost*), by which on thousands of pages of print it indicated its desire for freedom of speech, an uncensored press, public trials, open right of petition, and so forth.[2]

The fourth, very small general category of periodicals was composed of the various organs of the political Slavophiles, the *pochvenniki*, and the Dostoevskii brothers. All this group of publicists claimed to reject alien European theories in favor of what was truly and organically Russian. On the one hand, they typically supported such liberal-radical desiderata as freedom of speech and the press (for which they often suffered harsh censorship repression). Yet on the other hand, they took theoretically conservative positions such as approval of the legally unlimited power of the absolute autocrat. Consequently, contemporaries accustomed to view the intellectual scene through more-or-less European lenses could not precisely assign the enthusiasts of native custom and soil to an appropriate western political category.

Russian Speech was a liberal newspaper, and like a great many liberal publications it strove to avoid association with any one small group or narrow platform. In the all-important announcement of program which always accompanied the appearance of a new periodical and established its position in the spectrum from the first day of issue, the editor hopefully stated that *Russian Speech* would serve as an organ which could unify "all people wishing gradual and just progress in Russia."[3] The scope and nature of possible just reforms was made clear by the considerable space devoted to reports on the progress of the Sunday school movement for workers, descriptions of the miserable laboring and living conditions of artisans, and enthusiastic articles on the cause of female emancipation. On a wider political horizon the paper praised western parliaments and parliamentarians, defending them against the sneering hostility of the radical party. Thus when N. A. Dobroliubov devoted an article to the self-serving anti-democratic essence of the newly elected chamber of deputies of united Italy, *Russian Speech* countered with vigorous argument.[4] When *Russian Word* referred to Lord John Russell, head of the Liberal party in England, as a mental midget, the paper defended him as a veritable giant and friend of the people.[5] In general the liberals of the sixties found Great Britain most fascinating, while radicals found more material for pointed discussions in France and the United States.

Russian Speech evidently managed to unite very few gradualist-progressives. After less than five months of publication (January to mid-May 1861) financial difficulties dictated absorption of another paper in similar circumstances, the once successful *Moscow Herald* (*Moskovskii vestnik*). The latter, although privately owned, was regarded as an organ of Moscow University because of the number of professors who placed articles there. During its first year of existence its tendency was determined by a strongly Anglophile political survey written by M. N. Kapustin, a professor of law and collaborator with Katkov on the then leading liberal journal, *Russian Herald* (*Russkii vestnik*). For Kapustin, as for Katkov in this period, the *Times* of London was the highest court. Not all the contributors to *Moscow Herald* found this "ultra-English tendency" congenial; shortly after Kapustin wrote that the attempt of John Brown to free the American slaves was illegal and premature, the editorial staff was reorganized and the paper thereafter followed a broader (and more eclectic) liberal path.[6]

Suvorin's closest friend during his stay in Moscow was an editor of the perishing *Moscow Herald,* A. N. Pleshcheev, a condemned poet of the former Petrashevskii circle, newly returned to European Russia following Alexander II's general amnesty to political exiles.[7] In the early sixties, under the influence of Dobroliubov and Nekrasov, Pleshcheev was writing satirical verse for *Contemporary* on the self-satisfaction and social indifferentism of contemporary man. A vague socialist of no particular school, he seems not to have taken any further part in secret circles and revolutionary plans. Nonetheless, he was impatient with the inactivity of his liberal colleagues and considered that "the ideal of Chernyshevskii is wider than the ideals of all these parliamentarians."[8] In fact he was a personal friend of N. G. Chernyshevskii and acquainted, despite his long absence, with the literary figures of both capitals. Through him Suvorin met Ostrovskii, Saltykov-Shchedrin, Nekrasov, Lev Tolstoi, and others. When the inevitable collapse of *Russian Speech and Moscow Herald* left Suvorin without source of support, Pleshcheev found him literary odd jobs and finally helped him to obtain the position he held for eleven years with *Saint Petersburg Notices.*[9]

The social and political milieu which first influenced the young

Suvorin, newly arrived from the provinces, was both complex and typical of the times. *Russian Speech* had been founded by Evgeniia Tur, a writer of some reputation who maintained a well-known Moscow literary salon and most recently had been associated with Katkov's *Russian Herald.*[10] Connected by family ties or long friendship with most of the Westernizer circle of the forties, she managed for several decades to make her apartment one of the chief gathering places for the literary and scholarly intelligentsia of Moscow. In 1860–1861 while her son was involved in the student strikes at Moscow University, V. I. Kelsiev, P. E. Argiropulo, and other young radicals frequented her "Jacobin" salon. The countess herself, under the influence of aristocratic Polish friends, became at this time a partisan of the Polish national cause. As a onetime habitué recalled, her home became a gathering place for all sorts of people and all sorts of oratory about "freedom, equality, the necessity of struggle with the government, and so forth."[11]

Most of this radical passion remained oratorical. Kelsiev and Argiropulo, genuine would-be revolutionaries, had left when Suvorin arrived in summer 1861. By September Suvorin wrote to a friend that he was already tired of listening to the circle which surrounded his employer. All of them were well educated and well meaning people, but "completely useless at the present time. I know nothing worse than these constitutionalists, more inert, more monotonous. He who still has the instincts of life cannot live in harmony with them."[12]

Inert or no, Evgeniia Tur managed to attract to her paper a number of talented young men. The future nihilist V. A. Sleptsov, the chronicler of homeless wanderers A. I. Levitov, and the future alleged reactionary N. S. Leskov all worked with Suvorin on *Russian Speech*. Suvorin, Levitov, and Sleptsov used to help each other home late at night, loudly singing songs of peasant revolt to the shuttered windows of "quiet, patriarchal" Moscow.[13] Although Sleptsov soon left to write for *Contemporary* and to organize communal living in accordance with the prescriptions of Chernyshevskii, it may have been his influence as well as that of Pleshcheev which helped Suvorin to form comparatively leftist sympathies. Suvorin wrote to a friend at the end of 1861 that he could not adhere to the desire of *Russian Herald* and *Russian Speech* for an aristocratic constitution with a House of Lords. Although he did not share the socialist tendencies of *Contemporary*, he sympathized with its democratic strivings, its opposition to aristocracy, and its wish for a "government such as, for example, that in North America."[14] Suvorin strongly defended *Contemporary's* personnel, regarded by many of his colleagues as insincere and uncultured (rude, *nevezhlivye,* was the favorite word). It is worth noting that when I. S. Turgenev's *Fathers and Sons* appeared (February 1862), Suvorin immediately praised the nihilist Bazarov as magnificent, regretting only that the fictional man was so much better than any of the real people who had thus far arrived on the scene.[15] Nonetheless his general principles of democratic constitutionalism were in no way distinguishable from that left wing of gentry liberalism which petitioned at this time for the abolition of all class privileges. Even the aristocratic anglophobic readers of Katkov and the Slavophile partisans of an advisory assembly were, of course, in opposition to the existing autocratic state structure.

Russian Speech and Moscow Herald closed with the first issue of 1862. Suvorin undertook to support himself by his pen, mainly by writing historical pamphlets for popular reading. Both the reexamination of Russian history and the cause of popular literacy had become active concerns of educated society several years earlier. Writers sought through historical accounts to propagandize democratic ideas and to demonstrate that autocracy, the privileged position of the ruling classes, and the depressed condition of the peasantry (the younger brother, the people) were all of recent and artificial origin. As the historian of the Third Section (political police) complained in his entry for 1862, "our publicists turned largely to historical criticism: in the pre-Petrine era they pointed to village courts . . . to assemblies (*sobory*), to the Novgorod town meeting (*veche*) as examples of the political originality and self-government of the people, and they especially emphasized the election of Mikhail Fedorovich as sovereign with a 'compact,' which they consider the same as a limitation of power."[16]

Suvorin's first historical venture was written in simple language for one of Count Lev N. Tolstoi's short-lived twin journals named for his country estate. A burning question of the early sixties was the problem of education: what to teach and how to teach it. Generally speaking the whole oppositional intelligentsia agreed that there should be more education for more people, and that more of it should be scientific and practical. (Some radicals did refuse to take part in the famous controversy over secondary school curriculum, on the ground that the popular masses did not attend secondary schools anyway.) But all avenues were open with respect to purely practical questions of methodology. Numerous specialized pedagogical journals began to appear. Tolstoi experimented in a school for the peasant children of his own estate and became so enthusiastic that he founded two periodicals to further his theories of informal and disciplineless instruction: a pedagogical journal and a series of booklets for elementary reading.[17] Suvorin, who evidently fully shared Tolstoi's educational views, published an account of the life of Patriarch Nikon in the latter series. Connected as it was with both the origins of the religious schism and the problem of the relationship between church and state, the subject of Nikon was politically perilous. Suvorin avoided explicit treatment of the second problem but met the first head-on by assuring his young readers that the schismatics were sincere and good people, but misguided. The Orthodox clergy, in contrast, were shown as very ignorant and often venal. Nikon himself and the purpose of his reforms emerged in sympathetic light, although his overwhelming pride and harsh methods were faulted. Russian society seemed to consist of a basically evil aristocracy and higher clergy. Nikon was brought low by scheming boyars, jealous bishops, and money hungry foreign patriarchs. Both tsars were pious and benevolent but deceived by lying courtiers and clerics.[18]

Suvorin's next commission came from the Moscow Society for the Dissemination of Useful Books, a women's philanthropic group established in 1861 to "develop and strengthen sound moral understanding" by supplying educational books "for all classes and ages of Russian readers" at the cheapest prices possible.[19] In addition to picture alphabets, primers, and Bible stories, the ladies published descriptions of distant travels, introductory works on natural history (e.g., *Does the Sun Move Around the Earth?, How Does a Person Get Diseases Through Food?*), and a series of lives of outstanding people. The society maintained a bookstore in Moscow and stocks of books in the provinces. In its first three years alone it published almost fifty books of small format, at prices from 8 to 50 kopecks. Standing committees for book selection were advised by male experts, including professors of Moscow University; chief advisor to the society was Professor Kapustin, the sometime ultra-anglophile of the Katkov school.[20]

Present-day references to the society are invariably condemnatory, based on Dobroliubov's hostile review of two of its more unfortunate productions.[21] Dobroliubov used this review to voice his opposition to religious education, to optimistic notions about a new era of reforms, and most of all to the suggestion that the people must "have patience"—all of which errors he managed to find in two books. He enlarged the scope of his implicit revolutionary message by pointing out that the members of the society, those who urged the common people to be patient, were all ladies of the Moscow higher nobility.[22] It is true that the society encouraged a religious outlook, that its conscious aims were anything but revolutionary, and that the list of founding members consisted almost entirely of countesses and princesses. (But in what other strata of Russian society in 1861, especially outside Saint Petersburg, could one find a sizable number of women with the education, funds, and initiative to establish a large charitable enterprise of this type?)

Nonetheless, one ought not to dismiss the entire work of the society on the basis of Dobroliubov's partial message in a single review. In fact *Contemporary* at first greeted the organization with cautious enthusiasm, taking it as an example of increasing social activity by women and explaining that even among the upper classes there may be talented people who can do something useful, however small.[23] The society did contribute over a number of years to the cause of popular literacy, and in the context of the early sixties any program for mass education was, if not necessarily oppositional, at any rate not conservative. The society's title-list betrayed strong liberal, westernizing, and modernizing currents; by no means were all its publications of religious-moral content. Whatever its motives, it in effect responded to the nihilist demand for intellectual development through the natural sciences by providing in simple language at low price a variety of popular-scientific titles for self-study. One might even argue that the society was objectively in some ways more progressive than Dobroliubov. Its little books on scientific facts and home improvement encouraged a machine-conscious change-oriented outlook at variance with the traditional mental habits of the peasantry. It may be noted that among the society's volumes on outstanding men were *Fulton the Inventor of the Steamship* and *Robert Stevenson the Famous Engineer.*

Suvorin wrote three historical booklets for the society, *Ermak Timofeevich Subjugator of Siberia, The Boyar Matveev,* and *A History of the Time of Troubles.* The last was rejected by the censor and never saw the light of day.

Ermak Timofeevich is a straightforward nationalistic adventure. The implicit moral seems to be that the initiative and courage of ordinary Russian people won the vast Siberian land for the use of ordinary Russian people. *The Boyar Matveev,* despite its simple style, is a more complex book. Artamon Matveev (1625–1682) was one of Russia's first conscious westernizers. He introduced western European manners, gadgets, and theatrical entertainments into the court of his friend and confidant Tsar Aleksei Mikhailovich. The account of his life provided Suvorin an opportunity to contrast the narrow, ignorant, backward and oppressive milieu of old Russia with the new enlightenment, religious tolerance, scientific knowledge, and personal dignity which slowly entered Russian society from the time of Matveev. The philosophy of government had also changed. The present government, which gave freedom to the serfs, recognized that "all the powers of the state should be based on the well-being of the people." In the past, however, the government had spent all its energies on extracting the greatest revenue possible and otherwise had paid no attention to the people. "The provincial governors robbed them, the land owners oppressed them, the government did not pity them."[24] Peasant uprisings were the direct result of injustice and extortion. As before, Suvorin did not blame the rulers themselves, with the exception of cruel Ivan IV. The tsar himself, Matveev, and two others were the only honest men at the court of Aleksei Mikhailovich.

Amazingly, *The Boyar Matveev* was among those books selected by the Ministry of Education (under the comparatively liberal A. V. Golovnin) for distribution in village schools, but it was quickly withdrawn after numerous complaints. The archbishop of Chernigov prepared a detailed denunciation, a syllabus of Sovorin's errors: the Greek Orthodox faith is not the only true and real faith, other Christian confessions are not God-opposing heresies, the knowledge of medicine is more useful than that of the psalms, the submission of wife to husband is an intolerable violence, and so forth. Worst of all, in the archbishop's view, was Suvorin's description of the relationship of government to people during the reign of Aleksei Mikhailovich. For, as the archbishop pointed out, if such was the situation under the "best and kindest tsar, then every villager will conclude that now the people are just work horses for the government"—and such a conclusion will lead to insubordination and riot.[25] Unfortunately it is impossible to say which inference Suvorin wished his readers to draw: the essentially liberal position that life in Russia was progressing (even if too slowly) as it approached the western model, or the radical thesis that even the best autocracy was intolerable.

Within several years Suvorin was issuing popular educational books through his own publishing enterprise. Meanwhile he continued to write short stories and tales, managing even to place one, "The Soldier and the Soldier's Wife," in *Contemporary*. He also published in *Notes of the Fatherland,* the thick journal made famous by Belinskii and the Westernizer circle in the forties but in the sixties condemned by radicals as a "decaying corpse" (D. I. Pisarev's phrase) and representative of the worst sort of vague liberalism. One of his stories was accepted by F. M. Dostoevskii for his *Time (Vremia)*, an organ of the anti-western and anti-nihilist *pochvenniki;* however, the issue in which it was to appear was seized and destroyed by the police when they closed the journal.[26]

Any Russian radical, confronted with such an ideologically eclectic placement of published works, would at once conclude that their author totally lacked "principles" and a "unified world view." It may be suspected that Suvorin in fact had no strong principles. But it is also true that even among men now admitted to the circle of the democratic-sanctified, there were those who occasionally slipped for the sake of a living or because they did not understand that only a few journals would turn out in retrospect to have been progressive.[27]

In all these tales Suvorin continued to draw upon his knowledge of provincial dialect and rural superstitions to produce anecdotal descriptions of peasant ignorance and casual brutality. While his work lacked the starkly desolating effect achieved by others, including his sometime friend Sleptsov, it is clear he was attempting to meet the radical demand for fiction of a new and different type.

The radical editors and critics of the sixties, like their spiritual descendants to the present day, made quite definite demands on artistic literature. Chernyshevskii and others insisted that the value of a work of fiction lay in its oppositional ideological content. Fiction must unmask the shortcomings of existing society and indicate, however cryptically, the path to a better life. The largest part of the population of nineteenth century Russia, and clearly the most downtrodden part, was the peasantry. Consequently one of the foremost means of criticism was the tale of rural life. In the second quarter of the century the characteristic genre had been the philanthropic story, the most renowned examples of which may be found among Turgenev's *Sportsman's Sketches* (1847–1852). This sort of story depicted simple people in a sympathetic, even sentimental manner, often contrasting to idealized peasants the stock figure of a brutal landowner or a callous official. Although philanthropic fiction continued to abound into the sixties and even beyond, radicals began to insist upon harsh, unvarnished truth in representation of the peasantry. Only absolute realism could bring about genuine emancipation. Sentimental gloss may have been helpful in the thirties, they held, but it was positively harmful in the sixties.[28] Hence the belles lettres departments of *Contemporary* and *Russian Word* came to be filled with appalling descriptions of poverty, exhausting work, superstition, and easy cruelty —little distinguished from the serious articles on labor conditions and village life which appeared in other sections of the journals. The nonradical intelligentsia, including most of the men of the forties, often accused the younger generation (euphemism for radicals) of distortion and jeering at the people. Polemical exchanges over the question of who loved the people more became another way in which radicals and liberals differentiated themselves in censored print.

Meanwhile, however, the first fine intellectual rapture of the turbulent decade of awakening came to an abrupt end in the summer of 1862 with the arrest of Chernyshevskii and the suspension for eight months of both *Contemporary* and *Russian Word*.

*   *   *

Suvorin stayed in Moscow little more than a year altogether. After involved negotiations, early in 1863 he became secretary to the editorial staff of *Saint Petersburg Notices.* He was hired by the liberal publicist V. F. Korsh, who on the first day of that year acquired Russia's oldest newspaper by rental from the Academy of Sciences.[29] One of the youngest westernizers of the forties, Korsh had already proven his worth as an editor by considerably enlivening *Moscow Notices* before that newspaper was taken over by Katkov. Under his direction the hoary *Saint Petersburg Notices* became an outstanding political and general daily newspaper, as well as the leading organ of what came to be called zemstvo liberalism.[30]

After several years of apprenticeship in arduous but anonymous editorial tasks for *Saint Petersburg Notices,* Suvorin took over the Sunday feuilleton, a regular column of light comment on events of the day. Within less than a decade he became the most widely known feuilletonist in Russia. Even S. A. Vengerov, who was hardly friendly to Suvorin, wrote in retrospect that his "brilliant talent first gave great importance in newspaper publishing to this sort of feuilleton."[31] Hence, it would be appropriate at this point briefly to describe the nature and development of this journalistic genre. The entire bottom third of the front page of a typical nineteenth century Russian newspaper was marked off by a special border and reserved for the daily feuilleton. Different days of the week might regularly bring different types of writing, as for example the musical feuilleton on Tuesdays, the literary feuilleton on Saturdays, and so on. During the sixties a general or unrestricted type of feuilleton became an important feature of every newspaper; this so-called Sunday feuilleton is the precursor of the usual twentieth century representative of the genre.

Russians consider the newspaper feuilleton to be one of the important and characteristic features of their journalism, although precisely what is and what is not a feuilleton is hard to say. At present it may be stated at least that it is a short informally written article employing satirical methods of topical criticism. Definition presented greater difficulties in the past. When the word was introduced into Russia from France in the early nineteenth century, it somehow attached itself to a physical location (the lower section or back pages) rather than to a genre. This inferior department was traditionally given over to assorted light anecdotes and topical allusions whose banality and triviality made the term feuilletonist an insult to the intelligentsia of the forties. Yet that same intelligentsia employed an analogous section, often called hodgepodge (*smes*), for less superficial banter of their own. Among both philistines and progressives, individual writers increasingly wove the hodgepodge together into a single digressive monologue on literary and other matters of current interest. Under Russian conditions any discussion of literature, or even of foreign travel, became publicistic and disputative. O. I. Senkovskii, the first journalist to achieve renown specifically as a feuilletonist, hastened the sobering of his genre when he used it to attack Belinskii, whose supporters then replied in kind and in feuilleton. The literary-social feuilleton, crushingly sarcastic in tone, became a chief polemical genre; within its anecdotal and inclusive limits, journals expounded their views and confounded their enemies. The mixed heritage—principled and frivolous—of the term explains the curious circumstance that many publications used it both approvingly and scornfully. M. E. Saltykov-Shchedrin, for example, spoke of his own works as feuilletons and yet called Suvorin, when he wished to dismiss him as wholly unimportant, a "feuilletonist in the full sense the word."[32]

The relative importance of the feuilleton in the Russian journal decreased during the last third of the nineteenth century. As its star sank in the journals, it rose again with the rising newspaper press. In the old days, as Suvorin said, a newspaper feuilleton consisted of "gossip about charitable balls and concerts, about high-society parties." At its best it was a chatty account of exhibitions viewed and theaters visited. Such writing by no means vanished. From the sixties, however, Suvorin and his successors developed the genre as one of the most publicistically important and certainly the single most enjoyed feature of the serious Russian newspaper—as it still is, it seems, today. This genre, while now characteristic of the newspaper, grew out of the sarcastic polemical monologue of the oppositional journal; in adaptation to frequent appearance, it acquired even more immediately topical themes and if possible an even livelier style, which often imitates the forms of fiction to dramatize its socially critical message. The newspaper feuilleton of the Russian type, as it was often termed in the nineteenth century, is in fact a microcosmic political pamphlet. Thanks to its informal personalized style and humorous tone, it is the easiest to read of all political pamphlets. It is also undoubtedly the major concession of serious Russian newspapers to the short attention span and light-minded desire for entertainment so often manifested by the average newspaper reader—the rough equivalent of large headlines and prize contests. In the Russian milieu such a concession was ideologically informed and didactic in purpose. As Suvorin explained:

> The feuilleton reinforces the lead article and, for the busy person weighed down by the trifles of life, repeats in light form what he has no time or inclination to read in serious form. A feuilleton is a popularization of those ideas which newspapers try to disseminate by means of lead articles[33]

Repeating in "light, soaring rockets" the liberal ideas of *Saint Petersburg Notices,* Suvorin by the early seventies acquired a significant following of readers. The censor A. V. Nikitenko called him "almost the sole living stream in the newspapers."[34] When Suvorin published two volumes of old and necessarily somewhat stale feuilletons in 1875, they sold out in a few days, a rare event in the annals of Russian book publishing up to that time. His first public renown came a decade earlier and unexpectedly, however, when his first such collection was seized and burned by the censor for harmful radical tendencies.

chapter three

Suvorin as Nihilist

> *A book has perished! It was already*
> *Entirely ready—suddenly it perished!*
> . . . .
> *I am sorrowed, I am sorrowed*
> *And it may be that all Russia*
> *Will share my grief with me.*
> — *Nekrasov*

A leksei Sergeevich Suvorin's name first came to the attention of a wide public in April 1866, owing to a book few people had a chance to read. Two days after the unsuccessful attempt by D. V. Karakozov to assassinate Alexander II, the censorship authorities seized all copies of a feuilleton-novel by Suvorin and accused its author of extremist and socially dangerous intentions. To a great extent he was the victim of poor timing. A month or two earlier, to judge from the success of others, his book might well have passed the censors without incident. Karakozov's shot threw an already nervous administration into panic, and moreover served as occasion to introduce several notably reactionary high officials in place of comparative liberals. Numerous suspected radicals were arrested. The whole journalistic world of Saint Petersburg sat tensely waiting for police search.[1] In such an atmosphere it is not surprising that the censors grew cautious; at least fourteen books were seized in the capital during the rest of the year, while none had been held in the first three months.[2]

Suvorin had already attracted the notice of the Third Section for other literary activities, however. The political police ascribed to him a leading role in a publishing partnership, that of E. O. Likhacheva and A. I. Suvorina, which began in 1865 to issue generally educational volumes. Both the partners were active in the causes of literacy and female emancipation. Likhacheva, the wife of a jurist, later wrote extensively on the female question for the radical *Notes of the Fatherland* and helped to organize the famous Bestuzhev courses of higher education for women. Suvorina, who was Suvorin's first wife, made a number of translations from French writings of the useful sort.[3]

In an era when democratic ideals and natural sciences were considered to go hand in hand, the partners concentrated their attention on progressive poets and natural facts. Their first officially "harmful" venture, a translation of Jules Verne's *Voyage au centre de la terre,* included an article by Suvorina entitled "An Outline of the Origin and Development of the Earth, with Sketches of Primeval Plants and Animals." This essay was judged injurious to children and the book was forbidden to all school libraries.[4] They next offered the public an inexpensive volume for children, consisting of several dozen varied selections from the "leading authors of the day": Herzen, Dobroliubov, Nekrasov, A. I. Levitov, Thomas Hood ("Song of the Shirt"), the condemned revolutionary M. L. Mikhailov (recently dead in Siberia), to name those most likely to alarm the timid. Self-appointed literary police of the journalistic world, then beginning to appear in numbers, denounced the book as nihilistic. Radical bibliographers hailed it as a model textbook. The minister of internal affairs pronounced it "entirely immoral in its tendency" but nonetheless within the letter of the new press law.[5] That same worthy found their translation of François Auguste Mignet's *Histoire de la révolution française* (1824) to be "propagandizing revolutionary ideas and methods."[6]

Despite the harsh tone of the authorities in the months immediately following Karakozov's shot, Likhacheva and Suvorina emerged unscathed. Perhaps it was because their books had all spent the required three days with the censorship and passed into public light before April. (From that time the government began not only to scrutinize every book more carefully, but also to design restrictive amendments to the Temporary Regulations.) Or perhaps it was because after all the ladies were not very dangerous. After the flaming inauguration of their partnership, Likhacheva and Suvorina almost ceased to publish until 1870 and then largely confined themselves to translating travelers' accounts; in 1874 one of their last editions even gained a place on the list of books approved by the Ministry of Public Education for school libraries.[7] Nonetheless, their offerings of 1865–1866 were at least as dangerous to public order as most of the books suppressed after 4 April. The latter, like the "nihilistic" editions of Likhacheva and Suvorina, fell mainly into three categories: scientific expositions which seemed to cast doubt on such Christian doctrines as the simultaneous creation of all animal life or the existence of the immortal soul, writings of any sort by those already officially regarded as revolutionaries or about them, and histories of foreign revolutions, especially in France.

To Suvorin alone in his family, then, fell the honor of martyrdom for the printed word. The censored book, *All Sorts; Sketches of Contemporary Life,* was a feuilleton-novel. In 1865 Suvorin began to write a series of feuilletons on the social temper of the moment for *Saint Petersburg Notices.* Within a thin narrative framework he told anecdotes about public figures and let them speak on contemporary questions. Excitement was added by now obscure polemic attacks on other journalists, slightly disguised under transparent aliases. The whole effect was that of a picaresque novel, although of dinners rather than adventures. The hero and heroine wander from restaurant to restaurant, pointing out prominent personalities to each other and gossiping about them. These youthful diners belong to the student literary milieu. Between restaurants they hint at past circle activities and conduct an inconclusive romance. Near the end of almost every episode a strange woman appears with a cryptic message or an unknown man is seen spying from behind a potted palm; the mystery is resolved the following week. It should quickly be noted that it was not for this work that Suvorin won his reputation as a feuilletonist.

Operating under the system of preliminary censorship, the newspaper printed sixteen weekly episodes of *All Sorts.* As time passed, however, the author's sallies against the censors and against reactionary aristocratic elements became steadily bolder. After September, when the paper passed under the regime of the Temporary Regulations and received its first warning almost immediately, the editor accepted only four episodes in four months. When the feuilleton characters began to note a widespread desire for a central zemstvo of zemstvos, the paper dropped the series altogether. Not wishing to see his literary labors wasted, Suvorin gathered together published and unpublished episodes, added a few extra chapters, worked up the plot a bit more fully, and had it printed as a book.[8]

Considered as a novel, *All Sorts* bears the indelible stamp of haste and journalistic origin. The plot is needlessly complex, diffuse and rambling. The principal action, concentrated in the second half of the book, has no intrinsic connection with the topical chatter of the previously published first half. Minor characters flit in and out, to vanish forever. More than one mysterious messenger is abandoned without explanation. It is easy to believe the author's courtroom contention that when he began the novel, he had no idea how it would end. The judges, however, were not interested in the artistic merit of the composition.

The major protagonist of *All Sorts* is one Peter Vasilevich Ilmenev, described as the son of a free peasant. Having finished his education in a provincial seminary, Ilmenev came penniless to Saint Petersburg, entered the Medical Surgical Academy, and after years of semi-starvation, by dedicated hard work became a doctor. During the course of the novel he rarely has a chance to practice medicine because he is constantly moving about the city just ahead of the police. Although the nature of his crime is never revealed, he is obviously well acquainted in nihilistic circles. He is sheltered by a succession of poor students, former students, and wives of exiled students, and assisted by the urban poor, his former patients, all of whom love him dearly.

In his own student days Ilmenev received encouragement and assistance from a remarkable literary personality, honored and esteemed by all who knew him, Nikolai Gavrilovich Samarskii. This was a man who lived simply, rarely slept, and devoted all his energies to his work. Calm in the strength of his convictions, he always argued effectively. Once he had taught Russian literature in a school with a strict curriculum, but he overcame that limitation by reading aloud

"Pushkin and Gogol Gogol Gogol" to the pupils. Suvorin described this man of principle with rare lyricism:

> It would be hard to find a man more honest, more ready for every good deed, more devoted to those convictions which he tried to introduce into his literary activity and to which he adhered in life. With a good man he was ready to share all; for a talented youth he paved the way. (113)

Unfortunately, an unspecified fate overtook Samarskii after a certain Telomarov prepared an expertly forged letter. As the censorship committee at once realized, all this was an "apotheosis of a state criminal"—Nikolai Gavrilovich Chernyshevskii, arrested in 1862 and convicted in 1864 on the formal evidence of a letter forged by Vsevolod Kostomarov.[9]

As Ilmenev rushes about Saint Petersburg (perhaps engaged in political propaganda?), he pauses from time to time for weighty but cryptic conversations with his friends. The censor complained with reason that Suvorin had a tendency to finish his hero's thoughts and sentences with meaningful suspension points. Consider, for example, the following exchange between Ilmenev and a young woman who has been bemoaning her husband's lost strength, wasted in prison without the slightest good result. Ilmenev discourses on "struggle," which has at last been introduced into Russian life after long years of smoothness and blissful sleep: "and struggle is a glorious school."

> [Young wife]—I understand struggle in this [Darwinian] sense, but why must you go into a frenzy, why save the moon, why imagine yourself, like Poprishchin [protagonist of Gogol's *Notes of a Madman*], to be Ferdinand VII?
> [Ilmenev]—What can one do? That's the rule, that gunpowder must flash.
> —But you see that it is flashing into the wind . . .
> —Never mind—let it flash into the wind, it will still blow up the ground at least . . . (151)

Several slightly different meanings could be read into this typical conversation. Ilmenev might be doomed by his nature, elsewhere described as honest and sincere, to flash out and perish in vain in a Russia which he himself saw was still too backward for struggle; or he might be a John the Baptist, preparing the way in the wilderness for others yet to come. Even with the most charitable will, it would be hard to suppose that Suvorin had nothing more in mind than a discussion of gunpowder.

For all these young people the purpose of life is work, a word they mention often. In only one case is the work clearly defined. The emancipated female Liudmila Ivanovna, another of Ilmenev's conversational partners, organizes numerous cooperative institutions to improve the life of poor working girls and women. Liudmila Ivanovna lives alone, with bobbed hair and simple clothing, and supports herself by making translations. The projects in which she is involved include a school for girls, a seamstresses' organization, a small notions shop, and a savings bank for women. For the future she plans apartments for women and an exclusive female printing press and journal. Although her undertakings are in some unexplained way cooperative, they are not organized along pure artel principles such as were employed by Vera Pavlovna (heroine of Chernyshevskii's account of a cooperative sewing enterprise). Liudmila Ivanovna had found that workers' collectives of that type could be lasting only when the members were of the same trade and received the same earnings. Moreover, she insisted that her cooperatives remain exclusively female; although many nihilists truly devoted themselves to women's rights, she had encountered other men "for whom words were one thing, and foul passions quite another" (168). It was for these reasons that she refused to enter into a commune organized by acquaintances, educated men and women who proposed to live all in one house and pool a percentage of their earnings for a common economy. As she predicted, it did not last. Not only did the differences in wages of members lead to its rapid demise, but the commune itself gave all sorts of fuel for slander to those from the "sphere of routine" who were only too ready to find depraved aims in it.

Suvorin returns again and again to criticism from those routinists who oppose all aspects of female emancipation. When the universities and the medical academy closed their doors to women, the routinists rejoiced; when women then flocked to special obstetrical lectures, the routinists trembled lest girls no longer remain in poetic ignorance of their own internal organs. These people of routine might be compared to the former serf owners. They know very well that the present situation of women is abnormal, but it is more convenient for them, just as life was more convenient for landowners under serf-dom. But the director of the Chief Administration of Press Affairs leapt to too hasty a judgment when he wrote after a personal exam-ination of *All Sorts* that its author denied the necessity of marriage. In fact Suvorin described marriage as a great and holy thing, when based on knowledge and freedom of choice. The routinists have made of it "simply a trap and a game of chance" (171), a judgment the censorship committee termed "most cynical."[10]

The climax of Ilmenev's wanderings comes one night as he walks disconsolately through the silent city and reviews in his mind the events of the past. A whole era of the development of the Russian intelligentsia passes before him in a few remembered scenes: a student procession to the grave of T. N. Granovskii (as proxy for his pro-scribed friend Herzen, October 1861); great fires raging in Moscow and the terrible accusation leveled at the younger generation (May 1862); the ceremony of "civil execution," performed in the rain be-fore a large and silent throng (the civil execution of Chernyshevskii, May 1864).[11] To anyone who had lived through these events, it would have been clear to what Suvorin referred. It should also have been clear that these were stages in the developing relationship of the state toward radical youth: nervous toleration, uncertain persecution, and ruthless repression.

Mixed with scenes from the social movement are Ilmenev's personal memories of his youth: his sister seduced by their former owner, his father lashed with the knout and sent into exile for killing the man, his mother following her husband to Siberia and dying there. It is clear that Ilmenev knew of what he spoke when he told a friend that one must "struggle one's whole life, struggle . . . for every piece of bread, for every thought" (149).

Ilmenev's midnight meditations build to spiritual crisis as he considers the short and ineffectual life span of his generation. Staring across the river at the dark walls of the Peter Paul Fortress Prison, he reflects that he and his kind expended their best strength, ruined themselves, and lasted less than ten years—all for the sake of the passive masses, eternally submitting to the force of circumstances, eternally concerned only with their daily bread. And the masses did not know them, the masses rejected them. "Just what are we?" he exclaims bitterly:

> Are we pioneers? are we the last of the Mohicans? . . . No one will dare to deny us honesty, nobility. But did we understand what is needed . . .? Where is our impartial judge? (222)

The voice of Life intervenes to urge that the shattered generation of the sixties prepare bold strong sons who will serve the people. "Fill them with intense love for their native land, tell them that evil is shattered not by the sword, not by . . . deceit, but by love" (224).

Purged of his self-confident pride, Ilmenev goes to visit a good, honest, open young friend, whom he discovers putting the finishing touches on a poem exhorting the emperor to an heroic exploit of compassion—"be merciful / to stray children and by a word of pardon / summon the fallen to a new life" (226). The would-be saviour of the masses looks into his friend's honest open eyes and takes him by the hand, thus ending a chapter entitled "Strength Expended in Vain."

As an answer to Ilmenev's despairing questions and a resolution of the crisis of his generation, this strange servile denouement is neither intellectually nor emotionally satisfactory. The censors did not believe in it. They concluded that although Suvorin had attempted to escape accusation by including in his work various loyal judgments, nonetheless the purpose of this key chapter was to develop the idea that the only fault of certain political agitators lay in the prematurity of their generous hopes. "In this way the reader himself should reach the inescapable conclusion that the endeavors of these persons were not in essence criminal and that if they had been supported by the people and had achieved success, then these same persons who now are exiled and prosecuted could have been called benefactors of the people."[12]

To judge from his subsequent actions, Ilmenev was not really converted by a single handclasp to what he earlier called the "sickening uniform of loyalty" so many were willing to don. In fact even before his dark night of the soul he had decided to follow the example of several minor characters and go to try his strength, ax in hand, on the virgin forests of America. En route to the New World, he stops by Siberia and rescues his father. The last pages of the novel depict them standing together at the railing of a ship as it docks in San Francisco.

Suvorin submitted his book to the Saint Petersburg censorship committee on the morning of 4 April. The student Karakozov fired his ill-aimed shot that afternoon. Two days later the police visited the printer and seized the entire edition of 1,500 copies.[13] The director of the Chief Administration of Press Affairs declared it "propaganda of communist, socialist, and materialist theories." The head of the Third Section called it anarchist and reported that the author was a known political extremist.[14] By the time the case came to trial, however, the language and tone of the indictment had been moderated considerably.

Like all press and political cases, the trial of *All Sorts* and its author attracted widespread interest in educated society. This particular case, moreover, occupied a distinctive position as the first press case to be prosecuted under the Temporary Regulations and the first to be heard in the reformed law courts established by the Judiciary Statute of 20 November 1864.[15] Thanks to publicity of proceedings, a principle embodied in the new judicial system, verbatim reports from the trial could be published by all the serious daily newspapers. Transcripts also appeared in several legal reviews which came out that year, in the first flush of happy expectation aroused by the prospect of equal justice and rule by law.[16] The open proceedings were well attended. The idolized civic poet N. A. Nekrasov was present for at least one session and composed a rhymed lament for the perished book (see epigraph of this chapter).[17]

The main points of the indictment, as brought into the Saint Petersburg district court, charged Suvorin with sympathetically representing the activities of state criminals, shaking society's trust in the government, and arousing hatred for the upper classes. Not only had he painted Chernyshevskii and various fictional nihilists, male and female, in the bright colors of martyrdom, but he had also let drop a number of unacceptable characterizations of official institutions. For example, he depicted the censorship authorities as stupid, the Temporary Regulations as more onerous than the old, and the secret police as swindlers and debauchees. At one point an agent of the police was made to boast of vile tricks and regret the passing of the days when torture was admissible during a search. The accused missed no opportunity to insult the noble rank. Referring to the Time of Troubles, he contrasted the popular assemblies to the nobility and ascribed to the former all the honor of saving the motherland; in speaking of Minin, he failed to mention Pozharskii. In short, the entire book should be destroyed.

Still the author was not so dangerous as one would suppose; the public prosecutor asked for only three months' imprisonment. Suvorin pleaded innocent, arguing that an author cannot be held responsible for the thoughts of his fictional creations. K. K. Arsenev, his defense attorney and in later years a leading representative of zemstvo liberalism, developed at length the thesis that no crime had been committed. Since the book had been seized before publication, the possibility of harm had never existed and the author's deed was at most a preparation to crime. The district court rejected this notion, but the next highest court (*sudebnaia palata*) accepted on appeal a middle position, that a crime had been attempted, but not committed.[18] Suvorin's sentence was reduced to three weeks in the local jail, while his book went into a police bonfire.

The Saint Petersburg regional court heard only one more press case of a political nature, that of the editor and author of an unsatisfactory article in the last issue of *Contemporary*. They too received only a three-week stay in jail, plus a fine of 100 rubles each. In December 1866 the minister of internal affairs managed to transfer press cases to the *sudebnaia palata* as court of first instance. From 1872 such cases were altogether removed from the competence of the courts.[19]

*   *   *

Notwithstanding a judicial verdict that *All Sorts* was written "in order to shake society's trust in the government," Suvorin's true intentions remain a puzzle. Despite his frequent protestations of objectivity and purely reportorial "photographically truthful" impulses at his trial, it is impossible to avoid the impression that none of the author's affinities lay on the side of constituted authority and the preservation of the status quo. Not a single sympathetically delineated member of the bureaucracy, the higher aristocracy, or conservative literary circles appears, although representatives of all these groups are subjected to considerable abuse by author and characters alike. Of the fictional roles, only one very minor part goes to a gentry liberal of the type with whom Suvorin was professionally associated. Stripped of its excrescent layers of gossip, *All Sorts* is a novel about the "new people," a genre which in the mid and late sixties, in several mutually hostile variants, filled the pages of literary journals of all shades of opinion.

Thanks to the ambivalent attitude of his creator, the famous iconoclast Bazarov of *Fathers and Sons* (1862) was in some sense the progenitor of all those armies of nihilists—heroes and demons— who thereupon began to troop through Russian literature. As interpreted by Pisarev, that brusque physician was accepted in the editorial offices of *Russian Word* and its successor *Cause* as a model for scores of scientifically minded fictional radicals. By rejecting Turgenev's creature as vicious caricature and libel, *Contemporary* was forced to counter with its own models, provided in abundance by Chernyshevskii's final exhortation from his prison cell. His fictionalized tract, a complex utopian novel entitled *What is to be Done? Stories about the New People,* established a whole school of literature about new men and new women.[20] Simultaneously, from the other end of the political spectrum anti-nihilist novels of varying degrees of intelligence and originality rushed to struggle on the literary front against barbarism, separatism, and revolutionary intrigue.

The censorship authorities, with considerable cause, identified *All Sorts* as a product of the nihilist camp. Indeed, it has many points of similarity in characters and themes with Chernyshevskii's novel: the radical medical student of plebeian origin, the emancipated female busy with communal schemes on behalf of the poor, the idle idiotic pastimes of high society youth and the spoiled uselessness of people from the higher circles in general, and lesser parallels. In describing his heroine's sewing cooperative, Suvorin explicitly stated to his readers that she had improved upon a similar establishment of the heroine of *What is to be Done?* On the other hand it must be admitted that all these copyings become next to meaningless when weighed against the greatest divergence of *All Sorts* from the nihilistic norm—its almost complete absence of ideas.

The radical chroniclers of the new people stuffed their novels with theories, or at least with references to the holders of theories. Their heroes and heroines exchange meaningful books, reject certain authors, and recommend scientific studies (to develop an empirical and materialist outlook). There are long pedagogic, hygienic, physiologic, and sociological conversations. By means of dreams Chernyshevskii himself managed to set forth at length both an environmental theory of personality and a precise preview of the socialist future.

In contrast to all this didacticism and intellectual name dropping, *All Sorts* contains one passing reference to Darwin and several descriptions of the personal excellences of Chernyshevskii. Where *What is to be Done?* contains usable precise directions for the establishment of a workers' artel and school, Suvorin's book sketches a whole network of institutions in a few vague lines and offers a bit of advice on the impracticability of communes. *What is to be Done?* recommended communal living and cooperative production as a higher form of social organization, a link with the masses, and a school of revolution. Can Suvorin really have thought that practicality was a prime consideration? Perhaps so. At a time when young women struggled to study medicine in order somehow to serve the people, he ascribed all their industry to the desire to live independently or to help their husbands financially (172). But then, even Suvorin's nihilists are very down-to-earth people. Ilmenev, he tells us, "looked at life in a more practical way [than did Chernyshevskii], was better acquainted with people, and saw in them more bad than good" (114). Liudmila Ivanovna, champion of the poor and of female emancipation, was "in general not carried away by bookish theories, but wished to establish only what promised genuine success" (167). Several years later, in the course of a general polemic against the aimlessness of Suvorin's feuilletons, the radicals of *Cause* reviewed *All Sorts* posthumously. They concluded that its author, having no convictions of his own and anxious to neither praise nor blame too much but to preserve his middle-of-the-road tendency, had produced a meaningless mish-mash of current phrases.[21]

If judged, as Suvorin publicly urged, as a photograph rather than a tract for the times, *All Sorts* emerges more successfully. Many of the concrete activities of the younger generation of the sixties are faithfully reflected in its pages. The female question and attendant women's activities receive full and most accurate treatment. In Saint Petersburg at that time there really was at least one Society of Inexpensive Apartments and Other Benefits for Needy Females.[22] Young women really began to study, to write, to set type. Suvorin's own wife studied midwifery and published useful books, both very popular activities. Under Chernyshevskii's inspiration sewing centers and student communes blossomed.[23] Sleptsov, for example, organized a communal home for young people, most of them women. Among the members were well-known figures of the movement for female emancipation, who at the same time established a comparatively long lived all-female translating and publishing artel.[24] It was no doubt Sleptsov's commune, which gave rise among the routinists to many snickering comments about free love, that prompted Suvorin's gratuitous suggestions on organization.

Suvorin himself once proposed yet another interpretation of *All Sorts*. Some days after Karakozov's shot he attempted to salvage his book, or at least save his skin, by writing to assure the minister of internal affairs of his good intentions. According to this letter, *All Sorts* was really an unusually clever and persuasive example of the anti-nihilist novel. The chief character, Ilmenev, was one of those who had been attracted by socialist theories. But when society met them with indignation, he voluntarily renounced these theories and recognized that he was himself a superfluous person.

> A harsh attitude to such people, as in some literary works, would not accomplish my aim, since it would irritate even people who did not share their line of thought. It seemed more advisable to represent an honest man, sincerely devoted to his convictions, and in him show all the futility and undesirability of the theories dear to him.[25]

The minister ignored this, perhaps because he could not find many people "deeply devoted to the sovereign" whom Suvorin claimed to have contrasted to the discredited radicals. But even if taken seriously, this explanation leaves unanswered Ilmenev's bitter questions. Is he just a flash of powder in the pan, or is he a premature phenomenon, a failure because, as Turgenev wrote of Bazarov, he only "stood on the threshold of the future"?[26] Whose is the "new tribe, not such as we," whom Ilmenev urges a friend to "survive and raise up" (204)? Just what did Suvorin mean to convey by the epigraph from Pushkin, which confirmed the censors in all their darkest suspicions, "Some are no more, and others far away" (title page and 201)?[27]

If the same interpretive energy and ingenuity were devoted to *All Sorts* that have been given to some other books of its period, Suvorin might well achieve a reputation as the first to propound in fiction—however obscurely—what came to be called the philosophy of small deeds. In the late sixties and early seventies there flourished a whole subcategory of radical novels whose heroes occupied themselves preeminently with peaceful construction and explained in detail to readers the workings of country schools, cheese artels, and other devices to serve the people.[28] While it is true that *All Sorts* contains no blueprints, it seems to make clear that the grandsons ("bold strong sons" of the sons) must be raised to "serve the people" (224). The nature of the service is far from explicit, but since Liudmila Ivanovna remains behind when Ilmenev leaves—and even seems to be prospering—it may be presumed the future holds a place for her not-quite-communal cooperatives and her envisioned network of self-help schemes. More striking is the sudden appearance in the last chapters (with Ilmenev doubtless well on his way across the Pacific) of an elaborate contrast between the meetings of the Saint Petersburg zemstvo assembly and the assembly of the nobility. Liudmila Ivanovna, in the company of a knowledgeable guide, visits both but finds intelligence and activity only in the first. The zemstvo delegates are debating the desirability of a central zemstvo of zemstvos, which several eloquently defend.[29] As Suvorin wrote to the minister of internal affairs, he belonged to "that literary party which in the [Emancipation] Statute of 19 February and in the Zemstvo Statute sees great guarantees for the future development of Russia."[30] Perhaps *All Sorts* can best be classified as a curious hybrid, an extraordinary blend of radical-constitutionalist views. In the following years its author moved decisively toward zemstvo liberalism, small deeds, and enthusiasm for industrialization under enlightened capitalist auspices. Soon he could write that he had "not sympathized at all with the extremely one-sided theories of *Contemporary* in the best years of its existence."[31]

chapter four

Suvorin as Liberal

> [Moscow did not make] my heart beat
> patriotically, probably because
> "Mother" Moscow to me always
> somehow resembles a priest's wife, fat,
> greasy, submissively informing her
> husband that she is content.
> —Suvorin (1870)

Following his brief imprisonment as author of *All Sorts,*
Suvorin returned to work on *Saint Petersburg Notices.*
In the course of the next eight years he perfected his skill as a political
feuilletonist and became in time one of the paper's most important
contributors.[1] During part of that period he also wrote regularly for
the monthly *Herald of Europe.* In the decade around 1870 these two
periodicals were the chief press representatives of western political
liberalism in Russia and held a place among the most widely read
publications of the era.

Herald of Europe, one of the longest-lived and surely the most
scholarly of all Russian thick journals, appeared with famed punctuality from March 1866 to March 1918. For its first two years it was a
historical quarterly; from 1868 it became a historical-political-literary
monthly. By 1872 it had a circulation of 8,000, about the same number as the then leading radical monthly *Notes of the Fatherland.*
M. M. Stasiulevich, the founder and until 1909 publisher-editor, was

a former professor of history who left the University of Saint Petersburg in 1861 as a protest against the illiberal handling of student disturbances. Initially at least, most of his close collaborators came from the same university milieu, including B. I. Utin, A. N. Pypin, K. D. Kavelin, V. D. Spasovich, and N. I. Kostomarov (the first four left when he did). Some others, such as the lawyer K. K. Arsenev, who wrote the internal survey for many decades and became editor in 1909, were active in the free professions that became significant on the basis of the Great Reforms. The journal always had a serious, objective, professorial character; even in the most heated polemics, for example, it shunned harsh invective and often even avoided naming its adversary.[2]

In a historical spirit *Herald of Europe* took its title from the earlier publication of Karamzin, Russia's first thick journal. The title also testified to the journal's self-conscious position as heir of the Westernizers in the struggle against the new phase of Slavophilism that appeared in the seventies. While the opening issue announced that Russian society had outlived the era of definite journalistic directions, it nevertheless emphasized the universalism and anti-nationalism of its outlook. "There is no people so great that it could not consider mankind its second motherland, and the higher the destiny of any people, the closer and more lively is its relationship with humanity."[3] The opening statement also called attention to the new public courts and zemstvo organizations as "schools of society." Indeed, the chief preoccupation of the early *Herald of Europe,* as of all Russian liberals in the mid-sixties, seems to have been the extension and strengthening of the zemstvo responsibility. To reach this goal publicists reported exhaustively on the activities and sessions of individual "organs for local self-government," as the zemstvo assemblies were optimistically termed. Even as a historical quarterly, *Herald of Europe* always found room for a zemstvo review in its chronicle department (which in theory ought to have chronicled the world of historical societies and archeological expeditions).

From the moment that it achieved political status, *Herald of Europe* devoted itself with energy to the defense of the Great Reforms. As Arsenev explained many years later, indecision and incomplete implementation threatened (without actually abolishing the reformed institutions) to return society in fact to the past. So-

called amendments (in reality curtailments) were continually proposed. Hence the "task of the journal, defending the good and
striving for the better, consisted above all in elucidating as clearly as
possible the merits and inadequacies of the new institutions."[4] During
the years of Suvorin's association with the journal, for example, hardly
an issue appeared without an article by Arsenev on the new judicial
system and independent bar associations, by A. A. Golovachev (of
the famous Tver zemstvo) on the still brief historical development
of the reformed institutions, or by a host of writers on the zemstvo
question and the post-emancipation problems of the peasantry. Pypin's
studies on intellectual currents in the time of Alexander I, so easily
equated with constitutional yearnings under Alexander II, caused a
stir of excitement among readers. Even the distant past had its uses.
Kostomarov provided eminently scholarly articles on the Tatar origins of Russian autocracy. He later explained that he had "attempted
to derive the character of Muscovite dominion from the very history
of its formation." And thus month by month over many years, as
another contributor wrote, *Herald of Europe* placed its dark red
monthly booklet, "like a little brick, on the slowly and arduously
erected structure of social rights and consciousness."[5]

If *Herald of Europe* represented professorial liberalism, *Saint
Petersburg Notices* under Korsh stood for a more eclectic strain. The
editor himself was a late blooming Western flower of the forties.
The foreign editor, the positivist E. K. Vatson, had formerly directed
the external political department of *Contemporary;* the regular
writer on economic questions, K. A. Skalkovskii, was a deep-dyed
"bourgeois" who urged state support for private industrialization.
V. P. Burenin, the literary critic, divided his time between *Saint
Petersburg Notices* and the radical satirical journal *Spark (Iskra)*. In
external questions, by which a Russian periodical's direction could
usually be determined, the liberal paper extended equal sympathy to
Thiers, Gambetta, Proudhon, and the Paris Communards. Nevertheless, as already seen, it became one of the first important daily newspapers in the empire and achieved a circulation of 11,000 by the
time Korsh was relieved of his franchise at the end of 1874.[6]

Saint Petersburg Notices always presented an easier and more
attractive target for radical polemic than did *Herald of Europe*.

Periodicals that stood further to the left could clarify their own positions by attacking the alleged vacillation, equivocation, and facile optimism of the liberal publication. *Notes of the Fatherland* sardonically characterized the paper's whole direction as "on the one hand, but then on the other hand." *Cause* wrote of Korsh that " 'peace and harmony' was the motto of his journalistic muse." Saltykov-Shchedrin, who produced a topical satire almost every month over many decades for a succession of oppositional journals, always caricatured the paper as "Oldest All-Russian Cream-Skimmers," a title intended to suggest both superficiality and bourgeois greed. Like *Herald of Europe, Saint Petersburg Notices* itself directed its own heaviest polemical attacks against the publications of Katkov; *Russian Herald* and *Moscow Notices* presumably served, among other things, as convenient substitutes for those high government officials who intended to amend the Great Reforms into ineffectualness. The Katkovian camp, in its turn, had no doubts about the oppositional character of the liberal newspaper. *Russian Herald* lumped *Saint Petersburg Notices* with the radical journals as part of the Saint Petersburg tendency which denied for the sake of denial, derided for the sake of derision, and claimed to have high ideals but never could explain what they were (all typical anti-left phrases of the time). Katkov's journal summed up Korsh's paper as a "daily twelve-year feuilleton."[7]

Korsh himself, in a farewell statement to readers, defined his aim as "service to society" by means of a political publication entirely independent from any government department or partisan influence —a clearly liberal volley against the right, the extreme left, and the bureaucracy.[8] His newspaper, like *Herald of Europe,* supported the reformed institutions and the principles of self-administration which were supposed to lie at their base. From the moment of promulgation of the Zemstvo Statute in 1874, the paper defended local self-government and urged its extension. The editorial offices became an unofficial headquarters and information clearinghouse for zemstvo members visting the capital. During the mid-sixties the paper received much unwelcome attention from the censors; according to the government, it was engaging in censure of the administration in general and in hostile comparison of the latter with the zemstvo organizations, whose significance and role it persisted in misinterpreting. In April

1866, for example, it was warned for a particularly sharp article in which it not only detailed the systematic opposition of various official organs to zemstvo units, but also made plain to its readers that the bureaucracy was in fact hostile to the imperial intentions and thought only of enlarging its own independent power; if the "patriotic temper of the time" were truly understood, it would be plain that the zemstvos alone were devoted to the sovereign. Continued infractions in this vein led to suspension, after which the paper calmed down considerably. In general, however, disappointment with officially imposed limitations created a decline in interest in the zemstvo movement on the part of educated society during the period around 1870.[9]

During the early seventies the educational question replaced the zemstvo question as the single most burning issue in the liberal press. Early in 1871 *Herald of Europe* went so far as to say that the struggle against the classical curriculum of Katkov and D. A. Tolstoi was the "most important matter of the present moment."[10] When Korsh lost his license to edit *Saint Petersburg Notices,* it was for his paper's constant attacks on the minister of public education and his so-called system of Greco-Roman bondage. Ultimate ownership of the newspaper was transferred from the Academy of Sciences to the Ministry of Public Education, as part of a plot to let Katkov take it over as a colonial outpost of his empire. The plan failed when Korsh sold the remaining years of his publisher's lease to the banker-publisher F. P. Baimakov. The paper declined rapidly and never again assumed social significance.[11]

Not the least of links between the two liberal publications was a certain duplication of personnel. Suvorin, Korsh, Vatson, and other newspapermen contributed at some time to *Herald of Europe,* while Arsenev, Stasiulevich, and the historian M. P. Dragomanov found time to write occasionally for *Saint Petersburg Notices.* When Korsh lost his newspaper, he briefly joined the journal before attempting to launch another periodical of his own. By that time, however, Suvorin was no longer associated with *Herald of Europe.* Despite the enthusiastic recommendations of Ivan Turgenev, Stasiulevich failed to invite him to resume work.[12]

*   *   *

When Count E. A. Salias took over direction of *Saint Petersburg Notices* on the first day of 1875, the entire staff of writers departed with their former editor-publisher. As Suvorin explained, the total freedom and moral independence Korsh had given his writers had also spoiled them for work under other conditions. The very first issue under the new editor (and erstwhile Jacobin) hurled verbal missiles at the zemstvo, the new courts, and other products of the Great Reforms to which the Korshites were so devoted.[13]

Although the new year brought Suvorin the distress of temporary unemployment, it marked the apogee of his acclaim as a liberal publicist. He was the object of formal ovations. In March two volumes of his stories and feuilletons appeared; by April they had gone into a second printing. Even the populist journalists—or at any rate some of them—managed to find a sympathetic word for Suvorin. Since he had held no public office or administrative position, all of Suvorin's reputation rested on words. Not only had he provided feuilletons and theatrical reviews to *Saint Petersburg Notices* for almost a decade, but for three years he had also written book reviews and articles for *Herald of Europe*. He and his publishing associates had continued to issue a small number of uplifting titles: a translation of Samuel Smiles, for example. From 1872 he had begun to publish an annual calendar of the now common sort which gave more space to statistics of social and economic life than to religious fast days and the phases of the moon. It achieved immediate success.[14]

Suvorin was not a man given to theoretical speculations. His liberal writings were distinguished more by easy wit and vivid reportage than by any sign of systematic social analysis or deep thought. Even his longest and most serious book reviews—as on works of John Stuart Mill and Saltykov-Shchedrin—lack the philosophical atmosphere of a review by Belinskii or Dobroliubov, or even by his hated contemporary and rival, Katkov. If we accept Suvorin as a mirror of his era, as did the radical populist N. V. Shelgunov, then we must agree with the latter's dictum that "that intelligentsia, which once in former times thought and wished to think consistently and theoretically, has already vanished."[15] Nonetheless, it is possible to distinguish in Suvorin's work certain leading

themes and concerns, and even to give them some systematic arrange-
ment, without gravely misrepresenting the nature of his publicistic
activity.[16]

As a liberal publicist, Suvorin wrote on behalf of reason, freedom, education, public hygiene, and progress. He despised reactionaries, quack spiritualists, and bloated plutocrats. One of his favorite
words was civilization, a shorthand term for everything associated
with modern technology, western European social development, and
Russian small deeds liberalism.[17]

Although Suvorin repeatedly cautioned his readers that grovel-
ling self-abasement before other nations was as baseless and harmful
as the more common notion of some special Slavic mission was
fanciful, implicit in all his other advice was the idea that the light
comes from the West. He accepted as self-evident the proposition
that certain historical phenomena—civil liberty, capitalism, the proletariat—appear sooner or later inescapably in all "modern countries."
But the bitter truth was, as he reported ruefully after his first trip abroad
in 1870, that Russia was far behind Europe and would have to work
very hard to catch up, especially since Europe was not going to wait
for Russia.

In his analysis of the Russian historical experience, Suvorin presented a paradigm of every Slavophile's nightmare. Once, in the
Russian lands, all had been darkness, ignorance, and degradation.
Peter I brought the light of day when he undertook to educate the
previously barbarous gentry. Slowly, over the period of a century,
"the best part of the gentry freed themselves from their slavish
habits and began to resemble Europeans." In the recent past, the
Great Reforms had introduced a new phase of the same enlightening process; the remaining estates were set free and European or
Europeanizing institutions established (reformed law courts, zemstvos,
widened educational opportunities). The old calm and sleep had been
broken forever. But all this did not proceed without opposition. In
fact, there was much similarity between Suvorin's own time and the
epoch of Peter I:

Then as now the social forces were divided into two camps and
struggled with each other, sometimes openly, sometimes secretly—the

camp of sympathizers with the reforms and with the influence of the new life, and the camp opposed to them.

The enemies of the new life, according to Suvorin, came chiefly from the conservative gentry who had never accepted the principles of 19 February 1861 and were trying by every means to reverse or at least to nullify the social changes inaugurated by emancipation. In the late fifties the intellectual atmosphere had been so liberal that these unreconstructed serfowners hid themselves in silence or even waxed sentimental over human brotherhood and the Russian peasant, although "this affection did not prevent them from depriving the peasant of his best lands and inventing uprisings, and demanding troops for their suppression." In the soberer sixties the conservatives surfaced again, alternately reminding the government of their devotion and threatening unspeakable dangers on the horizon. These self-styled sincere and incorruptible sons of the fatherland early discovered the nihilist as a convenient new Antichrist and the source of all calamities. Now, from (short-sighted) economic motives, their spokesmen were producing all sorts of projects for restoring their former power: organization of a new class of larger land owners to replace the old noble estate, judicial control by the rural gentry over the peasantry, and so forth. But, Suvorin asked, should the government "preserve and reward those who strive to arrange the security of their little group at the expense of the poverty of millions, and who suspect even philanthropy as revolutionary propaganda?"[18]

Suvorin answered his own question in the negative and took it upon himself to expose the illogicality, hypocrisy, and malice of these apostles of reaction. In his opinion the danger from the right was very real. The enemy was energetic and scheming, and sufficiently clever to mask its opposition to the Great Reforms under attacks on radicalism, peasant drunkenness, and the alleged fall in agricultural productivity.[19] Hence he devoted much effort to wiping away the moderate and loyal colorations from their statements, to reveal the serf-owning world-view which lay behind them. He kept careful check on their newspapers. He attentively followed the proceedings of provincial zemstvo assemblies and assemblies of nobility, especially in the two capital districts, and analyzed important developments in them, which were chiefly verbal in nature. In his newspaper feuilletons he exposed the impudent machinations of the aristocratic party as it attempted to gain control of those lawful deliberative bodies. In literary reviews he ridiculed the "reform" proposals and political maunderings of such men as Prince P. N. Trubetskoi and Grigorii Blank, of reactionary zemstvo renown, or General Rostislav Fadeev, of a certain Yacht Club party—which, according to Suvorin, had "decided to form a powerful class of rich people, on the model of the English aristocracy, and to take all power exclusively into their own hands."[20] In fact, he often hinted that the enemies of the new life were to be found preeminently among the wealthy and highly placed. For example, he repeatedly linked them to the arrogant young generals and half-witted princes, all of the highest society, in Turgenev's famous acidic portrait of Russia's would-be oligarchs *en pique-nique*.[21] More than once Suvorin pointed out that he opposed any sort of coup d'état, even of the cultured classes, fully as much as he would oppose the horrors of a Russian peasant uprising.

The cornerstone of all reforms, and the chief target of reactionary scheming, was the liberation of the serfs. Suvorin's foremost defense of peasant freedom lay in pointing out in a hundred subtle ways that emancipation had become the law of the land and those who opposed it were in opposition to the government, an institution he apparently considered to be independent of the nobility and non-class in character. Cunning reactionaries now tried to show that the liberated peasant had grown lazy, disrespectful, and depraved; he was a wild child who needed the control of a stern and just father, the former serf-owner. Suvorin entertained no illusions about the coarseness of village life; rather he argued that, first, the situation had been even worse before 1861, and second, the cure for centuries of slavery is not further "guardianship" but its opposite. He attributed rural impoverishment not to sloth and strong drink but to insufficient lands, heavy taxation, and especially the failure of the gentry to educate the peasant and open for him new sources of productivity and wealth. Peter I had created his new nobility on the sacrifices of the peasantry; now both justice and intelligent self-interest demanded that the nobility enlighten the peasantry. As for the confusion and dislocations arising from the emancipating law itself, the solution lay not in amendments or alterations but rather in "realizing the consequences which logically arise from this statute."[22] Although the precise nature of these logical consequences was not elaborated, they clearly included three proposals that Suvorin warmly supported: abolition of class privilege, increased scope of activity for the zemstvo assemblies, and equalization of the tax burden (preferably as zemstvo delegates might work out). Rarely, and only indirectly, did he hint at the possibility of a national assembly or a fundamental organic law.[23]

Although dangerous, the aristocratic party (or *barstvo,* as Suvorin also liked to call his adversary) was small in numbers. Most of the gentry, including many ancient families, allied themselves with the zemstvo party, the party of those who understood their enlightening task. These people willingly participated in the new courts and the zemstvo assemblies. The best of them selflessly strove to establish literacy and to cover Russia with trade schools, inexpensive books, and better agricultural methods.[24]

At first Suvorin hoped for great accomplishments from the zemstvo, especially in the field of education. With the other writers of *Saint Petersburg Notices,* he publicized the activity of the assemblies and defended them from their ill-wishers. In the late sixties he attempted to organize publication of a reference calendar for popular dissemination of "independent ideas." One of the chief ideas was to have been an ardent apologia of the new institutions for self-government.[25] Whether owing to the disillusionment with heavily restricted zemstvo "autonomy" which Suvorin shared with other liberals in the early seventies, or for some other reason, that institution occupied only a comparatively modest position in the calendar by the time it finally appeared in 1872. Suvorin pointed out that zemstvo activity had been successful only in three provinces which enjoyed especially good relations between the zemstvo personnel and the provincial administration. Not only were zemstvo responsibilities restricted and activities generally constrained by administrative control, but also limited means hampered action even in permitted areas. Making his customary unflattering comparison to foreign conditions (in this case, English and Prussian rural self-government), he concluded that an income tax constituted the "only just and rational" way to finance the zemstvo.[26]

As might be expected, Suvorin saw the greatest threat to the zemstvo in the so-called aristocrats and in the imperial administration, although he could only hint at the machinations of the latter. Even if he never explicitly said so, he would seem generally to have subscribed to the dictum, "no enemy on the left." In Suvorin's own era, under Peter I, and presumably at other times too, there existed only the two basic camps of progressives and reactionaries. "Each camp, of course, consisted of several divisions, separated from each other not so much by inherent as by outwardly perceptible signs."[27] Despite frequent attacks on him from the radical press, he confined most of his own direct literary onslaughts to the struggle against reaction.[28]

An outstanding exception to this rule was the sharp criticism Suvorin several times leveled against the mordant social commentaries of Saltykov-Shchedrin, then writing in *Notes of the Fatherland* and hotly defended by his colleagues and by the politically sympathetic satirical weekly *Spark*. Suvorin praised his wit and accusatory talent, promising him a future place among the Russian classics. He especially admired Saltykov-Shchedrin's representations of certain heritages of serfdom: arbitrariness, predatoriness, bowing before rude force. He was delighted by the "pioneers" of his *Provincial Letters* (1869), new people "distinguished by their ability, discretion, and independence of conviction." But he could not let pass without challenge Saltykov-Shchedrin's mockery of both the zemstvo men and the Russian common people (*narod*). The chief cause of this ill-timed, misdirected, and even harmful humor, Suvorin found in the satirist's lack of a definite positive philosophy. Unable to base his work on the firm soil of an "established, deeply thought out political or social teaching," he too often fell into vagueness, light skepticism, and transitory caricature.[29]

Interestingly enough, this is the same argument as that periodically advanced against Saltykov-Shchedrin by the strict utilitarians of the Russian Word-Cause school of radical criticism—although not in order to defend the zemstvo. Pisarev established the critical tradition when he attacked the satirist for wasting his talent on idea-less humor and laughter for the sake of laughter, or on situations already a part of the past. His attack constituted one of the chief volleys in that battle between the two principal radical journals of the early sixties which Dostoevskii promptly dubbed "the raskol of the nihilists." Saltykov-Shchedrin himself, writing later about similar accusations by Suvorin and others, claimed that Pisarev's allegation sprang from personal hostility. In fact, as Pisarev's original article clearly states and his entire intellectual position at that time supports, he criticized the satirist for failing to provide Russian youth with positive models for present and future activity. His ideological heirs on the staff of *Cause* continued to find Saltykov-Shchedrin socially useless.[30]

It is difficult to assess Saltykov-Shchedrin's political position. He certainly attacked certain institutions and strata of society more often and more virulently than others. One scholar found throughout his work basic recurrent themes, among the most important of which were the mirage of reforms from above and the essential kinship of liberalism and conservatism in Russia.[31] Saltykov-Shchedrin also decried industrialization and the development of a class of capitalist entrepreneurs; at the same time, he heaped scorn on the populists and the peasantry. Thus, the objects of his positive support are problematic.[32] Part of the problem may lie in the obscurity of the satirist's famous Aesopian language. Whatever the value of his other thoughts on Saltykov-Shchedrin's work, Suvorin certainly was correct when he pointed out that in ten years most of it would be as hard to read as the works of mystics and Masons.[33]

Suvorin and at least one of Pisarev's heirs moved along parallel tracks in their distress over Saltykov-Shchedrin's widely acclaimed *History of a Certain Town* (1869–1870). The satirist painted in detail and with many grotesqueries (including the famous governor whose head was made of sausage) an unrelievedly cheerless portrait of the town of Foolsburg (*Glupov*), a locality whose history is remarkably reminiscent of the Russian Empire during the last half of the eighteenth and the first quarter of the nineteenth centuries. Suvorin devoted a special long review to analyzing the errors of this bleak little book. First, he found, it divided the entire population of Foolsburg into capricious, exploiting masters and passive, exploited *narod*. Hence it failed to note certain positive elements of the period; for example, the Russian encyclopedists and Voltaireans of the time of Catherine II. In other words, it omitted all mention of that progressive company of enlightened, reforming people, necessarily from the privileged classes, whose representatives in every possible era and field of activity—Nil of Sorsk, Antioch Kantemir, M. M. Speranskii, even Iurii Samarin—Suvorin was accustomed to hold up before his readers as positive examples and living contrasts to the benighted reactionary *boiarstvo*.

In fact Saltykov-Shchedrin had not found a single ray of enlightenment or wind of change worth mentioning in all of Foolsburg. This was not because he subscribed to any sort of populist faith in the pristine folk. Suvorin's second and even weightier accusation found the satirist occupying a "historically and artistically false" position in his view of that folk. Specifically, Saltykov-Shchedrin depicted them as totally passive and feebleminded.

> His Foolsburgers are so stupid, so thoughtless, so idiotic and worthless that the stupidest and most worthless master [must] seem to them to be a higher being whose equal they cannot imagine coming from their own ranks. The thought naturally comes to the reader that the Foolsburgers should thank God even for the masters that they have . . .

Assuring his readers that he was no Slavophile and had no intention of bowing down to the Russian peasantry, Suvorin nonetheless affirmed his own esteem for the *narod* and his faith in their creative powers, past, present and future:

> We esteem this people and see in them every inclination for development. Thanks to these people a state was created. Thanks to them there appeared the intelligentsia, literature, art, and various other comforts of life.

The famous satirist, on the other hand, was simply mocking the people.[34]

A venomous but not always enlightening polemic, typical of the literary battles continually raging in Saint Petersburg, followed upon this criticism. Saltykov-Shchedrin reacted immediately with an angry letter to the editorial board of *Herald of Europe,* in which he asserted that his satire was not of a historical but of an ordinary nature. If the conditions and habits he described had vanished along with the eighteenth century, there would be no reason to attack them today. Hence Suvorin's objections, based on an erroneous understanding of the author's purpose, were all false or irrelevant. Furthermore, the word *narod* must be understood in two senses, "the historic people" and "the people as incarnation of the idea of democracy." One ought to extend sympathy to the former only to the degree of their own effort to achieve consciousness. Contrary to Suvorin's assertion, compassion would be entirely out of place in satire, since the readers would not know which elements were truthfully represented and which were softened by misplaced magnanimity.[35] As the satirist expected, the editors of *Herald of Europe* deemed it unwise to publish such a statement.

Saltykov-Shchedrin presented an elaboration of the last elements of the above argument to the general public. In the next issue of *Notes of the Fatherland* he incorporated an attack on the "conciliatory" theory of humor into an anonymous review of the works of N. A. Leikin, a second rank writer who specialized in the unattractive life of small tradesmen. Briefly touching on the dishonesty, drunkenness, and ignorance of these people, Saltykov-Shchedrin pointed out with his usual tortuous obscurity that they nonetheless regarded themselves as pillars and foundation stones of property, family, religion, and public tranquillity. They were "not at all defenseless orphans, as sentimentalizing lovers of the people imagine them," but rather dangerous men who blocked achievement of consciousness. If history oppressed them, one must also admit they oppress history. Consequently, there can be no question of compassion; try to embrace them and they'll just bite you. The theory of a "certain critic" that humor ought to lower the great, raise the lowly, and comfort the afflicted, would lead to an incorrect description of society, confusion on the part of readers, and consolidation for all time of the forces of the mighty.[36]

Suvorin replied, equally anonymously, in his own review of Leikin's work. Where Saltykov-Shchedrin hailed his ethnographic realism, Suvorin questioned the exactness of Leikin's descriptions and found his stories no more than accusatory. Suvorin evidently based this opinion more on his antagonist's review than on Leikin's original work, since he proceeded to explain that the true artist learns to know the people and represents them realistically, without worrying that they may bite him. Only "rather shallow satirists and too elegant gentlemen" accuse the oppressed man and explain to him that in his turn he oppresses history. The noblest feature of the present period, the high task of progress, lie alike in striving to remove from the *narod* the heavy yoke of an unjust history. If, however, literature lashes the oppressed with the whip of satire and represents them as uglier than the oppressors, it will fail to gain sympathy and even prove harmful. The satirist cannot serve two masters—the oppressors and the people.[37]

It should be noted that all Suvorin's objections were ultimately practical, since he as well as his radical opponents accepted without question the notion that literature ought to have clear and immediate social purpose. Not only was the passivity and worthlessness of Saltykov-Shchedrin's *narod* false objectively, but also it demonstrated his incomprehension of the correct task of the writer. Ivan Turgenev, Charles Dickens, and Harriet Beecher Stowe had all understood the necessity of truly knowing the people and even at times of idealizing them, for in the service of eternal truth a degree of idealization can be true and just. Moreover, he who would evaluate the historical people must deeply know them and distinguish between their original nature and the modifications produced by historical conditions and oppressors. Hence Suvorin felt himself justified in asking to what extent Saltykov-Shchedrin could have correctly evaluated the people,

> if he represents the governors as better than the peons, and if he knows that his work is read not by the people but by governors and candidates for governor, and if he attaches any value to the moral influence of his satire on contemporaries?[38]

Suvorin received no answer to his question. In fact, on this issue he found himself isolated. His own newspaper, along with all other press organs which in any way aspired to be thought progressive, praised *History of a Certain Town* as yet another brilliant book by Russia's greatest contemporary satirist. Support from several minor aristocratic publications can hardly have been welcome; important conservative periodicals, such as those of Katkov, usually did not deign to note the appearance of a new work by Saltykov-Shchedrin. *Cause* also refrained from comment during these years, but its editor G. E. Blagosvetlov was heard to exclaim angrily about those who were calling the satirist a new and better Swift. "Allow me to ask you, lovers of the people—whom does your great Shchedrin mock? The government? No, not the government, but the Russian people."[39]

His profound esteem for the "historical people" did not blind Suvorin to the development of new socio-economic formations in Russia. Unlike the Slavophiles, most of the populists, and many official censors, he clearly saw as early as the late sixties that the "development of manufacturing, the formation of capital and of its strength" were already irretrievably under way. The (industrial) worker question already existed, and in time would assume in Russia the foremost position it already occupied in the West. In fact, he asserted, society was becoming more and more conscious that the whole structure of social life was connected with the worker question. Nevertheless, Russian journalism usually ignored the issue at home, although it often dealt with the worker movement in the West. The needs of the future demanded careful and thorough study of Russian factory conditions, strikes, artels, and so forth. Starting later, Russia could profit by the experiences and solutions of others. Consequently, although the worker question was far from being his major preoccupation, Suvorin occasionally took time in his reviews to welcome new studies on such subjects as German trade unions or the life expectancy of the Russian working class.

In Suvorin's opinion, the advantage of foreknowledge lay in the opportunity to choose reconciliation rather than revolution. The chief means for peaceful improvement of the worker's living standard he found in association—not only organizations to extract higher wages from the capitalists, but also such devices as savings and mutual credit associations or medical aid societies. He praised the artel, the native form of production cooperative. He went so far as to agree with the populist V. V. Bervi-Flerovskii that it would be more rational for the state to hand over the working of the Siberian goldfields to workers' artels than to a privileged class of monopolists (granted the monopolists in question were foreigners).[40] If Suvorin thought the teachings of the utopian socialists threatened him and his kind, he gave no public sign of it. Thus, he expressed regret that Ernst Becher's *Die Arbeiterfrage* (1863) gave so little space to the theories of Saint-Simon, Fourier, and others.[41] He cited with approval the same author's conclusion that a strong state power was necessary to support the workers against the capitalists, although he either would not or could not draw the inference desired by the Russian editor, that such a government will be effective only when it is in the hands of the workers. A short time later he recommended for the mass of the reading public a sympathetic outline of socialist systems as propounded in France for more than half a century.[42]

If column inches form a valid indicator of concern, Suvorin was far more interested in the pursuit of civil liberties than in the problems of the working classes. Like his fellow liberals, he supported freedom and freedoms. As a reviewer of serious books, one of his major preoccupations was with the harmfulness of censorship. Russian writers, he pointed out, had a tendency to die young. The implication was that censorship and official harassment were responsible. Freedom of the press was necessary not only for national literary development. Only a free discussion of governmental administration could keep the bureaucracy honest and active. Editors of the local press knew more about deeds of local bureaucrats than did the higher authorities—as the latter were well aware. On a higher level, the colossal plundering that led to the tragic debacle at Sevastopol (to take an example Suvorin used more than once) would have been impossible without censorship. Hence publicity was as necessary to the ruler as to the ruled. In his enthusiastic account of Mill's *On Liberty,* Suvorin gave particular attention to the English philosopher's analysis of those dangers a ruler faces from his civil servants, who can by simple passivity impede all his reforms and in fact control him. The unchecked bureaucracy enslaves the ruler, the ruled, and its own members. Austria and France, he pointed out, had fallen behind their neighbors in recent years and lost the power of initiative, precisely because opinion and criticism had been suppressed.[43]

Economic development as well as administrative efficacy would result from increased civil liberties. One of Suvorin's boldest and most notable feuilletons, according to his admirers, was that in which he explained the true causes of prosperity to the Russian industrialist V. A. Poletika. At a speech in celebration of the launching of a warship built by his shipyard, Poletika had complained that the whole of Europe was milking Russia; the imperial government favored foreign entrepreneurs, while it should favor Russians. To this Suvorin replied forthrightly that European economic advance derived from the area's "freedom of economic and civil life." The Russian people were as gifted and hard working as any other but would gain little even if the government gave millions of orders to Poletika's factory. Russia would achieve economic progress and economic independence when its inhabitants enjoyed economic freedom. The success of an undertaking ought to "depend exclusively upon our own energy, our own diligence, our own enlightenment." As for the future of the working class, Europe again showed the way as Suvorin returned once more to his familiar theme of social reconciliation through worker association:

> At a time when we are just beginning to organize companies of capitalists, Europe is already covered by associations of workers . . . there are already examples of the capitalist and factory owner who is not limited by the worker's daily pay but gives him a share in his enterprise . . . [*sic*][44]

The spiritual side of life was another important area requiring liberty for its fullest and most satisfactory development. The intolerant tradition of Joseph of Volokolamsk and his followers, which had passed into the whole organization of the Orthodox Church, was doing great harm to the cause of the spirit. The rigid religious censorship, which refused to allow works that the civil censor might pass, inhibited the most pious and moral men from discussing the condition of the clergy or from attempting to reconcile the Church with science and the enlightened demands of universal brotherhood. Only freedom of discussion within the Church and freedom of conscience for all men could permit true religion, "based on the great foundations of the Gospels," to penetrate among the masses.[45]

The Josephite tradition lay behind the continued legal persecution of the *Raskol* (Schism). As Suvorin liked to point out, Protestants, Catholics, and even Moslems enjoyed greater rights than schismatics. Yet the disabilities of *raskolniki* were illogical, inhumane, and in fact seemed to strengthen the most extreme and anti-government elements among them.

The sixties witnessed the birth of a great historical-sociological interest in the numerous and highly varied sects of the so-called Old Believers. Suvorin devoted considerable review space to publicizing some of the fruits of this interest and summarizing their more or less scholarly findings at length. He sternly refuted those writers who found the schismatics lazy and hostile to enlightenment, while he praised confessional freedom, civil marriage, and universal education. Although he recognized the "ignorant fanaticism" of some Old Believers (an early off-shoot from the same Josephite intolerance), he noted with sympathy the striving of others for a simple evangelical life, as in the earliest days of Christianity. To the other religions of the empire's peoples, he gave no attention.

A second depressed group whose legal disadvantages aroused the attention of the press in the sixties was that of women. Their access to higher education constituted the most pressing aspect of the female question and the only one to which Suvorin in this period applied himself in earnest. In the late sixties he was so unwise as to express reservations about female aptitude and about the strength of motivation of the young women who—their path blocked in Russia —were traveling to Switzerland to study medicine. By the early seventies, however, he could assure his readers that he had always admired the Russian woman—be her hair long or bobbed. After examining the experience of female students at the University of Zurich during a decade, he reported that women had proven themselves entirely capable of higher education and in fact were well suited to the tasks of medical practice. On a wider plane he enthusiastically seconded Mill's argument in *On the Subjection of Women* that women have a right to education and are no doubt fully as capable as men of professional and administrative work.[46]

Whether from comparative lack of interest or because of the dangers inherent in such a delicate matter, Suvorin had little to say about nationalism, Russian or non-Russian, within the empire or in Turkish or Austrian lands, except as it bore on his running polemic with the ultra-nationalist foe to the right.[47] He repeatedly held up to ridicule the grotesque discovery, allegedly made by Katkov in 1863 and urged by him ever since, that all evils came from the Poles (or from nihilist intriguers). Katkov's trumpetings had made thousands of separatists where once there were only hundreds, in addition to laying a "firm ground for reaction and demoralization." Suvorin several times exposed the falsity and chauvinism of works on Poland of Katkovian tendency. In one such work he did find a few "healthy thoughts" put forward, such as freedom of conscience and the introduction into the western provinces of "all the institutions existing in Russia" (presumably he meant chiefly zemstvo organizations).[48]

This "police-patriotism" of the right unfortunately cropped up from time to time elsewhere as well. Thus, Suvorin wrote with regret that his friend Nikitin's early verses, written in the mid-fifties, had "knuckled under to that patriotic-drumming clatter . . . heard at the time of the Crimean War from even such an uncommon poet as Maikov."[49] It must be noted that Suvorin entertained a certain suspicion of standing armies and the whole brotherhood of military officers.

Similarly, Suvorin refused to be drawn into the clamor against the Baltic Germans, whose alleged separatism was agitating the ultra-nationalist press. He went so far as to write that Samarin's famous denunciations gave a one-sidedly black picture of the situation. This, however, in no way blinded Suvorin to the fact that legally free peasant tenants in fact were held in debt slavery. He pointed out the hypocrisy of German apologists who spoke of the great sacrifices they had made when they freed their serfs, without land, half a century before, and who now tried to justify economic oppression as the price of freedom. At any rate, the Baltic barons and their Katkovian foe had much in common. As Suvorin once pointed out, the reactionary party revealed itself at various times in various ways, "now with a primordial Russian [Slavophile] hue, now with a Baltic hue, now with an English aristocratic hue."[50]

On the Ukrainophile question he was serene and conciliatory. All the accusations of separatism simply proved that the people of the southwest were no more than devoted to their own songs. Further,

if they write in Little Russian, others write in German; if they want to teach the people literacy in Little Russian—well, it makes the transition from a local dialect to the Russian language easier.[51]

This contribution to the philosophy of the golden mean was written in 1874, at the height of polemic by conservative periodicals in Kiev and Moscow against Ukrainophile literary activity and against the suggested use of the Ukrainian language in popular elementary schools. Both *Herald of Europe* and *Saint Petersburg Notices* came out firmly on the side of the Ukrainophiles, largely through the articles of the historian Dragomanov, their regular writer on questions concerning the "political situation of the so-called South-Western Region."[52] Suvorin, as may be seen, upheld the position of his colleagues; yet his own interests lay more in the civil rights of Russian educated society than in the national rights of minority peoples.

*   *   *

Before considering Suvorin's relationship to other "journalism parties," it would be well to define his own place as he saw it in the Russian social movement. The intelligentsia of each generation early developed a cult of ancestors and conducted a running analysis of their own place in the history of the intelligentsia. If Suvorin indulged in such retrospective self-measurement, the conclusions have not come to light. Nonetheless, it may at least be said that he thought himself enough the heir of the oppositional past to defend its leading figures on occasion. Thus, he praised Belinskii's beneficial influence on society and exposed the exploitation of the ailing critic by his editor, Kraevskii. (True, Suvorin was at that moment engaged in polemic with publications controlled by that same Kraevskii.) He defended Chernyshevskii from the slanders of Leskov and from the greed of speculators who endangered the exile's position by printing his works abroad.[53]

Throughout his writing in this period Suvorin displayed many of the standard signals that ordinarily identified the left. He venerated George Sand, considered the nurturing mother of the generation of the forties. He detested Leskov, Vsevolod Kostomarov, V. P. Avenarius, and other anti-nihilist novelists. He praised the historian Friedrich Christoph Schlosser and despised the despot Napoleon III. Most of all he loathed the journalists of the ultra-nationalist and aristocratic camps—with whom, however, the genuine radicals usually concerned themselves much less. Even when his enthusiasms paralleled those of the left, the political content and intent may have been quite different. For example, Suvorin, the accusatory authoress M. A. Marko-Vovchok, *Notes of the Fatherland, Cause,* and the anti-nihilist monthly *World's Work* (*Vsemirnyi trud*) all published translations of *L'Homme qui rit* by Victor Hugo in the same year, almost simultaneously.[54] The radicals undoubtedly admired this novel for its democratic sympathy with the oppressed English masses and its exposure of the empty pretenses which passed for law and government in the cradle of liberalism and capitalism. Suvorin's interest, on the other hand, most likely derived first and foremost from his preoccupation with the plots and schemes of native would-be oligarchs. *L'Homme qui rit* was another weapon in his struggle against Katkov, whose English proclivities were well known, and against all those who dreamed of aristocratic oligarchy. Hugo had revealed the "dark side of the English aristocracy, ordinarily concealed by its glitter." He had depicted the world's best such body of men, and thereby had demonstrated "that even the best aristocracy, by all its merits, does not redeem the humiliated position of the people."[55]

As already noted, Suvorin expected literature to contain definite ideas and habitually judged literary works by their social usefulness. For intellectual nourishment he recommended the modern authors, from Gogol on, and stated firmly that earlier writers were irrelevant. At the same time he evidently considered himself a sensitive judge of artistic talent and achievement. He would explain at length that some novel had a feeble plot or weak characterization, only to conclude by recommending it "for its humanitarian thought" or "as a program for those who wish to be useful." He condemned harmful ideas and writers who failed to serve their calling well. For example, he criticized *Anna Karenina* not only as a rejection of the intellect and a modern version of the sentimental literature of shepherdesses and lambs, but also complained that a serious writer should not be so narrow and so egotistical as was Tolstoi. "The private person . . . may build himself such an ideal of the vegetable life, but the novelist should stand higher than that."[56]

It is true that he criticized the stereotyped action and characters of the plebeian school of writers, all of whose heroes seemed to be perfect in every way, "born fresh like Adam."[57] Although he noted the one-sidedness of this "literature of the sons," as well as the greater talent and even objectivity of the best of the fathers, this was not, it seems, because he wished to approve conservative themes or condemn the ideals of the "new people." Indeed, most of the plebian literary product of that time was less accusatory than instructive, and if heeded, would have led to the organization of schools, production artels, and similar culture-bearing projects of the sort Suvorin himself urged. Hence he wished not to discontinue the product, but to offer advice on its improvement. An idea, to be effective, must be presented in a palatable setting—neither dull, nor obscure, nor unbelievable. Artistry, as praised in his reviews, seems simply to be an objective and realistic representation of life; accusatory writing, on the other hand, easily fell into caricature, distortion, even falsehood. Thus, when he wrote that the time for accusatory literature had passed, he was not only defending the zemstvo and *narod* from untoward attack. When he urged the greater usefulness of ethnographic description, he was not only upholding moderation against radical extremes. In the final analysis, he meant that the most truthful book was the most effective.

For Suvorin the forties had been a time of high ideals and magnanimous impulses, mingled with absence of initiative or perseverance. He once likened the period to the French forties of Gustave Flaubert's cheerless exercise in pitiless realism, *L'Éducation sentimentale*—and not only because both generations ended under the harsh vengeance of reactionaries.[58] But for the sixties, "the spring of liberalism," the "time of young enthusiasms" and the time when he himself was young, Suvorin always retained a special affection. He defended the memory of those years from the renegade accusations of Leskov. One might speak about them only "in a tone of benevolence and love." It was a time of long and emotional arguments about constitutionalism, socialism, Fourierism, and similar seemingly important matters—a time when even the wisest of men were "carried away by impossible fancies."[59] And it was precisely this question of impossible fancies that in the final analysis separated Suvorin the liberal from those further to the left. The new people, no matter how much they might seem to be consuming their energies on the management of cheese artels, never lost faith in the possibility of great and abrupt political changes in the near future. If only the right tactic, or the right organization, or the right contact with the masses could somehow be found, the revolution could be made. Suvorin's hopes for the forseeable future seem to have gone no further than "small deeds" and the defense of reforms already granted. Nor did he share the talismans of the radicals. He was capable of publicly dismissing the theorists of utopian socialism as insignificant. In a "Philosophical Dictionary" which breathed hatred for aristocracy, plutocracy, and bureaucracy, he defined the sacred word Revolution as a "French expression, consisting in taking a step forward and two steps back."[60] Probably he agreed with a once celebrated *Herald of Europe* article in which Arsenev explained the fruitlessness of secret political societies under Russian conditions. History revealed the impossibility of radical upheavals that did not arise from already altered intellectual conditions and realignment of social forces.[61]

*   *   *

The radical journals conducted an almost constant polemic against Suvorin, presumably more to make clear their own position to their readers than to persuade their target of the error of his ways. These verbal barrages seem to have been far more important to the left, and especially to *Notes of the Fatherland* under the editorship of Nekrasov and Saltykov-Shchedrin, than they were to Suvorin. It must be remembered, however, that Suvorin was usually denounced as a representative of his publication and in connection with regular campaigns against Russian liberalism, particularly as it was made manifest in the pages of *Saint Petersburg Notices,* which in turn employed specialists in polemic to reply in kind and launch counter-charges. Suvorin played no role, for example, in the fierce exchanges of mid-1872 between the satirist Burenin and a whole field battery of regular contributors to *Notes of the Fatherland*.

Another periodical with which Suvorin and his newspaper colleagues exchanged frequent volleys—more of small-arms fire than of heavy artillery—was the eclectically liberal, occasionally chauvinistic, always combative daily *Voice*. Its editor-publisher Kraevskii also controlled *Notes of the Fatherland*. When Nekrasov and his associates from *Contemporary* took over editorial control of *Notes of the Fatherland* in 1868, they had to agree to refrain from attacking *Voice*. Given the lofty scholarly tone of *Herald of Europe, Saint Petersburg Notices* remained as the only important journalistic target against which Saltykov-Shchedrin could regularly hurl his anti-liberal fulminations.[62]

The Slavophiles—to turn to another journal party—were few in number and during most of the period in question lacked a press organ. Suvorin gave them almost no attention, although he agreed with *Herald of Europe* that there were a few honest and sincere (if naïve) men among them, like the Aksakov family, who should not be lumped together with the crowds of cheap pseudo-patriots who flattered the "bad instincts of the masses" to gain readers. For his work in the freeing of the serfs, his devotion to justice, and his support for freedom of confession, Suvorin pronounced Iu. F. Samarin to be the best type of Slavophile.[63]

Among the cheap chauvinists who whipped up pan-Slavism to serve their own interests—indeed, at their head—stood, in Suvorin's view, M. N. Katkov and company. Throughout the period of his liberal activity Suvorin's single main target of attack remained the so-called Thunderer of Strastnoi Boulevard. As already noted, Suvorin saw no essential distinction between reactionaries in the purest literal sense and ultra-patriots of the school of *Moscow Notices* and *Russian Herald,* Katkov's daily and monthly voices. Both groups were hostile to the zemstvo party and the cause of progress. Nevertheless, the large following the Moscow publicist had attracted and his seeming power over certain sectors of the administration made him far more dangerous than the unreconstructed serf-owners of *News,* the absurd Prince Meshcherskii of *Citizen* (*Grazhdanin*), and the clumsy bigots of *Kievite* (*Kievlianin*), taken all together. That is not to say that Suvorin neglected these worthies. In fact he boasted that it was he who had made Meshcherskii famous as a public figure of fun.[64] But all these were purely negative in their reaction, while from the alternative center of power on Strastnoi Boulevard emanated an immediate threat of deformation to the Great and small Reforms.

As in regard to the entire aristocratic party, Suvorin's strongest charge against Katkov lay in the argument that he was less than loyal to the law of the land, that is, existing administrative arrangements and the expressed will of the emperor. According to Suvorin, Katkov somehow had gotten the idea that *he* was Russia, and that anyone who opposed his attempts to arouse hatred between estates, nationalities, and even generations, was guilty of "intrigue and treason." Many naïve patriots still believed that he had saved the Russian state at the time of the Polish uprising, although in fact his chief services lay in driving many thousands of peaceful people into opposition and in gaining glory for himself. The Polish question remained unsolved, while Katkov's love for classical education showed only that he was unable to understand the "genuine needs" of the country. His unchanging and mindless talisman, "treason, separatism, and nihilism," was no more intelligent than the belief of the ignorant that the cholera epidemic of 1831 was caused by evil men pouring poison into wells. His vacillations of policy and journalistic name-calling had made it clear, moreover, that his true purpose was to divide and rule.[65]

The "Greco-Roman bondage" of the Russian gymnasium curriculum, inspired by the Thunderer, began only in June 1871. During the preceding several years the polemic between liberal and Katkovian publications became particularly intense. *Moscow Notices* especially thundered out at all opponents of the Katkov-Leontev plan to eliminate nihilism by strictly classical education for the future administrative elite and strictly technical education for future technicians. The newspaper raged continuously against *Herald of Europe,* threatened everyone, and went so far as to accuse Suvorin, along with Shelgunov of *Cause* and V. A. Genkel of *Week,* of standing at the head of a proposed party of nihilists. "Nihilism is conscious of its strength and adopts the bearing of a party in power."[66]

Suvorin and his colleagues endeavored to expose the failings and ambitions of Katkov by a multi-genre attack. In a noted open letter Suvorin reviewed the record at some length and demonstrated that Katkov had met "all the *most important reforms* of the present reign . . . waveringly and sluggishly." In a fictionalized flying survey of the national and international scene at the end of 1870, he pictured Katkov threatening to "hammer out an article" if the "people in Saint Petersburg get uppity and don't do what I want"—to which the Thunderer's alter-ego, P. M. Leontev, replies with a smile, "They will be frightened and do it."[67] At the same time *Herald of Europe* was spelling it out in editorials like the one that accused *Moscow Notices* of adopting a peculiar super- and anti-government position, in which it identified itself with Russia (the latter in a subordinate position) and called all others traitors.[68]

Suvorin's analysis of his enemy's place in the movement of ideas, while persistent, was somewhat contradictory. On the one hand, Katkov was ambitious in the manner of Caesar, yet on the other, lacking any ideas of his own, he "regularly subordinated himself to the views of the crowd or the administration." If he went in front of them, it was not in order to lead society, as in the best tradition of the Russian press, but only to develop their ideas to absurdity. Moreover, although Suvorin spent a large part of his time defending Russia from the Thunderer, he early began to assure his readers that that peculiarly "privileged patriot" had passed his peak and like the Roman Empire soon must fall.[69]

While Suvorin condemned Katkov as a man of emotion rather than of ideas, his own criticism of the enemy was less than strictly ideological and relied heavily on felicity of phrase and innuendo. In one feuilleton he even clearly hinted that Katkov must be accepting bribes from various dishonest and profiteering railroad contractors (whom he named, in accordance with his announced resolve to warn the public openly on such matters).[70] Whether owing to censorship or to the limitations of his genre and his analytical powers, he did not undertake to explain in depth the disadvantages of Katkov's schemes or to expound the concrete virtues, for example, of an alternative educational method and purpose.

At the same time, Suvorin let no chance go by to assert his

opposition to classical education. Hence it may well be that he was only leaving the detailed analysis to his colleagues, the writers of formal editorials. He sharply criticized the claimed indifference of *Notes of the Fatherland* to the whole educational debate.[71] Looking back over the struggle several years later, in a savage obituary attack on Leontev, Suvorin noted that in the height of battle only *Saint Petersburg Notices* and *Herald of Europe* had stood firm against *Moscow Notices* and for a correct development of technical education. Certainly, he himself had seized upon every likely and unlikely review topic—a traveler's account of Japan, an outline of German pedagogic knowledge, a history of the working class movement in Germany—to insert a word of praise for the *Realgymnasium* and a word of censure for so-called Latin wisdom. In a longer discussion he cited a French study of English schools to demonstrate that Englishmen and English triumphs were produced not by the classics but by a whole system of education, a system in which an important place was given to free time and learning to use freedom. The English had come to understand that classical studies were a waste of time and worse, since they took time away from the native language and literature (the latter of course being one of the subjects Katkov was most eager to eliminate from the curriculum). Equally as important, Suvorin had discovered, were British popular and adult education, both based on new methods which merited careful study:

Our opponents linger over the England almost of the time of William the Silent [*sic*], while we take note of the mighty and educated modern England which understands the new demands of the time and new conditions of social life.

Like his exposure of the English aristocracy through the pages of Hugo's *L'Homme qui rit,* this was an obvious attempt by Suvorin to carry the struggle into the enemy's camp and to render Katkov hoist with his own petard. Its effect on any wavering Katkovites must have been considerably vitiated by the fact that their master had long ago ceased to justify his plans by special reference to British example. Rather, his projects were arising logically from his notion of the root causes of that nihilism he singlemindedly sought to combat. Nonetheless, reference to English upper-class experience had become a standard code for those writing against Katkov, his publications and his proposals; as such, Suvorin's unmasking activities no doubt had a cheering effect on the already convinced liberal faithful.[72]

Another burning public question of the period around 1870 was that of army reform. Following the defeat in the Crimea, steps had been taken to correct the most obvious and unquestionable deficiencies of staff and field organization. However, the government made no final decision on amending the system of conscription—with all its potential repercussions on the social structure—until the early seventies. Finally, in January 1874 a military statute established all-class obligation and short-term active service followed by reserve status. During the preceding years the press discussed rather freely the respective advantages of professional or civilian armies, restricted or general liability to draft, and so forth.

Conservatives feared the revolutionary potential of a mass army, while reformers urged such an innovation for a variety of reasons. Unfortunately for clarity, the conscription problem became entangled with other points in debate. Throughout the sixties Prussia had been revealing itself as the most militarily effective power in Europe. Hence Prussian military organization came to be regarded as a model for others. The issue of Russian army reform unavoidably became enmeshed, at least in the press, with conflicting attitudes toward Prussia, Germans in general, and Russia's own future path of development. The events of the Franco-Prussian War further exacerbated the debate by seeming to display both the might and the cruelty of a Germany united under Prussia by Bismarck.

The longest and most important serious article of Suvorin's liberal period, on army reform and other social questions, appeared in the first months of the war and immediately raised a storm of controversy from all sides. As a convenient summary, sometimes even to exaggeration, of his favorite themes, this article would merit attention even without its comparatively clear analysis of the virtues of a people's army. "Visiting and at Home" constitutes the publicistic fruits of Suvorin's first trip abroad—to a Germany mobilizing for war. For him, as for many other Russians, the sights beyond the western frontier provided much food for thought. He reported to his readers that "every step abroad demonstrates that you are not in the motherland; every step presents you with material for comparison, unfortunately not to the credit of the motherland."[73]

Unlike some of his compatriots, he reacted with humility and eagerness to learn. He looked about him for the "expiring West" of so many reactionary Russian publicists, but found instead prosperity, liberty, honesty, and order. That famed German order of which Russians of left and right spoke with irony and disdain, turned out in fact to be the basis of a high standard of living, genuine patriotism, and an atmosphere of real trust between government and people. Order admittedly had its pedantic side, but the railroads ran on time and horses ate grain too good for people in some parts of Russia. But this German order constituted an inborn tenor of life; despite attempts by the Russian administration, it would not soon be introduced by decree. Suvorin made clear that it was inseparably linked with freedom. Freedom and order lay beneath the advance of knowledge, rule by law, public trust, general competence. Freedom of opinion and investigation made the German a solid, moderate, practical fellow. For example, biblical criticism and analysis had done what no police or censorship could do. If anything, it had strengthened belief, and on an educated and conscious level. Independence of spirit and initiative, together with civil service examinations, had created an able, energetic, honest bureaucracy. As one of the miraculously perceptive natives Suvorin met on his travels pointed out, in Germany "every civil servant is a servant of the public and his job; in your country every civil servant is the servant of his immediate superior, the immediate superior has his superior, and so a whole staircase."[74] Russian railroads, for instance, furnished a leading example of corruption, laziness, and disregard for law and for the rights of the public. Germans too incompetent to find work at home were to be seen everywhere in Russia in the employ of the railroads.

The same German conversationalist also thought that if Russians were as free as his own countrymen, they would no doubt be less "many-sided" but would do everything incomparably better. At every turn Suvorin exposed to blasts of heavy sarcasm the catchwords of Slavophiles, pan-Slavs, and nationalists—all those wishful sounds about the young, fresh, broad, original Russian (or Slavic) people, and the spoiled, tired, worn out, empty West. How much harm had been done to Russian society, he wrote with sorrow, by those who always laughed at parliamentarism and "self-government" (in English), who asserted that the Slavic tribes were a peculiar people with a special mission. Certainly the Russian peasant possessed great talent and ability, but it could avail him little as long as all the burdens of the state lay on him. Yet nowadays every dirty little newspaperman was boasting of the lofty Russian mission, because it was profitable and flattered the bad instincts of the masses. Certain organs of the press had learned how to please without exertion.

> You begin to persecute the Germans and give a Slavic exhibition with Czech, Galician, Slovak hymns . . . As intermezzo it's not bad to organize a deputation from the Slavs, who come to us in order to marvel at our might and well-being.

Nor was the left exempt from the lash of Suvorin's pen. Indeed, the populists had fallen into the same self-centered error as had the nationalists. "The most gifted part of our press was charmed, like the Slavophiles but from the other side, by the verbose "mission" of the Russian people, with its peasant commune, with its Great Schism."[75]

Yet the truth was, as another German conversationalist amiably explained, that the Russians were just plain not cultured. Russian life required constant struggle against the internal enemies of rudeness, backwardness, and ignorance—simply to maintain a balance of European civilization. To overcome backwardness, it was imperative to "imitate and study," especially Germany. In recent times Russia had turned to Paris for all things. The coincidence of the years of Russian progress and the triumph of Napoleon III led to such unfortunate borrowings as those in the spheres of police and press organization. Suvorin closed the first half of his article with a ringing appeal to a pre-Marxist classic. It was not an accident, he said, that Peter the Great had chosen Germany and Holland (rather than France) as his examples.

Taking up the same theme again a month later, Suvorin finally unmasked himself as an opponent not just of the Second Empire but of all that France stood for in Russia. He dismissed in a few words those critics to right and to left who were already accusing him of blindness to German faults, and proceeded to make explicit his dichotomy of the two national models. This was at base a contradiction between slow but steady progress on the one hand and rapid spurts coupled with sharp retreats on the other. During the past century France had moved again and again from military despotism to unlimited freedom and back in the other direction. The French role in the world had been by no means insignificant. Without the daring of the French, without their attempts to introduce all possible progressive ideas, other countries would move forward much more slowly. But the example of Germany showed that small gains taken step by step were the more durable. The Germans had their own sort of daring, according to Suvorin—the daring of the engineer who extends a bridge across a turbulent river. Of course it would be nice to fly across the river rather than bothering to build a bridge, but for the moment projects on flying should be left to those "passionate dreamers" who have not been "made wiser by the experience of history and the truths of mechanics." Such dreams might bear fruit in the distant future, Suvorin granted, but for the present one must do what one can—follow the Germans and bridge the river.

As might be expected, Suvorin found the chief catalyst of German progress in the principle of association. Europe had long ago come to realize, he wrote, that mutual benefit societies of all sorts, so far from being means of revolution as supposed in Russia, were in fact powerful means of peaceful non-revolutionary advance. And nowhere was association more highly developed than in Germany.

At times Suvorin seemed to offer a world of associations as either a substitute for or a precursor of a generalized Utopian Socialist world, at least as he understood it. As always, however, his precise attitude toward such "noble dreams" is unclear. He saw war and revolution equally as terrible scourges, but he did not automatically associate socialism and revolution. He found the socialist ideal of life, the "fiery plans" of Fourier for example, to be "quite narrow, the more or less equal distribution of food and labor." The communists intended to give to all mankind "good food, healthful living quarters, and peaceful physical and spiritual enjoyment." While Suvorin repeatedly assured his readers that the human race would not soon enter such a paradise, he was also capable of a degree of rhapsody of his own over the prospects which lay before Germany and her diligent pupils. To just such a paradise of plenty, of general well-being, the Germans were moving

> slowly and firmly, by means of mutual aid, by means of manufacturing artels, by *vereinen,* by order and personal initiative. They do not build anything like the communes of Fourier and Owen because they know that only that endures which creates the progress of an entire nation, and not that which creates the fantasy of one man, however noble it may be.[76]

Suvorin's ringing declaration that the future belonged to Germany fell upon Russian educated society at a time when almost every sector of public opinion sharply condemned the Prussian state and German qualities in general. Although the imperial government followed a policy of pro-Prussian neutrality during the war of 1870–1871, this was based entirely on the will of an autocrat who stood almost alone in his Prussian sympathies even at court. The "nationalist" press, led by *Moscow Notices,* had been alerting its readers to the dangers inherent in the rise of Prussia and the alleged separatist ambitions of the Baltic barons for half a decade. During the months just before the outbreak of war, the nationalists and even the official *Journal de St. Pétérsbourg* supported the idea of a rapprochement with France. The journalism of the left, more interested in universal principle than in national security, saw France as the source and symbol of advanced thought. *Notes of the Fatherland,* for example, recognized only two possible forces of contemporary French public opinion: the so-called unprincipled camp of political banditry headed by Napoleon III, and that French nation which was the bearer of progressive socio-political ideas. After the battle of Sedan the German armies were crushing not Louis Napoleon but the Republic of the French. As Saltykov-Shchedrin sternly pointed out to Suvorin, it was the French nation which had created "that arena of political and social questions into which step one after another all members of the human family." Such a nation would without doubt soon eliminate the causes of present failure, yet not sacrifice its universal aims to concentration on domestic details.[77]

No doubt many educated Russians not closely aligned with either of these journal parties were at first indifferent to the outcome of the war. But with the rapid defeat of the French regular armies and the terrible siege of Paris, sympathy swung to the side of France and distaste for German militarism and aggression became widespread.[78] After all, the nationalists had been pointing out the barbarous character of the Teutonic horde for some time. Only the liberal periodicals seemed to lag behind. Even in late October the editors of *Herald of Europe* were still assuring the world that the civilian and democratic character of the Prussian army precluded its use as an instrument of conquest.[79] Later, true, they became less confident on this score and even Suvorin tried at the end of the year to redeem himself with an imaginative word picture of masses of mangled bodies heaped on recent battlefields and German soldiers with gauntlets of blood keeping watch over starving Paris. How much suffering to how many millions, he exclaimed, had been caused by war and by "great men" such as Bismarck![80] Yet more than six months later *Spark* continued to hold up to scorn Suvorin's "famous article" in which he had proved—the radical satirists claimed—that Bismarck was a giant before whom all the principles of 1789 were worthless (an accusation manifestly not true, but in accord with the polarity that the editors of *Spark* wished to establish between bourgeois liberalism and true democracy).[81]

Even if Suvorin could not accept all its methods, the Prussian system of military organization aroused his boundless admiration. The advantages of that system, as expounded in "Visiting and at Home" and elsewhere, may be quickly summarized. An army like Prussia's, formed as it was of citizens continually being drawn from all classes for short periods of active duty, was genuinely a popular army in several senses of that overworked word. An army of the whole people not only bridged the gap between rich and poor, teaching honor for labor and introducing a "healthy democratism" into society, but also received the "respect and trust of its fellow citizens," the first characteristic of a good army. Honesty and thrift prevailed, for the soldiers realized they lived on the wealth of the people, contributed by their own families and by themselves when they would lay aside the uniform. Moreover, such an army became a school for the whole nation of order, sobriety, punctuality, firmness, and persistence in obtaining one's goals.

For Suvorin the two most appealing features of the Prussian military system were the all-class service obligation and the high educational level of officers and men. Universal obligation was far more just, he thought, than the situation prevailing in Russia, where the poorest strata of the population provided both the soldiers and their funds. If introduced everywhere, it would free Europe from "useless wars undertaken not in the interests of the people but to satisfy the personal desires of the rulers." When ministers and kings had to send their sons into battle, it would be hard to begin a war with a light heart, for dynastic reasons.[82] When war did prove necessary, modern conditions and modern weapons demanded educated, thinking soldiers. The Prussian army was the best educated in the world. Suvorin chastised the folly of the "privileged patriots" who, having finally realized that a people's army was far less revolutionary than one composed of professionals, now clamored for Prussian military organization just because they expected the great size of such a force to somehow secure the Baltic provinces against Bismarck. Without education—and, he hinted, without a sense of citizenship and civic participation—it would be impossible to transform soldiers from "living machines" into a national army.

Suvorin extolled the Prussian military model not alone for the civic virtues it taught. Russia had to imitate Germany in order to compete with Germany. As he pointed out, sooner or later the Russians would find themselves in combat with someone other than the inhabitants of Turkestan. During this period he repeatedly compared the situation of defeated France—with exhausted army, ill-trained officers, and corrupt bureaucracy—to that of Russia in the Crimean War. As Prussia had profited from observing Russian defeat, so must Russia add the lesson of Sedan to that of Sevastopol and never permit another such debacle.[83] While Suvorin's other views on the Prussian army system found parallels on the editorial pages of *Herald of Europe,* neither the liberal journal nor the radicals seem to have shared his obsession with the Crimean defeat. It may be noted that five years later, while Russia hesitated on the verge of war with the Ottoman Empire, Suvorin in the pages of his own newspaper exulted that Russia—humiliated by Europe twenty years before in the Crimea—now stood forth against Turkey and all the great powers for the sake of the suffering Slavs.[84]

A third topic of great concern to Suvorin in this period—although it aroused no real polemic—was the rising plutocracy. Russia's first great industrial boom in the late sixties gave birth to a whole host of financial entrepreneurs. Bankers, stock promoters, and directors of share companies appeared in Saint Petersburg and—according to Suvorin—conspired together to defraud the public and despoil the state treasury. All such people constituted a new social strata, the plutocracy, a term Suvorin liked to derive from the word *plut* (swindler). They heralded a new era, he wrote, in which the thirst for money was driving from society all its former high ideals and every serious thought or noble feeling. Literary people, lawyers, even school children, brazenly embraced plutocratic teachings and hastened to enrich themselves by deceit, bribery, and an orgy of stock market speculation.

As a class the plutocracy could do no good. When *Stock Market Notices* defended plutocracy as a comparatively "just" social division, thanks to its democracy of access, Suvorin argued at length that the new class was incapable of political ideals, knew no science but bookkeeping, and destroyed art on contact. At times, as he fulminated against the "Suzettes, Juliettes, Alphonsines" who represented the highest interests of plutocracy, against their Lucullan banquets and fantastic parties, their villas and balls and vulgar tastes, Suvorin sounded almost like Saltykov-Shchedrin or N. K. Mikhailovskii. At least from 1870, Suvorin undertook to chronicle the life and times of this plutocracy. Detailed accounts of its misdeeds constituted the most common subject matter of his Sunday feuilletons in the early seventies.[85]

The Russian government's program for rapid expansion of the railroad network lay behind the speculative fever of the era. The state granted concessions for construction and operation of railroad lines to private companies, which received in addition substantial subsidies and a guaranteed rate of return on their investment. Thus stimulated, foreign capital and foreign capitalists poured into the country. Native financiers did not lag far behind in forming banks and joint-stock companies to exploit the golden possibilities of the moment. Corruption flourished. Poor construction and mismanagement at great expense to the public coffers characterized even the more successful rail lines. Meanwhile, the middle strata of the Russian population hastened to invest in railroad and banking shares. Even before the industrial depression of 1873–1875, a series of crises, bankruptcies, and scandals visited the money manipulators who floated in the froth of the construction boom. Small investors invariably lost everything, Suvorin noted, while the plutocrats scampered nimbly from the wreckage of their companies and organized others.[86]

While Suvorin chronicled railroad wrecks, maimings, and fatalities (which he invariably ascribed to faulty construction and maintenance), his major concern was with the speculators rather than the builders. He took his readers within the walls of the stock exchange and laid bare its workings: a "gambling house" that had "developed its own laws, by which neither deceit, nor forgery, nor existence of a secret society clearly acting to the public harm is punished."[87] He took his readers with him to innumerable shareholders' meetings of investment banks and joint stock companies. There is a certain dismal sameness in his descriptions of these meetings, as glib directors and their bemedaled bureaucratic stooges sidestep embarrassing questions about solvency and persuade their meek shareholders to vote them larger salaries and enthusiastic thanks for robbing the government, the shareholders themselves, and the general public. How delightfully patriarchal such meetings were, he exclaimed sarcastically, like teachers with schoolchildren—or wolves with lambs. On all sides he denounced nepotism, favoritism, bribery, fraud, profiteering, stock speculation, and the arrogance of the newly rich plutocracy.

Suvorin's attitude toward the economic environment he chronicled seems somewhat contradictory. On the one hand, he condemned all financial speculation as robbery per se, quite apart from the other vices that flourished in speculating circles. The stock exchange, he urged, should be closed at once. On the other hand, he displayed sympathy for the bedazzled and bewildered shareholders— would-be speculators themselves, in the final analysis. Pointing out repeatedly that a joint-stock company was a pitiful parody of parliamentary government, he seemed to be urging the "honest and decent" shareholders to take courage and wrest power from the directors. He suggested neither dissolution nor government control of credit corporations but simply full inspection by independent auditors.

It would be as futile to expect a systematic program of economic development from the pen of Suvorin as to look for a reasoned statement on the nature of the state, the relationship of education to society, or any other abstract or speculative question. Within the context of his condemnatory chronicle of the plutocracy, however, he made clear that he rejected only unconstructive financial activity. As he wrote on another occasion, he wholeheartedly favored the "peaceful revolutions" of the telegraph and the railroad. The usefulness of capital and credit should be accepted, he thought, but capital had to be "linked with a high development of mind and heart" and devoted to the improvement of society. Under present conditions huge banking credits were expended not for industrial development but for playing the stock market. Part of the trouble lay with the banks themselves. As creations of plutocracy, they served plutocratic ends. For example, the numerous land banks—or banks for landlessness, as Suvorin liked to call them—performed a certain service to society by removing mortgaged estates from the possession of incompetents. Unfortunately, such lands usually passed to merchants who despoiled soil and timber for quick profit, rather than finding their way into the competent hands of the peasantry. When the government endeavored to aid the poor by means of savings and loan associations and small credit institutions, thereby freeing working people from dependence on the great capitalist and the kulak, plutocracy grew suspicious and spoke of concessions to socialism. And since the Russian plutocracy had its own laws and morality, it was left to the government to raise the social well-being of the masses.[88]

*　　　*　　　*

Thus in 1875, when Suvorin's liberal renown stood at its height, he was known to the reading public as an ardent champion of the Great Reforms, struggling for political and personal liberty within the framework of a universalized western European model. Non-bureaucratic institutions such as the zemstvo and the courts—however imperfect and restricted in the present—contained the seed of western independence and legalism. If the emperor could be held to his supposed original reforming intentions—that is, to limitation of his own power—and the bureaucracy could be excluded from arbitrary interference, educated men of good will and vision (the liberals) could gradually transform Russia into a *Rechtsstaat* that combined respect for individual rights with state-assisted economic and social progress for all classes.

Suvorin continued to champion the new institutions in some form or other during subsequent years. Yet within a short time his former associates came to regard him as a renegade and apologist for autocratic and bureaucratic tyranny—a transformation accomplished under the influence of militant nationalism and anti-universalism.

chapter five

A *New Direction at* New Times

*The boredom, the melancholy mood
that so many feel, the apathy that
makes people shrug their shoulders or
begets pointless irony, tell us that
people are waiting for something.*
—*Suvorin* (*February* 1876)

*A*fter leaving *Saint Petersburg Notices* and publishing
with such success his collected newspaper writings,
Suvorin briefly held the position of Sunday feuilletonist for the moderately liberal daily *Stock Market Notices*. Meanwhile, throughout
1875 he bent every effort either to join forces with a more important
periodical or to obtain his own publication. At last in February 1876,
in partnership with V. I. Likhachev, a jurist and liberal publicist,
Suvorin bought the political newspaper *New Times* from its previous
publisher for 30,000 rubles.[1] More precisely, the newly formed partnership bought the name, the obligation to satisfy existing subscribers
until the end of the year, and the printing equipment and supplies on
hand.[2] It was considered easier to gain official permission to continue
an existing publication than to found a new one. Likhachev, a man of
wide acquaintance, had managed to borrow the money from a Warsaw
banker. The rapid success of the new enterprise is graphically illustrated by the fact that, despite heavy outlays for a more modern

press, the debt was entirely repaid in a little less than a year. Unfortunately, thanks to several destructive fires, precise information on the financial aspects of the operation will probably never come to light. However, Suvorin's gradual acquisition of other enterprises, not all of them successful, and the increasing prosperity evidenced by his subsequent manner of life make it clear that *New Times* proved immensely profitable.[3]

Even in this period of the growing importance of the daily press in Russian literate society, there were many failures for every one publisher who prospered in the manner of Suvorin. The earlier history of *New Times* illustrates the elusive nature of success in the circular pond-life world of Saint Petersburg journalism. *New Times* was founded in late 1867 by A. K. Kirkor, a scholar of West Russian origin who supported the conservative and regional interests of Polish-Lithuanian landowners. In the next eight years it changed hands four times, coming in turn under the control of the liberal dramatist F. M. Ustrialov, the converted Jew and sometime philosopher O. K. Notovich, the economist-industrialist K. V. Trubnikov, and Suvorin. All five received censorship penalties of some sort. The first four gave up their efforts chiefly because they failed to gain sufficient subscribers, but in two cases the decision to close was forced when the government suspended publication rights for six months after a third warning—a crushing punishment Suvorin managed to avoid throughout his publishing career. All five publishers, as well as their editors, took an active part in other periodicals at other times and spent a large portion of their adult lives in journalistic work (although all were trained for some other profession and all but Suvorin at some time practiced that profession). Notovich and Trubnikov both obtained other daily newspapers soon after their failures with *New Times*. In fact, during the fifty years between the Crimean War and the Russo-Japanese War, Trubnikov published twelve different periodicals, with an average life span of four years each.[4]

In view of Suvorin's established journalistic reputation and recent renown as a principled martyr to the reactionary minister of education and to the schemes of the hated Katkov, it is not surprising that news of his purchase attracted the optimistic interest of literate society. As the liberal literary historian Vengerov cautiously expressed it, acquisition of *New Times* by a member of the progressive camp "aroused great hopes in literary spheres"—in other words, hopes that it would be a voice of at least some sector of the oppositional intelligentsia.[5] A police agent reported in alarm that the new *New Times* would take over the role of the former *Saint Petersburg Notices* and become the most important liberal organ, "around which the whole party will group itself and which, commanding vast contacts with the provinces, will have an enormous influence on youth and on all Russian society." Moreover, Suvorin was known to be a close personal friend not only of various well-known liberal publicists, such as Likhachev, but also of Nekrasov, the editor of *Notes of the Fatherland.* Another secret police agent reported a rumor current in late 1875 that Suvorin and Nekrasov, along with Saltykov-Shchedrin, planned to join forces in opening a bookstore for the distribution of "tendentious literature." Several months later the daily newspapers were speculating that Nekrasov would play an important role in editing Suvorin's *New Times.* Although the poet hastened to deny any such plan in an open letter to the most widely distributed paper of the period, he did take the occasion to issue a public blessing by wishing "complete success" to a newspaper "at the head of which are people I sincerely esteem."[6]

Popular rumor had ample reason to link Nekrasov, Suvorin, and *New Times.* Nekrasov and his associates had been trying to gain control of a newspaper outlet, in addition to their monthly journal, for several years. At one time Nekrasov had even thought of buying *New Times* from Ustrialov. In the autumn of 1874 *Notes of the Fatherland* sent five of its regular contributors, as colonists of a sort, to participate anonymously in *Stock Market Notices* and there to "introduce the views" of their journal. This was the paper for which Suvorin wrote in late 1875, although by then death and departure had already thinned the ranks of the radical colonists. Nekrasov had acted several times as intermediary in Suvorin's attempts to obtain a newspaper or an important editorial position. Moreover, at one point Nekrasov tried to find a place for Suvorin among the contributors to *Notes of the Fatherland.* His attempts failed, evidently due to the determined opposition of Mikhailovskii. Nonetheless, the new publisher of *New Times* could be regarded as a man well connected

in radical as well as liberal journalistic circles. It is remarkable that
the Chief Administration of Press Affairs saw fit to grant him the
necessary certificate of right to publish.[7]

*   *   *

The first issue of the new *New Times* appeared on 29 February
1876. Although the initial printing was only 3,000 copies, press runs
averaged 13,000 to 15,000 within a few months. Nevertheless, even
the publisher's closest friends assumed the paper was ephemeral and
would soon close.[8] Illustrious names were linked to it by rumor, but
none gave the paper great assistance. Nekrasov declined to participate.
Saltykov-Shchedrin, although at first willing to contribute, in fact
provided only one satirical article and soon, for mainly political reasons, turned against *New Times* and all its works.[9] Turgenev sent
two short stories before he quarreled with Suvorin over publication
rights and broke off relations.[10] The populist novelist N. N. Zlato-
vratskii offered to write stories and a review of zemstvo publications,
but his proposition evidently was not taken up.[11] Vengerov, then
quite young but already well recognized in literary circles, undertook
to provide a regular feuilleton of literary criticism; however, his
name disappeared from *New Times* after six months. Hence the
success of Suvorin's newspaper did not depend upon the aura of great
liberal and radical names which at first accompanied it. In subsequent years illustrious names of another sort appeared on the pages
of *New Times*—the names of pan-Slavic publicists like V. I. Lamanskii and distinctly non-liberal novelists like Leskov—but by that time
circulation had risen to that of its closest competitor, *Voice,* and the
continued existence of the paper was assured.

The permanent editorial staff, which was small, included the
onetime radical satirist V. P. Burenin, the economist K. A. Skalkovskii, and several lesser figures from Korsh's *Saint Petersburg Notices.*[12]
The two men named, along with Suvorin, determined the paper's
policies and direction for at least the first decade of its long existence.
It may be noted that the majority of the old Korshites, including the

most politically oriented, accompanied their former editor in his repeated efforts to keep alive a new newspaper on the old liberal bases.[13]

New Times soon attracted a number of other regular contributors, correspondents, and city reporters—more than one of them, in the Russian journalistic tradition, poor students working to support themselves at the university. Most of those who joined the paper in its first, presumably liberal, days continued there throughout their adult lives and evidently were contented members of the *New Times* family.[14] In view of the undoubted political conservatism and chauvinism that characterized the paper in its later days, it would be fascinating to discover that the *New Times* staff held a significant proportion of elderly Orthodox Great Russian landowners from the ethnic borderlands of the empire. In fact, most of the known contributors had Russian names, but this circumstance in no way distinguishes *New Times* from other Russian language periodicals of general, non-ethnic orientation at that time. As far as can be determined, they came from the same educated strata of petty gentry and *raznochintsy* (non-gentry intellectuals) as did the rest of the intelligentsia of the period. In contrast to many other journals and newspapers of the capital, however, no Jews wrote for *New Times.*[15]

Although a "responsible editor" (inherited from the previous two publishers) performed practical tasks and answered to libel suits or official displeasure, the real editor and guiding spirit was Suvorin himself. It is true that in the eighties and nineties he increasingly devoted his attention to the Russian stage, while his sons gradually took over the actual direction of *New Times.* At least as late as 1883, however, Suvorin was accustomed to look over and edit the whole paper every night—except when he was away from the capital, reporting on his travels through Russia and Europe.[16]

*   *   *

It may be worthwhile at this point briefly to describe the physical appearance of *New Times,* since in makeup and categories of coverage it was typical of serious Russian newspapers of that time. *New Times* of the late seventies closely resembled not only its contemporary competitors, but also *Saint Petersburg Notices* of the sixties and most newspapers of successive decades.[17] It consisted of one or one and a half large sheets, folded in folio to form four or six large printed pages. Before important holidays, additional advertising often increased its size to eight pages. Advertising usually occupied a fourth or a third of the total space. In the period under study the most prominent advertisements were those of publishers, patent medicine firms, and investment trusts. The paper cost five kopecks a copy or fourteen rubles a year, plus mailing charges, the usual price for large-format dailies.

Although Suvorin took pride in the liveliness of his paper, which he thought avoided both the allegedly boring long lead articles of his Saint Petersburg rivals and the antiquated composition of *Moscow Notices,* in fact *New Times* appears quite dull if compared with American newspapers of that time.[18] The type was small and densely set, with a minimum of white space. Even the lead articles were not always titled, while other sections bore standard titles (Chronicle, Internal Correspondence, and so forth) which gave no hint of a particular day's news. In view of the increasing importance of individual sales and the sharp competition between newspapers, it is remarkable that the Russian dailies failed to develop the bold display headlines already dear to the hearts of American newspapermen. Without headlines to attract purchasers, street sales must have depended upon the reputation of the paper and the vocal efforts of the vendors.

The day's editorial (*peredovaia* or lead article) occupied most of the center part of the front page, directly below an ornate masthead. It was flanked by a column of advertisements on one side and a column of telegrams (mostly from European capitals) on the other. The second page contained dispatches from abroad (External News) and extracts from the foreign press. Internal Correspondence, on the third or even the fourth page, contained communications from outside the capital and short news items copied from provincial papers; this section never occupied more than about a third the space alloted to foreign news. A third section, Chronicle, reported events in the city: although the public appearances of the imperial family, and even rumors of the impending retirement of diplomats and generals were recorded, no accounts of interviews with high government figures (so important to American reporters) ever appeared here. *New Times* kept close watch over the world of finance as well. Market Telegrams reported the previous day's prices for Russian state bonds and paper money on the exchanges of Berlin, Riga, and Odessa; Market Chronicle reported prices from the Saint Petersburg stock exchange, the grain market, and elsewhere. An extended analysis of the market situation appeared weekly. Other regular daily divisions were Governmental Orders (occasionally important decrees, but usually lists of persons officially honored, promoted, or retired); Court Chronicle (stenographic reports of interesting trials, presented in even smaller type than the rest of the paper), train departures, and a strikingly vague weather forecast. Like other newspapers, *New Times* was obligated upon request of a ministry or other government department to print articles directed against statements in the paper the appropriate officials thought incorrect; such "communicated articles" always appeared with a note explaining the legal basis for their publication.

In addition, book, art, and drama reviews, obituaries, announcements of meetings, special articles on historical subjects, short stories, and serialized novels appeared from time to time. Advertisements covered the last page rather than appearing with the text. All this material was arranged in parallel columns from top to bottom of the page, with only double spacing or at most asterisks to divide individual news items. The only exceptions to the columnar rule were large advertisements and the daily feuilleton; the latter, following tradition, covered the entire bottom third of the first or second page. Diagram maps of important battles and great fires appeared from time to time with the news, but more elaborate illustrations made their debut only in 1885. *New Times* boasted of its highspeed rotary press—the first in the Russian Empire—but this and other modern innovations served if anything to lower the quality of the finished product. It was often poorly printed, with smeared ink, unevenly inked type, and double impressions to the point of illegibility.

New Times introduced one novel feature into the practice of Russian journalism: a daily survey of opinion in the newspaper press, similar in aggressive tone and polemical aim to the surveys of journal opinion which were a standard department of thick journals and some newspapers. In the hands of Skalkovskii, this Among Newspapers and Journals department became from the first day of publication an important element in setting the direction of the paper.[19] It gave voice in the bellicose language of direct attack to the tendencies of thought presented formally in anonymous lead articles and informally in the feuilletons of Suvorin and Burenin.

Although we are concerned primarily with the spiritual progress of Aleksei Suvorin, it would be impossible to describe the evolution of his publicistic position and to understand the response of other "journalistic camps" without constant reference to the development of the paper as a whole and especially to its most polemical sections. The analysis below will concentrate on the signed articles of Suvorin and on anonymous editorials, most of which presumably he wrote; for the sake of clarity, *New Times* or "the editors" will be cited as the authors of unsigned statements of opinion. The polemical attacks of Among Newspapers and Journals, although presumably written by Skalkovskii except during his summer absences as traveling correspondent, will be treated as the collective work of the editors. This practice is justified by the close similarity on any given day between the content and tone of Skalkovskii's column, the editorial page, and Suvorin's own feuilleton. As noted, the column was considered a part of the policy statement of the paper. The most elaborate and intellectually ordered statements of opinion appeared over the signatures of occasional correspondents. While their precise views cannot be taken as those of Suvorin, the fact that certain categories of publicists (and not other categories) contributed to *New Times* can be regarded as an indication of the general direction of the paper and hence of its editor-publisher.

*   *   *

Every serious Russian periodical began life with an announcement of its program, in most cases carefully worded to convey a maximum of political inspiration and identity to its readers with a minimum of clarity of expression. The literary intelligentsia eagerly read the first issues of a promising new periodical and commented upon them at length in other organs of the press. In certain instances a phrase or word from the program became the standard shorthand symbol for the entire periodical, its editorial staff, and even its "party" of faithful readers. For example, the famous opening statement of *Voice,* "We are for *energetic reform,*" became the battle cry of its partisans and a target for derision by enemies from left and right. Prince Meshcherskii of *Citizen* was invariably referred to as Prince Full-Stop (*kniaz Tochka*) by his numerous journalistic opponents, for his statement that it was necessary to "put a full stop" to further re-forms. *Herald of Europe,* on the other hand, expressed itself in such abstract and scholarly tones that would-be satirists had to fall back upon its famed punctuality of appearance as a symbol of all they disliked about its brand of academic Westernism. "Every first day of every month: European moderation, punctuality, and liberalism" was its motto, Burenin wrote with withering scorn at a time when such terms had acquired entirely negative connotations in the vocabulary of *New Times.*[20]

The expectantly awaited first issue of *New Times* appeared on 29 February 1876. In addition to news and announcements, it con-tained a light-hearted Sunday feuilleton and a lead article entitled "Instead of Our Program," both by Surovin. The feuilleton, written in his inimitable punning style, rambled through a variety of sub-jects: the unusual date, the joys of a life in journalism (struggling for the "eternal principles of good and truth"), the social apathy of the era, the conviction that public opinion only waited for some un-known signal to awaken from its sleep, the duty of a newspaper to develop and support the best feelings of public opinion, the assurance that *New Times* would "serve honest people and honest aspirations, no matter whence they might arise," and so forth. It ended by urging any who found such a program slight and comic to laugh freely, for "we ourselves do not renounce laughter, and we shall see who laughs last."

The non-program editorial was if possible even less explicit. Assuring his readers that he "believed in Russian society," Suvorin announced that his direction would be "frank" (*otkrovennoe*). Since Russia had no parties, the press had to represent the views of literate society. Yet neither the press nor any other institutions of Russian life, new or old, was able by itself to move the country "forward into international competition" or arrange its internal life in such a manner that "all might live untrammeled." Nevertheless, Suvorin concluded optimistically that

> one may find everywhere shining personalities turning their gaze far beyond the boundaries of their own special interests and occupations. We would consider our aim accomplished if these best people responded to our modest summons and made our newspaper their *newspaper*.[21]

It is not surprising that the very serious populist organ *Week* concluded that *New Times* would be an "ultra-Saint Petersburg" paper (a negative term in the vocabulary of these friends of the Russian village) whose chief aim was to provide entertaining light reading.[22] Would-be satirists clung tightly to "frank direction"; perhaps nothing else was clear enough to lend itself to their special type of treatment. Mikhailovskii, for example, parodied Suvorin's thoughts:

> I began with the frank announcement that I would pursue a frank direction. I left it to your stupidity to guess whether I would limit myself to a frank description of the secrets of demimonde boudoirs, or in general would write as God moves the spirit, by revelation.[23]

The noted twentieth century historian of Russian journalism B. P. Kozmin pronounced Suvorin's program a "clear example of liberal twaddle."[24] Certainly the implied aspirations to progress, westernization, and personal liberty for all estates were well within the main currents of Russian liberalism. The evident desire—or pious wish—to ally all groups of the oppositional intelligentsia ("shining personalities," "honest people") by means of a single publication and even the refusal to adopt a definite program were not unknown to liberal periodicals. Thus, *Voice* had announced its refusal to serve any party or particular current of opinion. Katkov, then a reformist if not precisely a liberal in the western sense, had attempted to rally all shades of unofficial opinion in his newly founded *Russian Herald* in 1856. *Herald of Europe* had claimed that society had outlived the era of journalistic "directions." However all three publications, despite disclaimers and compromising words, at once made quite clear their support for the reforms of the sixties. *Herald of Europe,* for example, directed attention to the public courts and zemstvo assemblies as two new "schools of society."[25] The need to guard the new institutions from the attacks of repressive officialdom certainly had not passed by 1876, yet Suvorin made only vague and perfunctory references to the Great Reforms he had so recently and ardently defended. Another curiously non-liberal strain of *New Times'* opening statement lies in its emphasis on the apathy and melancholic mood of society. As Suvorin also noted in his feuilleton, liberals were calling the mid-seventies a period of stagnation. He dwelt on this theme with extraordinary insistence, however, harking back to it again and again in later issues and bemoaning his own boredom as well as that of others. The problem of boredom, together with the wish for a clear call to action, assumes greater significance in the light of subsequent developments.

Editorially *New Times* spent its first months explaining its position on the questions of the day. From the very beginning the editors devoted at least half their attention to international problems and to political developments in foreign countries. On the domestic scene, however, the lead articles and feuilletons continued to find important most of Suvorin's chief concerns of earlier years. Although the tone and evaluation remained liberal, the emphasis had changed. This may be seen most clearly in the case of the so-called institutions for local self-administration. The secret police agent quoted above need not have feared that *New Times* would recreate the role of *Saint Petersburg Notices* as a publicity center for zemstvo institutions in the provinces. Although the new newspaper conscientiously reported the debates and activities of both the Saint Petersburg provincial zemstvo and the city assembly, it otherwise limited itself to an occasional correspondence from the provinces and an occasional editorial urging wider zemstvo activity in such local spheres as the making of small loans to peasant producers.[26] Granting that this period before the Russo-Turkish War marked a lull in zemstvo political activity, one must also grant that Suvorin—a supposed liberal publicist—contributed in some way to that lull by failing to devote more attention to defense of the zemstvo.

The new courts fared hardly better, although an occasional article appeared to defend the reform from attacks by *Moscow Notices* and from rumors of impending retreat from the precious principles of public hearing, elected judiciary, and jury trial.[27] Freedom of the press received only fleeting glances, while educational classicism was never mentioned at all. On the other hand, no opportunity was missed to take a derisive slap at spiritualism, evidently rampant at that moment in Saint Petersburg.

Another typically liberal concern, freedom of conscience, was accorded comparatively greater attention. Concrete discussion of this principle was limited, however, to the case of the Russian Old Believers. *New Times* demonstrated at length that the schism would be weakened only when the state authorities at last learned not to intervene in religious affairs, that more schismatic marriages would be registered if their own clergy were empowered to do so (rather than the local police), that converts from Orthodoxy to sectarianism should not be punished for conversion, and so forth.[28] The problems of the other large non-Orthodox religious communities of the empire —Roman Catholic, Lutheran, Armenian, Jewish, and Moslem—found no notice in the newspaper. Presumably the first four faiths were subsumed in the whole nationality question, which did not as yet greatly concern *New Times.* A series of articles on the history of Polish political decline constituted a small exception, but the series stopped short of the nineteenth century. The major thesis of this series would seem to be that the Polish magnates and gentry sorely oppressed the Polish people while proving themselves incapable of maintaining the state.[29] Replying to criticism that the first articles were "not at all liberal," Suvorin explained himself to his readers in significant and ominous tones:

> We have grown up, and this growth is visible, among other things, in the way we have become more Russian, we have better understood our tasks. In a Russian newspaper there can be a place only for a Russian view on Poland.

In the sixties, he continued, some periodicals had favored the separation of Poland from Russia, but now everyone agreed it would be impossible to give up Poland "lest the Germans devour her." The Russians would never eat her up, since they had never done this to anyone in the past. In fact, they had displayed themselves incapable of such an action,

> and this incapacity is our great virtue, for it may be translated: live and let live! In this is the future of all the Slavonic tribes, if at some-time they should group themselves around Russia, and this will come to pass if Russia does not die, does not cease to live a European life . . . [*sic*].[30]

Although this argument betrays a certain unwillingness to recognize the nature of Russian administrative practice in the recently renamed Vistula Region, it may be noted that European-ness is still somehow essential to Russian leadership of Slavdom.[31]

The Moslem religion, as practised in Central Asia and in the Ottoman Empire, early became the object of almost daily attack. Islam, according to *New Times,* displays a very low moral development; its main task is the extermination of unbelievers. The Koran is "hostile to peace, science, love of neighbor, and progress." The fanaticism of the Central Asian Turks made the total pacification of the Turkestan region imperative. The Moslem peoples of European Russia—for example, the Volga Tatars, already subject to a campaign for conversion to Orthodoxy—did not interest the editors of *New Times.*[32]

Far more important than all the great traditional liberal causes put together, to judge from the space allotted, was the familiar denunciation of plutocracy, speculation, and railroad scandal. Suvorin continued to write indignant feuilletons about imperious railroad officials and dishonest bank directors. When the Moscow Society of Commercial Credit blamed the increased number of banks and the competition of foreigners for recent reverses, Suvorin scornfully invited its officers to reexamine their own claims to honesty, intelligence, and efficiency. While taking the waters in the northern Caucasus he reported to his readers that everyone seemed to be curing himself at government expense, thanks to the corruption of doctors who freely sold at low prices the tickets of admission intended for distribution to invalid soldiers.[33]

The cause célèbre of the year was the Strousberg case, the arrest and trial of the German-Jewish industrialist B. H. Strousberg and twenty other directors and officers of the bankrupt Moscow Loan Bank, all charged with a variety of dishonest financial activities at the expense of state coffers and private investors.[34] Long before the trial began, Suvorin reproached Strousberg's attorney for defending a guilty man. Although preoccupied with external affairs, *New Times* reprinted the entire transcript of the lengthy trial and commented continually if inconclusively on the proceedings. Suvorin fulminated against bribery, love of luxury, and the race for profit, all characteristic of the present era. At first he feared lest the accused somehow escape trial, and then complained while the trial was in progress that it was being ignored by the Russian public.[35] Evidently, no periodicals defended the Moscow Loan Bank. When *Stock Market Notices* suggested that stock market speculation had useful as well as harmful aspects, *New Times* denounced this view at length: only speculators, not society, can profit from the activity of the stock market.[36]

Although Strousberg and several others were frequently identified as Jews, there is no evidence that this was part of a general anti-Jewish campaign. Indeed, Suvorin himself showed much more anger over Strousberg's claim to immunity from trial as a German citizen than over his membership in the "Jerusalem gentry." In view of the excited attention given to the case, *New Times'* final recommendations for future improvement were slight and uninteresting: private banks should be required to make public a monthly balance sheet, and government officials (forbidden to serve in banks) should conduct a periodic inspection of their financial situation.[37] In general, the editors of *New Times* displayed far more energy, passion, and imagination in exposing the evils of the feverish growth of investment corporations than in proposing concrete means to minimize the evils or to find other ways to mobilize private capital for railroad construction and industrialization—both of which *New Times* regarded as essential to national well-being and national defense.

Both *New Times'* first censorship penalty and its first literary polemic were eminently liberal; neither, however, arose from

Suvorin's pen. The first censorship penalty came after less than three weeks of publication. A correspondence decrying the purge of Turgenev's "weeds" (*Fathers and Sons* and *Smoke*) from the secondary school library in Novgorod—clearly suggesting the reactionary nature of educational classicism and of the local school administration—brought prohibition of retail sales for several weeks.[38]

The first polemic involved the opposition of "Europe" and "the village," as supported by liberals and populists respectively. Although Suvorin contributed almost nothing to the exchange, it is worth recounting as an illustration of the range of views, against the background of which *New Times* was soon to define its own position. In the second half of the seventies *Week* was the outstanding organ of that literary and publicistic tendency which glorified the peasant commune and the "ideals of the Russian village"—supposedly unspoiled ideals of altruism and equality that made the commune the embryo of a future just form of production. According to *Week,* the Russian peasantry was the social and moral superior of the intelligentsia; the latter should merge with the peasant and learn from the truths of village life. This line of thought necessitated rejection of the radical heritage of the sixties, so called, and of the value to Russians of western socialist and materialist thought. *Week* pointed out a wholly separate and distinctly Russian path to the future good society, while denying the intelligentsia an independent role in hastening the advent of that society.[39]

Cause, while it yielded second place to none in its protestations of faith in the peasantry, also cherished the tradition of Pisarev's "thinking proletarian," the critically thinking individual intellectual who would eventually lead the people and influence the course of history. Hence, in the seventies *Cause* repeatedly protested against the idealization of the village, for fear the intelligentsia would become passive and rest illusory hopes on independent action by the peasantry. At one point Tkachev likened the views of *Week* to those of the Slavophile *pochvenniki* and expressed his bewilderment that a supposedly progressive organ should fail to recognize those features of European life worthy of imitation.[40] Into the fray leapt Vengerov, as literary critic of *New Times.* Tkachev, he wrote, had a right to feel bewildered; the nationalist direction of *Week* was so extreme as to border on chauvinism. Moreover, the educated ought to enlighten the peasantry rather than the other way around; civilization could not progress by moving backward to earlier forms, nor could the rude teach culture. The peasantry had finished one phase of their history and stood on the threshold of full participation in national life, into which they would be propelled by freedom and schools. This future moral and intellectual development would be, he predicted, "joined in the closest way with general European culture and civilization."

> The whole program of the present time, all our strivings, desires and aims, all the guiding principles of the seventies—in a word our whole *profession de foi* can be expressed in one word: Europe.[41]

Mikhailovskii, although himself a critic of the anti-intellectualism and idolatrous worship of the peasant typified by the romantic populism of *Week,* could not resist the red cape of Vengerov's *profession de foi.* From the pages of *Notes of the Fatherland* he pointed out that the word Europe had many meanings. One must choose among "the Paris Commune, or Thiers and the bourgeoisie, or Bismarck and militarism, or Caesarism and the Second Empire, or Chambord and legitimism." At any rate, the true program of the seventies was not Europe but "the Russian people (*narod*)."[42]

In a conciliating maneuver typical of literary liberalism, Vengerov replied by attempting to show that despite differences of vocabulary all the important thick journals, including *Notes of the Fatherland,* were in fact united in the aim of having Russia reach the same stage of development as other civilized nations. He continued to avoid a definite stand on the future of the peasant commune or the precise nature of freedom, which in the context of the debate could mean either communal freedom from exploitation (the populist dream) or individual freedom from the commune (the logical concomitant of increased Europeanization). At the same time Vengerov asserted that Mikhailovskii and his allies were armchair philosophers with no understanding of the genuine desires of the people for whom they claimed to speak.[43] Suvorin himself, who had already firmly informed his readers that the sixties were no more than past history, now dismissed *Week* as a musty relic of the sixties or even the forties, a pygmy eating crumbs from another's table, without so much as a hint of original thought.[44]

This polemic marked the last stand of unqualified westernism in *New Times.* Despite continued avowals of devotion to European civilization and science, within a few months the editorial columns began actively to defend the peasant commune against all those unnamed persons who would destroy it in the name of Europeanization and economic development. In view of the paper's growing attraction to pan-Slavism (the flamboyant and aggressive heir to the old scholarly Slavophilism of the forties), its new-found sympathy for the commune would seem to derive more from the right than from the left side of the sheepskin clad coin. But *New Times'* neo-Slavophile semi-populist tendencies retained a touch of liberal pragmatism. While the populists and Slavophiles discussed the moral values of the uncorrupted peasantry, Suvorin's paper argued in a more practical vein. For example, its editors seized upon Finnish cooperative successes to demonstrate that communal landowning promoted (rather than paralyzed) the improvement of agricultural technique. But the Finns were fully free to organize and manage their own farming activities, which led *New Times* to conclude in the Slavophile manner that a Russian commune cleansed of unnatural "historical excrescenses" could also raise its economic and cultural levels.[45] *New Times* especially feared lest the peasants fall into the hands of kulaks and other exploiters. Hence it applauded all efforts to organize low-interest credit schemes to help the peasants buy additional land or live through the winter; zemstvo organizations, the editors thought, should take a large part in such a system.[46]

An important long article entitled "Our Parties and Our Condition" summarized *New Times'* position in 1876 on pressing domestic matters. According to the editors, the essential question of the era—a transitional era between periods of development—was that of the fate of the Russian peasantry. The era was further characterized by a confusion of mottos between the two chief parties of Russian life. The conservatives had become champions of European social order, while "people of the opposing camp" sought to preserve national social characteristics—although not for the sake of abstract principle, as with the Slavophiles of former times, but for the sake of the people.

Thanks to peculiarities of historical development, Russia had neither an aristocracy in the western sense nor a powerful bourgeoisie. Hence Russian society tended toward equality. (The bureaucracy, being a parasitic growth, fortunately could not put down deep roots.) Yet now proposals were being heard to create a western bourgeois class and to break up the peasant commune, most of whose members would then be exploited by kulaks and the new bourgeoisie. Even otherwise perceptive observers proposed to bridge the gap between intelligentsia and common people by means of a third, middle estate. However, Russia could attain a European structure only by taking into account its own historical peculiarities. From western civilization Russians ought to expect not the destruction of peasant land security and the birth of a wretched artificial bourgeoisie, but rather strength for the educated classes to make creative use of the blessings of that civilization.[47]

If *New Times'* social analysis owed something to the generalized populist currents then in the air, its solutions wholly lacked the moral fervor and emotional intensity of genuine populists. Rather than seek salvation either among the people or in leading the people to some promised land, *New Times* recommended that the intelligentsia join with the people in an expanded all-class zemstvo. Freedom of resettlement and development of the spirit of independent activity would assist the peasantry to weather the crisis. *New Times* placed its greatest hopes, however, in reform of the taxation system. An income tax, by tapping the wealth of the possessing classes, would make possible some relief in the heavy burden borne by the common people. This in turn would decrease the economic dependence of the peasant on the kulak and give him the possibility of schooling. Throughout the period under study the income tax remained *New Times'* favorite solution for Russia's financial problems.

A final domestic development of great importance, in the estimation of *New Times,* was the "uniting" of Central Asia to the Russian Empire. Several weeks before Suvorin acquired his newspaper, Saint Petersburg had formally annexed the khanate of Kokand, thus crowning a series of conquests that gave the empire control over most of the settled states of the region and over the vast steppe to the north (now called Kazakhstan). *New Times* immediately welcomed the conquest, describing it as part of the elemental eastward movement of the Slavic-Russian nationality. The newspaper dismissed the apprehensions of "some people" who feared lest the new acquisition, distant, poverty-stricken, and too densely populated to allow Russian immigration, would prove another Caucasus to burden Russia with endless struggles and great financial losses. *New Times* admitted that intervening deserts made close economic union of Kokand and European Russia impracticable. As the southern region of Siberia, however, closely bound to that vast area by entirely feasible railroad and river routes, Kokand could complement and greatly stimulate the development of Siberia. The Siberians themselves instinctively understood this point, as their colonization of the intervening steppe was daily demonstrating.[48] *New Times* took a great interest in the problems of extending agriculture over the dry steppe and examined enthusiastically various plans for afforestation and irrigation. It was more skeptical about a scheme to connect the Azov, Caspian, and Black Seas.[49] At first it explicitly disavowed any interest in Central Asia as a land route to India; only at the end of the summer, when a defeated Serbia was suing for peace with England's ally Turkey and *New Times* trumpeted in the full grip of war fever, did its editors announce that new advances in Turkestan were opening a better path to England's greatest colonial possession.[50] By that time the editors had subordinated all other questions to the cause of their struggling Slavic brethren in the Balkans.

chapter six

Suvorin as Reactionary

> *The Slavic question is a Russian
> question, a question not only about the
> liberation of the Slavs, but also a
> question of our development and our
> liberation from the foreign yoke,
> which lies on us like a heavy weight
> and threatens misfortunes in the
> future. Alongside us grows the German
> world, which will make us its
> tributary if we do not use all our
> strength to unite in a broad Slavic
> union and free Europe from the Turks.*
> —*Suvorin (June 1876)*

Suvorin acquired *New Times* in the midst of a rapid intensification of the perennial Eastern question. The current round of popular uprisings in the Balkan peninsula had begun in the summer of 1875 with a chaotic rebellion by the Serbian Christians of Herzegovina. The revolt quickly spread to the neighboring province of Bosnia. The autonomous principality of Serbia and the tiny independent state of Montenegro seemed on the verge of war against the Ottoman government. On the international scene the entire winter of 1875–1876 was occupied with elaborate diplomatic maneuvers by the interested great powers, each fearful lest one of its rivals gain an advantage in the eventual disposition of the "sick man's legacy." By the end of February international tension had momentarily eased following acceptance by the Porte of the Andrássy plan, an Austrian program for reform of the Turkish government in the insurgent provinces. The Russian government at that time gave support to the Austrian plan, and hence to pacification rather than liberation of the South Slavs, in order to avoid the destruction of the *Dreikaiserbund.* Meanwhile the insurrection continued its bloody course and the Serbian government, confused by contradictory advice from various agents of Saint Petersburg, continued to vacillate between peace and declaration of war. Elements within the Russian government and even some individuals high in the diplomatic service —not to mention the heir apparent and his court—favored active intervention on behalf of their brother Slavs and Orthodox Christians. The policy of armed intervention gained ascendancy with the Russian emperor only later, after agreement with Austria on future arrangements in the Balkans guaranteed Austrian neutrality in the event of a Russian campaign against Turkey.

From late 1875, however, the irresolution of the imperial government made possible an unusually free press discussion of the situation and the expression of a wide range of opinion not only on the activities of allied governments but even, albeit indirectly, on the foreign policy of the Russian state. Press interest rose with the increasing sympathy of the Russian public to the plight of the Balkan Slavs. Although interest developed slowly at first even among the small proportion of educated society that consciously supported pan-Slavic ideas, by February 1876 public excitement was already great and continued its growth to eventual fever pitch during the rest of the year. By the time Suvorin took over *New Times* the Slavic Benevolent Committees of the two capitals had become energetic centers of sympathetic propaganda and fund raising activities on behalf of Serbian refugees, while the Red Cross, some newspapers, and various other unofficial organizations also took an active part in forwarding funds and encouragement to the inhabitants of the rebellious provinces.[1] Hence it is not surprising that the editorial columns of Suvorin's *New Times* immediately undertook to explain the paper's attitude to the current Balkan crisis and to the whole Eastern question.

At the same time Suvorin and his associates attempted to fill their pages with as complete and interesting information from the Balkans as possible, receiving their own dispatches from residents of the Balkans and sending their own correspondents to the scene. Even in the first four months of publication, before Serbia and Montenegro actually opened hostilities against the Turkish armies, almost half the newspaper's editorial space was taken up by discussion of some aspect of the question. As the year passed, both editorial and news coverage increased steadily; by the time Russia took up arms in April 1877, it had become difficult to find any long news item which was not somehow connected with the war, the Slavs, the Turks, or the attitudes of the other powers.

New Times' initial attitude toward the South Slavic insurrection, while distinctly sympathetic to the "heroic struggle of the Slavic handfuls," was calm and moderate in tone compared with later demands for a Russian crusade against the Turks. In the second issue under their aegis the new editors extended only faint hope for a happy outcome to the struggle for freedom: Austria, momentarily too weak to continue her historic task of Germanization of the Slavs, had consequently determined to preserve the Ottoman Empire and to aid in crushing the uprising. It would seem, the editors concluded sadly, as though the hapless Slavs were created to be slaves of the Turks or the Germans. Two weeks later they developed their thoughts further, citing the hypocritical futility of all Turkish promises of reform and the hypocritical disinterest of that European diplomacy which for the sake of balance of power denied freedom and human rights to oppressed Christians. Turning to the "Slavic idea," the editors found that it was in essence a Russian matter: only Russia could give it practical meaning, and the position of Russia had aroused national consciousness among all the Slavic peoples. Consequently, the Slaves had the right to hope that Russia would fulfill her historical calling, the precise nature and timing of which *New Times* left to the workings of History.[2]

Analyzing the attitudes of the Russian press, the editors expressed their inability to understand the trust and confidence being placed in the sultan's worthless promise to implement the Andrássy plan. Certain newspapers, headed by the widely distributed *Voice,* had formerly urged private donations to assist refugees and had greeted with joy each new insurgent victory. Yet, as soon as Austria announced five points for reform, everything changed. *Voice* expressed its indignation at the obstinacy of the rebels who did not trust in the sultan and lay down their arms.[3] The incomprehensible "cold-blooded objectivity" of *Voice* continued to manifest itself in reluctance to see Serbia and Montenegro enter the conflict lest full anarchy result. *New Times,* on the contrary, assured its readers that Serbia should and would take the decisive step, of whose successful outcome there could be no doubt.[4] The newspaper did not bother, however, to point out that support for the Andrássy plan, pacification of the insurgents, and containment of Serbia were official policies of the Russian state at that moment.

Not until early April did *New Times* undertake to explain more fully the role Russia should play in the Balkans. The paper announced that all the Slavs (except the Poles) concurred in their opposition to the Germans and Magyars; the Slavs wished to see Russia not as a member of the *Dreikaiserbund* but rather "at the head of the Slavic nations, as their protector who will be able to organize them into an independent union." This national (*narodnaia*) and organic idea, the editors continued, represented not only their own suggestion but also the policy of the "best people in the Slavic world." Comparing this policy to the historic gathering of the Russian lands by Moscow, the editors nonetheless were not wholly ungenerous to the smaller nations. "An equal union of Slavic peoples with the hegemony of Russia—this is our historical task," *New Times* declared.[5]

But Russia must seize the present moment, lest the Hapsburg Germans and the Magyars take her place and succeed in Germanizing all the Slavs. *New Times* identified the "rule of the stock market" as the chief internal hindrance to prompt implementation of the Slavic idea. The gentlemen of the stock market represented complete indifference to political matters and to important national tasks. Moreover, such gentlemen would insist that Russia lacked the means—to which *New Times* retorted that the true means of strengthening the state, the income tax, had not yet been tried. At this time and throughout the period under study *New Times* consistently underestimated both the practical ability of the powers to prevent a unilateral Russian solution in the Balkans and the fighting potential of the Turkish army. It was soon disabused, however, of its high hopes for the Serbian and insurgent forces.

It must be noted that this explanation of the Russian national task represented a high-water mark of sorts in the propounding of a general theoretical outlook in the anonymous editorial columns. Generally speaking, the regular editors devoted themselves to narrower and more immediate problems; grand vistas of the past and future of Slavdom were left to the pens of various pan-Slavic publicists whose signed articles began to appear in New Times in midsummer. The best known of these occasional contributors were the Slavicist V. I. Lamanskii and the literary historian O. F. Miller, both longtime officers of the Saint Petersburg Slavic Benevolent Committee.[6]

Meantime, in his Sunday feuilletons Suvorin complained of the indifference of society and of scandals among the plutocracy. In late April, after two months of bemoaning his boredom and hypochondria, he began to call for armed liberation of the Slavs by Russia, a "holy war which would elevate our spirits and would cleanse the atmosphere."[7] He could not understand, he wrote, those publicists who insisted upon peace in order (so they claimed) to develop industry and trade. He, Suvorin, saw only the development of banks and exploiters (*kulachestvo*) of all types; the industry and trade of which they boasted so loudly existed only in their plutocratic rhetoric. A war could sweep away all the petty squabbles, the scandals, the "trials at law which result in precisely nothing." Continuing his praise of war as social purge, Suvorin began to meditate on the "Slavic idea," and especially on the significance to Slavdom of the city of Constantinople. The Turkish capital, he wrote, was the key to Slavic life, and not only because its control would open trade routes. As Paris became the cultural center of western European civilization, so must Tsargrad become the center of an eastern, Slavic civilization. At any rate England was seizing Egypt, so "why shouldn't we seize Constantinople?"[8]

The editorial columns of New Times soon took up this theme on a regular basis, pointing out at length that Russia, for the sake of its own greatness as well as in the interests of Slavdom, must control the exit from the Black Sea. New Times's advice on the constitutional arrangements of this control varied. For example, one lead article reached the ringing conclusion that Russia's well-being depended upon a "free Constantinople in the hands of free Slavs, our allies, friends, brothers." Yet the body of that same article had developed at length the thesis that all leading states from classical Athens to modern Britain had become great powers and centers of knowledge and wealth in proportion as they rose to importance in international trade. All had made sacrifices on the road to peace, as for example the Greeks in their wars against the Persians. Now Russia must seize the moment and act for the sake of military and commercial greatness—a clear call for Russian rather than "free Slavic" administration of the Turkish straits.

If the precise shape of the future was less than clear, the need for action was immediate. The English, not the Turks, presented the greatest threat; fear that the whole Ottoman Empire would soon irrevocably pass under British control haunted the pages of *New Times.* Newspapers like *Voice,* by urging respect for general European interests in settling the Eastern question, endangered the interests of Russia and the whole Slavic world. If Russia followed the advice of *Voice,* England would soon buy up Constantinople, and then "the Caucasus will become an English factory, our ports in the Black Sea, English warehouses, the whole South Russian region a broad arena for their manufacturing activity." As for the fate of the South Slavs in the Anglo-Turkish Empire, they would remain "eternally hungry peons like the Irish and the Indians, and London, Manchester, and all the other stock owners will clip their coupons with profit." By prompt action, however, the liberated Balkan region could become Russia's best market for manufactured goods.[9] How the supposedly unproductive plutocratic exploiters of Russian industry could represent an improvement over British traders from the South Slavic point of view, *New Times* never attempted to explain. Presumably the close fraternal ties of Slavdom and Orthodoxy, so often referred to in the pages of that newspaper, would overcome all such minor difficulties. As the editors noted on another day, "Russia follows a more unselfish policy than any other European power and of course does not intend to make a milch cow of the Slavic lands. The Slavs know this."[10]

In May Bulgaria joined Bosnia and Herzegovina in rebellion.

The desperate Turkish authorities dispatched undisciplined irregular forces who joyously proceeded to destroy villages and massacre Bulgars. From the first news of the uprising *New Times* devoted great attention to this Slavic people "who in the course of centuries-long poverty" had not "learned hypocrisy and deceit," who had preserved the patriarchal commune while developing the fullest equality of individuals, and before whom lay a great future.[11] On the basis of dispatches from its own correspondent in Bucharest, *New Times* was among the first newspapers in the world to report on the "Bulgarian horrors."[12] More pacific Russian newspapers at first accused *New Times* of credulity and of arousing religious and racial passions, provoking the fierce retort that certain publicists forgot that they were writing "in a *Russian* paper, published in *Russia.*"[13] Thereafter throughout the summer almost every issue of Suvorin's newspaper contained a bloodcurdling account of the latest Turkish atrocity in Bulgaria.

Not every manifestation of the Balkan insurgents received the approval of *New Times.* When G. Veselitskii-Bozhidarovich (a mysterious figure who claimed to represent the Herzegovinians in Saint Petersburg) announced in favor of a modified version of the Andrássy reforms, he became the target of a concerted campaign by *New Times* to discredit him politically and personally.[14] In general any suggestion that Serbia and Montenegro ought not or could not go to war with Turkey was greeted with fierce scorn and accusations of Turkophilia: "Take off your mask!" *New Times* demanded of one lukewarm rival paper, "What nation do you belong to?"[15] When Serbia finally opened hostilities in late June, *New Times* was transported with joy and assured its readers that liberation for all Slavdom was at hand.[16] This woefully misplaced optimism derived not only from a false view of the respective strengths of the South Slavic and Turkish forces, but also from the extraordinary confidence the newspaper placed in General M. G. Cherniaev and the Russian volunteers in the Serbian army.

General Cherniaev, famed as the victor of Tashkent, had resigned from military service in 1874 in order to devote himself to spreading pan-Slavic—and at times pan-Russian—ideas in the pages of the nationalist daily *Russian World* (*Russkii mir*). Despite the emperor's disapproval and Russia's official position of neutrality, Cherniaev in mid-April 1876 succeeded in making his way to Serbia, where he soon assumed command of the principal army corps of that country. His presence and bellicose influence played an important role in Serbia's declaration of war and even more in prolonging the war after the inadequacy of the Serbian forces had been revealed. *New Times* enthusiastically supported Cherniaev's Serbian adventure from beginning to end and even beyond the end, when almost every other newspaper except *Russian World* condemned his incompetence, failure, and deceit of the public by news management. Suvorin boasted that he had been the first to announce that Cherniaev was going to Belgrade (although he had sensibly waited until the general reached the Serbian capital before making his departure public). Everything connected with the Russian capture and administration of Tashkent had already been for some years a standard butt of oppositional satire. Yet Suvorin now praised Cherniaev for his role in Central Asia and pointed out that if he had waited for instructions to capture Tashkent—rather than acting on his own and contrary to official policy, which was of course the situation with regard to the Serbian war as well—he never would have accomplished anything.[17] *New Times* reviewed the general's "almost legendary" military career and concluded that no matter what one thought about the significance of the Central Asian victories, one had to acknowledge the man's glorious heroism and historical importance. *New Times* defended Cherniaev from attacks by *Voice,* which at one point characterized him as one of "those condottieri to whom it is all the same where and for what they fight," by *Agence Russe Presse,* which hastened to assure the world that it did not approve of the "demagogue," and by other doubters and scoffers.[18]

From the outbreak of the war Cherniaev and his Russian cronies controlled news from the Serbo-Turkish front by means of a Correspondence Bureau which fabricated reports of nonexistent victories and explained defeat by Austrian and English treachery. Although *New Times* received its own dispatches from at least three correspondents with the Serbian army and from a dozen in Belgrade, the paper's news columns generally reflected the optimistic fancies of the Correspondence Bureau. Successive issues of late June and July placed

Cherniaev and the Serbian army deep inside Bulgaria, while in fact the Bulgars failed to assist the Serbs as anticipated and Cherniaev after less than three weeks of war had to abandon the offensive and retreat inside the Serbian frontier, closely pursued by the Turks. After several additional months of inconclusive fighting inside Serbia and a short period of truce, in mid-October Cherniaev was defeated at the disastrous battle of Djunis and soon thereafter left the country. Only immediate intervention by the Russian emperor saved Belgrade from the advancing Turks. His ultimatum to the Porte, accompanied by partial mobilization on the southwestern frontier, forced Constantinople to accept an armistice favorable to the Serbs.

During the summer of 1876 Cherniaev was, in the words of a specialist on the subject, "unquestionably the most popular man in Russia."[19] Even such skeptical organs of the press as *Voice* and *Stock Market Notices* wished him success, while he became a great military hero to millions of ordinary Russian people. *New Times* was at all times among the foremost in its enthusiasm for the general's adventures. For example, when Cherniaev in early September suddenly proclaimed the full independence of Serbia and gave its Prince Milan the title of king (to the dismay of Milan, of the Russian government, and even of the chairman of the Moscow Slavic Benevolent Committee, which financed Cherniaev), *New Times* responded with full support. When *Voice* denounced the proclamation as an obstruction of efforts to end the fighting, Suvorin devoted half his front page to suggesting that Kraevskii, its publisher, had openly entered the pay of Turkey. *New Times* favored not peace and great power diplomacy, but Russian intervention and the unilateral liberation of all the South Slavs, although at that time it avoided extended discussion of the implications of such a policy.[20]

It should be noted that censorship placed limits on press discussion of foreign policy even during this period of official indecision and wavering. So long as the upper levels of government continued to support the necessity of a general European solution to the Balkan problem, any very clear demand for military action implied criticism of state policy. Both *Russian World* and *Citizen*, the two periodicals most vociferous in their demands that Russian armies aid Serbia in its war against the Turks, suffered numerous warnings and eventual suspension for just such criticism. *New Times* presumably escaped punishment by the vagueness of its language. From the beginning of November, after Alexander II had rescued Serbia from defeat and had spoken publicly of Russian honor and "our sacred mission," the whole atmosphere changed.[21] During the following months almost every issue of *New Times* pointed out unimpeded that not diplomatic notes but armed force would save the Slavs—and the sooner mighty Russia applied that force, the better. As the Christmas Day editorial put it:

> Not by accident did the Divine Teacher say, "I came to bring not peace, but a sword" . . . Only by the sword can the Moslem yoke be cast off, only by the sword can peace be established.[22]

While *New Times* praised Cherniaev and war from afar, Suvorin acquainted himself with both at first hand. In early June he announced to his readers that he could not bear to sit in Saint Petersburg while diplomats chattered and Turks slaughtered insurgents. He would go himself as a correspondent to the theater of war. Following a circuitous route, he reported his impressions from every stop. In Kiev he stood on the bluffs high above the Dnieper River and meditated on the necessity of the Dardanelles to further Russian development. "As long as we have only the Baltic Sea, we will forever only sit by the 'window into Europe' and pay dearly for the light that comes through it." The whole Ukrainophile movement, then agitating the Kievan intelligentsia, he dismissed as "simply a literary quarrel," pointlessly raised by Katkov and his followers to the level of a political question. Although a handful of dreamers might think of the separation of Little Russia from the empire, the people had no such plan. As several years earlier, he argued that permitting Ukrainian reading in schools would assist literacy and eventually lead to greater acquaintance with Russian literature. But to introduce Ukrainian into the zemstvo and court, as some suggested, would be nonsense; if plain Russian were used, rather than fancy oratory, the Little Russian peasant would understand.[23]

In Odessa Suvorin found too many Jews and correspondingly little support for the Slavic cause. From Constantinople he reported on the backwardness and fanaticism of the Turks, the treacherous intrigues of England at the Porte, and the marvelous courage and love for Russia displayed by some Herzegovinians on their way home to join the fight. He praised the Russian ambassador N. P. Ignatev for his "faith in the calling of the Russian people and of the Slavs in the Balkans."[24]

In Romania the venality and corruption of the inhabitants shocked him; he attributed their failings to the gypsy element in their blood. But for the Bulgars, whose fierce courage and desperate plight impressed him deeply, he appealed to the Russian public for money and arms. He advised his readers to stir up the hearts (and pocketbooks) of the simple folk by fiery sermons in aid of the Christians.[25]

Even before he reached Serbia, Suvorin proposed that Cherniaev, as a Russian and thus non-partisan in terms of Serbian politics, take full power as commander-in-chief of all Serbian forces. Hearing of the general's reverses in the field, Suvorin finally admitted that "poor Serbia" alone lacked the strength to drive the Turks from Europe. Rescue lay in the arrival of more Russian volunteers and in the whole-hearted support of the Russian people. Without mentioning officialdom or army, he developed the idea that became the principal theme of his writing during the next few years—that the liberation of the South Slavs could prove the moral, emotional, and economic salvation of Russian society. All those who did not want to see their motherland the vassal of Germans and Britons ought to come to the aid of the Slavs. "All parties must unite, all think about one thing, all act in one direction," the lifting of the Turkish yoke.[26]

By the time Suvorin actually reached Serbia in mid-July, Cherniaev had already abandoned his initial offensive into Turkish territory. Nonetheless, Suvorin fell completely under his influence and attributed all his failures to outside factors, Magyar intrigue, British gold, Serbian cowardice, or Turkish fanaticism. Where two weeks previously he had praised the Bulgars, now he transmitted the general's negative view of Bulgarian fighting qualities. He called constantly for Russian soldier and officer volunteers, asserting as did Cherniaev that a few thousand more Russians in the Serbian army could win the war. Russia need not fear the disapproval of the powers; while western governments hated Russia and despised the Slavs, even in Turkophile England many decent ordinary people were beginning to oppose the official pro-Turkish stand, Suvorin thought. Moreover, much of the hostility of western public opinion could be attributed to the false reports filed by the foreign corespondents in Belgrade, most of whom, he discovered, were Jews.[27]

In August Suvorin returned to Saint Petersburg, where he continued to defend Cherniaev against a slowly rising wave of disillusionment, hastened by revelations in *Voice* of the general's attempt to deceive the public with false news. By the end of September, however, even more Russians were thoroughly disillusioned with the Serbs. Suvorin merely anticipated the general reaction when he began to ridicule Serbian fighting abilities and territorial pretensions; now he placed his hopes in the youthful vigor of the Bulgars.[28]

During Suvorin's absence a leadership crisis had arisen within *New Times.* Insofar as can be reconstructed from fragmentary and contradictory evidence, Burenin and Likhachev remained in charge while Suvorin went to the Balkans. Despite minor and short-lived personal reservations, Burenin attempted to preserve the "Slavic tone" and general position Suvorin had already established, which "so profitably distinguished" *New Times* from other newspapers.[29] Likhachev evidently viewed this whole tendency with something less than enthusiasm. When *Voice* accused him of partisan journalism unbecoming to his position as assistant chairman of the Saint Petersburg District Court, he published an open letter in *New Times* denying all responsibility for the paper's contents and direction. Meanwhile, *Voice*'s reporters in Serbia had managed at last to circumvent Cherniaev's watchful Correspondence Bureau and dispatch uncensored reports on the true military situation there. *New Times,* along with *Russian World,* denounced these reports as tendentious. Now Likhachev became involved in an obscure argument with *Voice* over its telegrams and *New Times'* denunciations; after several more open letters categorically denying responsibility, he left the paper and went abroad for a rest.[30] During the Russo-Turkish War of the following year, Suvorin persuaded him to return to the paper as a co-editor. In December 1878 he left again, irrevocably, and Suvorin bought out his share of their joint enterprise; neither he nor his wife ever spoke to Suvorin again. Unfortunately, it is impossible to determine to what extent Likhachev's departure was motivated by principle and to what extent—as Suvorin preferred to call it—by personal rivalry between them.[31]

The battle of the telegraphic dispatches continued. During the last two months of the year *Voice* exposed in detail Cherniaev's failings and falsifications in Serbia. It termed his bureau a "weapon of political blackmail" and called its chief journalistic voices (*Russian World, Moscow Notices, New Times*) criminals since, "by falsehood and deception, they hoped to involve Russia in a war with Turkey." *New Times* replied with cold fury that *Voice* had lost the last vestiges of "political and literary honesty." Suvorin's paper made no attempt to refute *Voice*'s facts; rather, it asserted once again it had always believed and would continue to believe it was the clear duty of Russia to liberate the South Slavs, by force of arms if need be. "In this there is nothing for us to repent and recent actions of Russia have given brilliant proof of the correctness of our view."[32]

The recent actions in question were the ultimatum to Turkey and the mobilization of six army corps in southern Russia. Through the winter of 1876–1877 the military systematically prepared for war while the emperor and his advisers, after a short burst of war fever in early November, once again hesitated and wavered. A diplomatic conference in Constantinople and numerous protocols and circular letters failed to find a means to satisfy Russian demands while preserving the Ottoman domain intact. Throughout this period, as noted, *New Times* urged immediate military action and attacked periodicals which did not follow suit. While *Voice, Journal de Saint-Pétérsbourg* (an organ of the Ministry of Foreign Affairs), and other papers expressed fervent hopes that the Constantinople conference would avert the threatening war, Suvorin wrote bitter satirical sketches on the duplicity of diplomats and the futility of diplomacy. A peaceful solution, *New Times* repeated daily in one form or another, was "on the basis of historical evidence, objectively impossible." When *Stock Market Notices* inquired whether constant appeals to "supposedly insulted national honor" were not misplaced, since in that paper's words pride and honor demanded rather that the nation "preserve the life of its sons and not begin a bloody and destructive war," Suvorin replied sarcastically that of course "for us the most important thing of all is stock market speculation," which certainly must be protected from any control, any criticism, any disturbing possibility of war. To the many worried voices raised to point out the precarious financial condition of the Russian state, *New Times* patiently explained that Russia's resources were great and that an income tax, by tapping the pockets of rich speculators, could mobilize those resources for the army. One especially interesting article sought to prove, on the basis of figures from past Austrian state budgets, that armed readiness for war was actually little cheaper than war itself; the drain on the moral well-being of the people might, in fact, be greater than during time of combat. Most important of all, however, were the immaterial gains of war, the "general animation and energy naturally associated with war in a healthy society."[33]

Thus, in less than a year Suvorin and his associates moved from a liberal position in which the liberation of the South Slavs was only one among many pressing problems, including further loosening of the bonds oppressing the Russian people, to a nationalistic position in which a war against Turkey to free the Slavs became the most important task of Russian society—a task, moreover, which in some mystical way was expected of itself to heal the ills of the Russian body politic. By the time Alexander II issued his declaration of war on Turkey early in April 1877, *New Times* well deserved Mikhailovskii's ironic accolade as the "most 'patriotic' newspaper" in the empire.[34]

*   *   *

Suvorin's shift in publicistic priorities did not escape the attention of the Russian journalistic world. As *Cause* noted, he "who not long ago laughed at the Slavs now appeared in their defense in the open field"; *New Times* itself reminded the radical journal of a military camp.[35] Although Suvorin's paper engaged in constant hostile skirmishes with other daily papers, their exchanges chiefly concerned immediate issues of the day. General ideological criticism, in contrast, flourished in the more reflective pages of serious weeklies and monthlies. Such intellectual periodicals generally gave little attention to newspapers; they reserved their blows for rivals in their own weight class. Suvorin and his paper, however, figured frequently in the polemical sections of radical and liberal journals during the time of the clamor over the fate of the Slavs. Indeed, the high point of Suvorin's importance to the oppositional intelligentsia—if measured by attention given him in print—seems to have occurred during the years 1876–1878. Certainly this was due in part to the wide circulation enjoyed by his newspaper. No doubt, too, the widespread support for the South Slavic cause on the part of Russian society during those years raised the fear that many others might follow the evolution of Suvorin from liberal sympathy for oppressed peoples to politically conservative support for pan-Slavic ideas and the power and might of the Russian imperial state. By the early eighties the oppositional literary world had already labeled Suvorin reactionary and gave his views only occasional attention. Perhaps by that time his greater political distance from them made him a lesser threat to constancy in the faith on the part of the lukewarm and the doubtful. Perhaps also his open support for the increasingly oppressive government of Alexander III made it more difficult to attack his opinions without great risk of a censorship penalty.

During the course of 1876 *New Times* and the liberal and radical journals moved in opposite directions. As the former grew more enthusiastic about the Slavic cause, the latter grew more hesitant and suspicious. Many elements of the left initially reacted with hopeful enthusiasm to news of the uprisings in Bosnia and Herzegovina. Among the first wave of volunteers to go to the aid of their Slavic brethren were Russian radicals, including several contingents of émigré socialists and anarchists.

Although Lavrov warned from Geneva that wars for national independence only divert the masses from the struggle against their exploiters,[36] legal radical journals inside Russia supported the insurgents as social revolutionaries. During the winter and spring of 1875–1876 *Cause* emphasized the contrast between the despotic Ottoman state system and the European system of rule by law; the source of Slavic hostility to the Turks lay in a "terrible government which constituted the cause and result of a still worse social structure."[37] At the same time the journal hinted at the possibility of yet a third path of development. For example, the regular foreign chronicler noted the naïveté of those English liberals who believed that the Balkan peoples need only copy the West. Does the East, he asked, need only the progress represented by railroad trains and stock markets? *Notes of the Fatherland,* although initially devoting little attention to the South Slavs, similarly expressed sympathy for their struggle against oppression. The liberal *Herald of Europe,* at a time when the government still sought a diplomatic solution, urged the Russian people to support Serbia in its approaching conflict with Turkey.[38]

The high point of liberal-radical enthusiasm for the Slavic cause came in the summer of 1876, especially as it became obvious that the Serbs alone could not stand off the Turkish army. *Cause* proposed a voluntary league to liberate the peninsula and demanded to know why the rich and the monasteries were not contributing money for the Slavs. *Notes of the Fatherland,* after neglecting the Serbs for some months, suddenly filled its July, August, and September issues with appeals for donations to the Slavic Benevolent Committee, indignant references to Islamic fanaticism, and lengthy paraphrases of books then current in a variety of languages on the past and present sufferings of the South Slavs. The internal chronicler exclaimed with passion that if only he were twenty years younger he would gladly shoulder a rifle for the "pure holy struggle," far removed from the "young liberals" concerned only with acquiring capital, the "former liberals" openly prostituting themselves, and the whole amoral Russian society which chattered about great ideals but in reality strove only for profits. As late as September the journal threatened to march against the Turks, with or without the consent of the European powers. The liberal-populist weekly *Rumor* (*Molva*) welcomed the beneficial aspects of war itself, which would "enliven the national spirit and carry off a lot of assorted trash that accumulated in the long period of peace." Thus during the summer much of the rhetoric of Suvorin and *New Times* found its counterpart in the leading oppositional journals. War fever gripped the intelligentsia. Not without reason did the émigré paper *Forward* (*Vpered*) ask in despair what had happened to "yesterday's liberals, radicals, social-

ists," now shouting, "To Moravia! To the Drina!"—while the real
enemy was to be found in Russia.[39]

Even before their government veered decisively to official support for Serbia, radical publicists began to regret their bellicose tone.
The spread of pan-Slavic concepts and the chauvinist tone of social
agitation worked contrary to their democratic political aims by chan-
neling attention away from internal problems and by encouraging
nationalistic all-class support for the state and army as potential
saviors of the Slavs. The cause of progress required popular liberation from below rather than liberation from above by a Russifying
autocratic government. As G. Z. Eliseev, co-editor of *Notes of the
Fatherland,* wrote to Nekrasov in late September, "the mood aroused
in the public by the Slavic war is wholly unfavorable to the ideas
that our journal is trying to spread and strengthen among the public."
Accordingly, in the next issue he "corrected" the journal's line. Bellicose articles about the South Slavs vanished, while its Internal
Survey pointed out that those who wished to help poor Slavs could
find plenty of them at home in Russia. *Herald of Europe,* which had
held aloof from the saber-rattling alarums of mid-summer, began in
August to emphasize the European future of Russia and the importance of internal over external questions. According to the liberal
journal, the theory of the vitalization of society by means of war was
entirely false; by war one only distracted attention from internal
reforms, as did the regime of Louis Napoleon, for example. If Russian
publicists wanted a livelier society, they should look around for things
to write about at home. Interestingly, although *Herald of Europe*
mentioned by name not a single periodical or publicist, *Rumor, Cause,*
and *New Times* all unhesitatingly identified this article as a polemic
against the last.[40]

Rumor agreed with *Herald of Europe* (although not until after
the radical journals reversed themselves two months later). The
populist weekly devoted most of an issue to attacking Suvorin and
the "familiarity, triviality, insolence, and conceit" of his newspaper.
If Suvorin continued on his present path, one author warned, he
would finish worse than *Moscow Notices.* Another article, by the
Ukrainian historian Dragomanov, assailed the "pseudo-Slavophile
opinions" of *New Times* under the meaningful title, "A Pure Cause

Requires Pure Means." This proved to be *Rumor*'s last issue, but Dragomanov (who had gone abroad after the most recent repression of Ukrainophile activities) continued the attack with an open letter to Suvorin in the form of a pamphlet printed in Geneva. As an émigré, he could write openly what others expressed in hints: that a "Turkish order" ruled in Russia as well as in the Balkans, that closer acquaintance with the Russian state and army would arouse not gratitude but hatred among the South Slavs, that the Slavs of the Austrian and Prussian Empires (whom the pan-Slavic publicists spoke of liberating next) already enjoyed more freedom than did members of the ruling Great Russian people in the Russian Empire. "It is impossible," he concluded, "to free others without freeing ourselves."[41]

Despite the ever-present censor, however, the thick journals managed to make their positions clear. *Herald of Europe* devoted many pages to the problem of Slavic unification as proposed by Lamanskii and others. This attention took the form of exhaustive demonstrations of the diplomatic, military, financial, and cultural impossibility of Russian hegemony in the Balkans. The journal emphasized the "historically separate development" of the Balkan peoples, citing, for example, the existence of a parliament in Serbia and the fact that that country enjoyed a greater number of schools, proportionally, than did Russia. To the pan-Slavic claim that the Russian people entered upon a "new life" by taking up the Slavic cause, *Herald of Europe* countered that the new era began with the emancipation of the serfs; to the Orthodox and anti-western exclusiveness of Slavophile utopias, it contrasted the universal and scientific civilization of western Europe. *Notes of the Fatherland,* starting with the December issue, published a series of articles on the disillusionment of Russian volunteers with the Serbian war, of the Serbs with the volunteers, and of everyone with Cherniaev. *Herald of Europe* praised these and other satirical revelations, noting that Russian failures in Serbia demonstrated the internal condition of Russian society. *Cause* managed to explain that the English opposed Russian intervention not from love of Turkish tyranny, but because they feared an increase in Russian strength to the point of influencing all European policy. Following the actual declaration of war by Alexander II, while *New Times* exalted the gallant army and its glorious victories, the oppositional journals fell silent about the Balkans and devoted most of their pages to other matters. In *Notes of the Fatherland* Mikhailovskii wrote of the South Slavic struggle in the past tense. As *New Times* later complained, some monthly organs of the press greeted the extraordinary political events of 1877 with indifference and even attempted to ignore the war while complaining about the alleged superficiality of daily newspapers; such "liberal equivocations" demonstrated the decline of the "former category" of monthly journalsim and the exhaustion of "formal liberalism."[42]

As *New Times* parted company with the oppositional journals, its course increasingly coincided with that of various conservative newspapers. During 1876 the pro-government press moved in the opposite direction from the anti-government forces. Generally speaking, conservative papers met initial reports of Balkan bloodshed with cautious concern for European stability and expressed hope for a peaceful diplomatic solution. *Saint Petersburg Notices* even warned that agitators of the Socialist International had sparked the Herzegovinian uprising and that the bellicose Serbian Liberals (then in control of the national assembly) were the enemies of Russia. By mid-summer, however, sympathy for the struggling Orthodox Slavs (or perhaps the possibility of Russian territorial expansion) melted the stoniest hearts. *Moscow Notices* urged voluntary—although not yet official— Russian assistance. *Saint Petersburg Notices,* reversing itself overnight, declared that the Serbs were "inspired by a great idea" and began to hint that Russia would enter the conflict if necessary.[43] While the Russian government prepared for war and the left rued its earlier belligerence, conservative organs adopted the language of pan-Slavism and breathed hostility to all Europe—as did *New Times* also. Hence, Suvorin found himself among unaccustomed allies. For example, in the first issue of his paper the new department Among Newspapers and Journals introduced itself by satirizing the reactionary "pathos" of *Citizen;* by the end of the year it was often quoting that paper's warlike outbursts with approval. Most frequently and most approvingly quoted by all departments of *New Times,* from early in the summer, was the ultra-nationalistic daily *Russian World.*

While certainly on the political right, *Russian World* did not follow the conservative evolution outlined above. As an organ of pan-Slavism, it supported Russian intervention in the Balkans, by any means possible, throughout the period. Clearly, its constancy in Slavic matters attracted Suvorin's sympathy; *New Times* did not refer to the internal political views of its strange new bedfellow. It was the only periodical in the Russian Empire in 1876 which Suvorin could never scornfully denounce as a "chameleon organ." Like *New Times*, it dared to call for war while the emperor and the minister of foreign affairs stood for peace. Moreover, it was the voice of "heroic" General Cherniaev. Yet *Russian World* harbored not only Cherniaev but also General Fadeev and other military-aristocratic reactionaries, against whom Suvorin had so passionately polemicized a few years earlier when his chief concern was the defense of the Great Reforms.[44]

During the Russo-Turkish War *New Times*, *Russian World*, and the more conservatively pro-government papers were united in enthusiastic and uncompromising support for the war and the commander-in-chief of the Russian forces Alexander II.

Although the journalism of the left and the right moved in opposite directions, their paths briefly converged during the widespread midsummer zeal for the Serbs. In contrast, as seen earlier in this chapter, certain of the more important Saint Petersburg dailies never fully shared the popular militancy. Rather, throughout the year they fairly consistently urged in one context or another the diplomatic and economic folly of Russia's involvement in any war, no matter how just. *Voice* emphasized diplomatic realism, or the practical necessity of acting in concert with other European powers in order to avoid formation of a hostile anti-Russian coalition; *Stock Market Notices* and lesser representatives of what *New Times* liked to call "stockmarket liberalism" pointed out the financial and industrial weakness of Russia, which in their view could neither successfully sustain nor quickly recover from a war.

Contrary to the accusations of *New Times* and the pan-Slavic publicists, *Voice* always made clear its sympathy for the South Slavs and its recognition of Russia's special interest in the Balkan peoples. Nonetheless, it is true that the paper responded to Serbian military reverses by calling for European diplomatic intervention (while *New Times* demanded Russian military involvement). Two days before Alexander II issued his formal declaration of war against Turkey, *Voice* was still advocating diplomatic efforts to preserve peace.[45]

The financial papers advocated concentration on internal economic development and attempted to demonstrate that national strength depended upon domestic manufacture and trade rather than upon military exploits in foreign lands. In addition to citing the poverty of the Russian people and the already precarious position of the ruble at home and abroad, they avowed themselves lovers of peace, horrified by the prospect of needless bloodshed which diplomacy could prevent. *New Times,* on the other hand, insisted that all their protestations concealed the speculator's fear that stock market prices might fall in time of war. *Stock Market Notices* pointed out to Suvorin that Russian shipping made little use of the Dardanelles not because the Turks controlled the passageway but because Russia had few ships and almost no foreign trade. *New Times* retorted not with reason or statistics but by asserting that its fellow daily was an "organ of plutocratic interests" and hence could have no feeling of national honor or national pride. Similarly, Suvorin's paper asserted that *Stock Exchange (Birzha)* would swing around to support of the Slavic cause as soon as Serbian bonds came to be quoted on the market.[46]

Thus on the Eastern question *Voice* and the financial papers took a stand which allied them with neither left nor right of the Rusian journalistic world. Contemporaries called them organs of moderate liberalism and it was as such that *New Times* railed against them. They displayed other hallmarks of liberalism as well: support for "Europe" and the Great Reforms, hostility to both chauvinism and radicalism, absence of populist assumptions on an exclusively agricultural future. While in spring and summer their prescriptions on foreign policy coincided with those in favor at court, by the end of the year they had acquired an oppositional character. Late in the following year, when the Turks halted the initially successful Russian advance through Bulgaria, they began at once to suggest a negotiated peace (while *New Times* gnashed its teeth and called on all loyal Russians to rally around emperor and army for an all-out effort to win). *Voice* in fact acquired in the mid-seventies a reputation as the most liberal daily paper in the capital and the nearest thing to a replacement for Korsh's *Saint Petersburg Notices.*[47]

*   *   *

Thus Suvorin, by championing the liberation movement of the South Slavs to the extent of unconditional support for armed intervention by the Russian state, found himself alienated from his former friends and allied with his former enemies. A few years earlier he had written with sorrow of an old friend who succumbed to the patriotic clatter of the Crimean War era, and with scorn of newspapermen who boasted of a lofty Russian mission in order to flatter the crowd and make money. Now his onetime colleagues, with some reason, accused him of the same. His enthusiasm for unilateral military action led him to denounce not only European diplomacy but whole European peoples, which brought him close to rejection of the symbolic Europe that summarized the aims and dreams of Russian liberalism. His new-found passion for Slavic peoples, in whom he had demonstrated no previous interest, united him with the pan-Slavic theorists whose articles began to appear in his newspaper. His own writings took on a neo-Slavophile coloration, although to a greater extent in subsequent years than in 1876. As a passion with necessarily military overtones, it also brought him close to certain so-called aristocrats whom he had once denounced as would-be oligarchs.

It is impossible to determine Suvorin's private thoughts and intentions in 1876. Probably he still considered himself in the tradition of the oppositional intelligentsia. Writing privately to Dragomanov during the course of their public polemic, Suvorin told the Ukrainian historian that "no matter what the government may be like, I am ready to give it my soul if it will go liberate the Slavs." He further explained that he was trying to separate the aspirations of educated society from those of the Ministry of Foreign Affairs in order to awaken a spirit of independence in society, or at the least to arouse some awareness other than the "spirit of money-grubbing and corruption." In October Saltykov-Shchedrin bluntly told him that he had no literary allies left except *Russian World* and Katkov's *Moscow Notices*—to which Suvorin replied with cheerful indifference, or so at least the satirist reported. Those who knew him in later years found he fell at times into short-lived fits of melancholy, brought on by accusations that he had sold himself and turned traitor. His diary, for all its trivialities, shows clearly that throughout the nineties and the first years of the twentieth century, while his newspaper seemed to give unquestioning support to repressive autocracy, Suvorin himself scorned the "degenerates" of the ruling spheres of bureaucracy and loathed his own servility toward them. This did not hinder him from moving to a conservative pro-government position by a process which began already in 1876 when he praised the liberating powers of the Russian army. By the late seventies a survey by the censorship authorities found *New Times* to be the "most moderate and loyal of all the newspapers in Saint Petersburg." By 1881 the bureaucracy thought well enough of Suvorin to turn to him for assistance in popularizing the official point of view. When the philosopher V. S. Solovev raised a public stir by urging Alexander III to spare the lives of his father's assassins, the minister of internal affairs sent a high-ranking emissary to persuade Suvorin to write an article "in the spirit of the government" against clemency.[48]

Despite the existence in 1876 of more thoroughly rightist organs like *Russian World,* Suvorin and his newspaper provided the chief target for journalistic hostility to "liberation from above" by the Russian state power, and all that it implied. *Cause,* for example, placed *New Times* at the head of all the "Tashkenters of theory" who were trying to divert public opinion from serious internal questions to noisy chauvinism.[49] Yet that same journal constantly described *New Times* as a caprice, wholly lacking in consistent direction, and Suvorin himself as a witty but idea-less feuilletonist who had strayed far out of his element when he took up politics. And *Cause* was not alone in this judgment. However, Suvorin was an apostate, as others were not, and moreover, publications like *Russian World* never gained many readers. By the end of its first year under Suvorin's direction, *New Times* was one of the two most widely circulated periodicals in the empire. Early in September Suvorin announced he was printing as many copies as *Voice* (about twenty thousand a day). As Eliseev noted bitterly, Providence seemed to have arranged the Serbian war just for the sake of *New Times.*[50]

Whatever the precise figures, circulation and therefore readership of *New Times* soared strikingly in less than a year. The immediate material success of Suvorin's newspaper has sometimes been explained by the fact that it managed to obtain quantities of exciting and comparatively fresh (if not always accurate) news from the theater of war and insurrection. In addition to correspondents engaged from among those already in the area as combatants or onlookers, almost every member of the permanent editorial staff—including Likhacheva, although not Likhachev—seems to have gone to the Balkans at some point during the year. But the "authorized historians" of *New Times* preferred to emphasize that their newspaper supported the struggling Slavs when its rivals, and especially *Voice,* did not; hence *New Times* rose and *Voice* fell in importance. As Suvorin and his associates put it on so many occasions during that stormy year, the public would judge between them—and the public chose the Slavs and *New Times.* However, available figures do not bear out the constant assertion that society was rejecting *Voice.* Its retail sales were always somewhat greater than those of Suvorin's paper, while subscriptions to both rose still higher during the following year (1877). The true explanation would seem then to be that events in the Balkans aroused a great hunger for war news; but it is also likely that the aggressive and optimistic nationalism of *New Times* touched a responsive chord among many readers. Whatever the reservations of the oppositional intelligentsia, police reports show that the idea of war with Turkey to save the Slavs enjoyed great popularity among all strata of at least the urban population during the second half of 1876 and the first months of 1877.[51]

*   *   *

Following its dashing debut during the Serbian war, *New Times* continued its course as a nationalistic paper favoring an aggressive foreign policy in line with pan-Slavic aspirations. The basic characteristics of this policy may be more clearly delineated in reaction to defeat than to victory. As noted above, when the emperor declared war in April 1877 and his armies poured across Romania and over the Transcaucasian frontier into the territories of the Ottoman Empire, the Russian press either supported military intervention or spoke of it as little as possible. At first the Russians moved forward rapidly; many papers duplicated Suvorin's raptures over each new success of the "great Russian tsar and his people, true help and patron of all the oppressed."[52]

In mid-summer the Turkish forces rallied. The main Russian strength was halted before Plevna early in July, while advance columns which had crossed the Balkans were driven back again. After three sanguinary and disastrous attempts to take Plevna by storm, the weary and decimated Russians settled down to starve out the Turkish garrison. In Asia Minor, meanwhile, the Turks forced the Russians to abandon their gains and retreat behind their own frontiers. The elite Guards regiments left Saint Petersburg for the front, amid wild rumors of rout and ruin. Revelations of scandal in the commissariat and breakdown in the medical service, added to enemy blockage of the southern ports, depreciation of the ruble, and failure of the latest state bond issue, further dampened enthusiasm for the war.

By September, after the last and bloodiest repulse at Plevna, the pent-up discontents of almost every sector of the Russian public were bursting the bonds of customary caution. Pan-Slavs openly attacked the army leadership. Zemstvo liberals, many of whom had hoped from the beginning of the war that a ruler who liberated foreign Slavs might also liberate Russians, prepared petitions on civil rights and spread rumors about constituent assemblies. Revolutionary circles multiplied their activities. In the autumn the famous public prosecution of 193 young populists (arrested after they "went to the people" in 1873–1874) climaxed a series of show trials intended to demonstrate the dangers lurking on the left. Contrary to official hopes, the trial aroused widespread sympathy for the accused. The serious periodical press began again to stress the primacy of internal over external questions and the need for full publicity of social ills. To Suvorin's disgust, liberal newspapers cast longing eyes at the idea of an armistice or even a negotiated peace which would leave the Ottoman Empire intact below the Balkan range. The western press freely predicted the collapse of autocracy. From London, Karl Marx rejoiced that in the East the revolution was at hand.[53]

New Times responded to the historical moment by attacking every suggestion of armistice and by reminding its readers that the "terrible sacrifices the present war demands from Russia place us all under obligation not to consider peace until the Turkish horde is driven back into Asia." Citing reports in Europe that Russia had bled herself white, Suvorin's newspaper called upon the Russian press to abandon its alleged apathetic silence and to counter the western lies with all the united moral strength of Russian society. To proposals that the army winter in Romania, the paper retorted that only the dynastic armies of the past could thus retire from the field; a national army with national aims had to continue the struggle in all seasons.[54]

Suvorin continued to praise the regenerative powers of the great common struggle in the Balkans. He could not, he wrote, understand those who opposed the war. But many had not lost their faith in the mission of the Russian people and still believed that Hagia Sofia in Constantinople would be Christian again. "No one will crush the Russian people, no one will stop it, not Turkish pashas, nor Hungarian and Polish magnates, nor all the forces hostile to us in the whole of Europe; this is not boasting—our whole history is for this . . . [*sic*]." Indignantly rejecting suggestions that army and economy stood on the verge of collapse, he urged the "stock market interests" to make a few sacrifices for once, to give up their champagne and expensive French mistresses, rather than let the whole weight of the war rest on the simple people and on the middle strata from which the officers came. The war, he reminded critics and waverers, was not yet at an end—"Wait two or three years"![55]

New Times joined in the widespread press demand for publicity; unlike the oppositional press, however, it emphasized the necessity for full discussion of inadequacies to improve military efforts. Besides, the paper noted in a typical strain, foreign so-called allies had already told so many lies about Russia that there was no need to worry lest the truth make a bad impression abroad. In aid of truth, *New Times* painted heartrending pictures of the wounded lying cold and hungry in the open fields and pleaded in almost every issue for aid to the Red Cross. It made no attempt to discover the reasons for the poverty and inadequacy of the medical service. The paper gave only brief attention to the zemstvos. It proposed that the zemstvo organizations of southern Russia take over provisioning the army on a non-profit basis, so that the food would be fit to eat and the money would go to the Russian people rather than to swarms of Jewish contractors.[56]

New Times' chief contribution to the demand for publicity lay, however, in the revelations of its editor-publisher about the Greger, Gorvitz and Kogan Corporation, a firm supplying food under contract to the army in the Balkans. Along with a host of other newsmen, Suvorin spent most of the summer in Bucharest, talking with wounded Russian heroes and fuming against the ingratitude of the pseudo-French Romanian intelligentsia with its stupid dreams of retaining Bessarabia. In September he suddenly denounced the commissary contractors. Their office in Bucharest was the New Jerusalem Temple, their hotel Little Vienna, and thence to worship came hordes of dishonest, profit-greedy Yid subcontractors in strange greasy clothes. The food they provided was overpriced, underweight, usually spoiled, and often did not reach the troops anyway. Suvorin strongly implied that the root cause of all these failures lay in Jewishness, although he also hinted at a significant link to hostile Austria.

Several days later, replying to unnamed challengers of his blanket indictment, he added that the Yids of the commissariat kept Viennese Yid newspapers and Turkish spies informed on all Russian troop movements. When Rabbi S. Z. Minor of Moscow protested against the "anti-Jewish agitation" and especially the last accusation, adding that he wrote in *Moscow Notices* because the Jews lacked a press organ of their own, *New Times* demanded to know what prevented the Jews from founding a paper, "rather than the taverns, pot-houses, banking counters, and in general other 'philanthropic' institutions which the Jews keep for the exploitation of the Russian people?" Suvorin's newspaper hastened to add, however, that it did not intend to attack the whole Jewish people or any other people. Jews fought and died with Russians in the army, but the worst of Jewry also played a role in the present campaign. No more was said about spying.[57]

Beyond doubt the commissariat was dishonest; its peculations and those of others were widely discussed at the time. Saltykov-Shchedrin satirized such profiteers and their highly placed protectors in *Notes of the Fatherland.* The underground press accused the grand dukes of involvement. The liberal and radical periodicals, however, attacked not Jews but exploiters in general. As *Cause* sternly pointed out to Suvorin, "pure-blooded Russians" were involved as well. *New Times* disregarded this criticism and continued to couple the words Yid and food contractors as it followed the government's inconclusive postwar investigation of the company; the names of Greger, Gorvitz and Kogan assumed a dishonored place in the standard rhetorical vocabulary of the paper.[58]

After four months of gloom and tension, the military situation once again changed dramatically. At the end of November the Turks at Plevna surrendered. Resistance in the Balkans collapsed and the Russians moved over the mountains toward the Turkish capital. Adrianople fell early in January and the Porte sued for peace. An armistice took effect a week later, but peace negotiations were delayed and ended only on 19 February. The resultant Treaty of San Stefano included, among other provisions, creation of a large autonomous Bulgaria under initial Russian supervision and military occupation. Fearing to provoke British attack, the Russians made no effort to capture the straits. Even before the armistice took effect, Britain and Austria-Hungary protested against the terms of peace. The following months were filled with diplomatic maneuvers to avert an Anglo-Russian war and to bring about a revision of San Stefano which would be acceptable to all the European powers. Part of the Russian army remained encamped near the Turkish capital, but the emperor was forced at last to recognize the futility of any attempt to take the city by storm. A British fleet occupied the Dardanelles.

The immediate threat of war ended when all the powers accepted the invitation of Bismarck (acting as self-styled "honest broker") to attend an international diplomatic congress. The Congress of Berlin met throughout June 1878 and resulted in a general reduction in the gains made by Russia and her presumed clients, the South Slavic states. Most important was the division of the San Stefano Bulgaria into three parts, of which only the northernmost became autonomous. To balance Russian gains, Britain occupied Cyprus and Austria occupied Bosnia-Herzegovina. The position of the straits remained as before.

From the surrender of Plevna to the Treaty of San Stefano, *New Times* in increasingly emotional tones insisted that the Russian army must occupy Constantinople and seize control of the straits. Typical of its lead articles from this period was one which explained that Russia did not really *need* Tsargrad; rather, the Russian army and Russian hearts demanded it as the "aureole of Russian glory" and the powerful uniting symbol of the Slavic people. Although the paper finally admitted the unpleasant condition of the national economy, it grossly overestimated Russian military strength; moreover, it asserted, the "moral atmosphere" had become cleaner and all but a handful of the fainthearted favored a war to the finish. Like Ivan Aksakov and other ardent voices of the pan-Slavic spirit, *New Times* refused to believe that victorious Russia could not defy the European powers and divide European Turkey as it wished. The paper continually warned the government to disregard the empty threats of Slav-hating western governments that sought to restore the power of the sultan. The editors recognized neither military nor diplomatic impediments; for example, when English warships appeared off Constantinople, they wrote that this action removed the last reason for the Russian army not to move into the city. As *Cause* pointed out, for *New Times* the opinion of Europe had ceased to exist; the paper proposed not a foreign policy but a common provocation.[59]

In mid-March Suvorin's paper began to prepare for war with England. Almost to the eve of the congress, its lead articles discussed the "coming conflict" under such headings as "What Means of War Will England Choose?" (raids and diversions, as in Portugal against Napoleon I), "The Strategic Significance of the Bosporus for Us in the Coming War" (seize the shoreline now before England digs in), and so forth. It may be suspected that *New Times* positively looked forward to settling scores with Britain. It rapped *Stock Market Notices* for failure to understand why there should be war between the two countries, even as it praised *Russian World* for writing that the time had come to topple hypocritical and tyrannical England from the pedestal it had occupied so long and from which it had insulted so many peoples.[60]

In mid-April *New Times* began to publicize the volunteer fleet, a scheme under the patronage of the heir apparent to purchase ocean liners by popular contribution and refit them as armed privateers to destroy British shipping.[61] From that time to the end of August almost every issue carried in the center of the front page an account of the latest contributions and of benefit entertainments in aid of the new fleet. After the congress, however, the "primary theater of struggle" against England shifted from the Sea of Marmora to the Afghan border area where, as *New Times* noted hopefully, the "preponderance of strength is on the side of Russia." In addition to endlessly analyzing military preparations and prospects in Central Asia, the paper began to dwell on the suffering and starvation of India, "on whose blood juices England lives." Strangely enough *New Times*—preoccupied as it was with agitation against Britain—gave comparatively little attention to the bloody insurgent struggles which accompanied the Austrian occupation of Bosnia-Herzegovina in the autumn. It would seem that Russian control of the straits had become more important than the independence of the South Slavs for whose sake the war supposedly had been waged.[62]

The concessions made to the European powers before and during the Congress of Berlin disappointed all sectors of Russian society. However, the liberal and radical press, out of opposition to pan-Slavism, to chauvinism, and to further war, responded to the congress by tepid support for the principle of international settlement coupled with satirical sallies against the type of furious nationalist outburst which brought *Citizen* temporary suspension and Ivan Aksakov exile to his country estate.[63] *New Times,* although indignant, managed to moderate its tone and avoid even a warning.[64] Rather, it poured out its ire against other publications, for example, *Herald of Europe,* which haughtily pointed out that if Russia had asked for less it might have ended with more.[65] In attempting to analyze the causes of Russia's diplomatic defeat, *New Times* gave first place (after the general hatred of European rulers for Slavs) to the alleged failings of Russia's diplomats, especially the "cosmopolitan type of eternally smiling diplomat" who was "master of the phrase" and indifferent to the interests of his fatherland. *New Times* was particularly incensed by the discovery that Russian diplomats corresponded among themselves in French; it continued to hark back to this for some months, urging diplomats to learn to speak the language of their own country. Pointing out the abnormality of a situation in which a chancellery, regiment, or ministry could be filled with men from the Baltic provinces who hardly knew a word of Russian, the, paper nonetheless scorned "certain organs" that claimed to see danger in every German name—Totleben, for example, the victor at Plevna, had a German name but was beyond doubt a real Russian.[66]

Despite its acknowledgement that Bismarck had done less for Russia at the congress than Russia had a right to expect, *New Times* held aloof from the press campaign against Bismarck and Germany that many Russian newspapers conducted during late 1878 and 1879.[67] It even poked fun at the excessive alarmism of such papers as *Saint Petersburg Notices,* which announced that Germans controlled not only the German Empire but also all the hospitals of Russia. But at the same time Suvorin's newspaper glorified the Russian drift into diplomatic isolation, surely another manifestation of persistent overconfidence. It rejoiced that Russia was now free of all diplomatic debts to Germany or any other state. Again and again the paper emphasized that Russia had tested its allies—Austria in the Crimea, Germany at the congress—and found them wanting; hence Russia could depend only upon herself and her "hands should be free from all obligations."[68]

Throughout the Russo-Turkish War and the protracted aftermath of peace settlements, for *New Times* the most dangerous enemies were not the Turks but the Turkophile Magyars, and even more, the perfidious English. The Russian blood spilled in the Balkans lay on the heads of the lords and gentlemen who directed British policy.[69] The English were generally depicted as intriguers and profiteers greedy for gain, although the paper sometimes distinguished the Tory aristocrats from Gladstone and the basically decent pro-Slavic English people; the Magyars were an undifferentiated mass of fanatics impelled by hatred of Slavdom (and assisted by English gold). Unlike the thick journals or the hated *Voice, New Times* made little attempt to probe the inner mechanisms of international diplomacy or to unravel the complex motives of the contending powers. Suvorin and his colleagues evidently saw the world as a cockpit of mass emotions. It must be admitted that they sometimes showed ingenuity in discovering slightly more rational if equally unlikely motivations within their vaguely neo-Slavophile framework of thought. Thus, they printed excerpts from Disraeli's novel, *Tancred, or the New Crusade,* which demonstrated, they wrote, not only that the prime minister of England admitted Europe had lived out its time, but also that he saw in the peoples of the East a healthy, renewing element for civilization; hence he loved the Turks and naturally was an opponent of Russia and Slavdom (in which *New Times* saw the "renewing element").[70] The reader of the oppositional press during this period was exposed to a world of rational political calculation to a far greater extent than was the reader of *New Times.*

As the Russo-Turkish War receded in time, the oppositional press redoubled its attacks on *New Times* for neglecting internal questions —with some reason. Suvorin responded with furious denunciations of "doctrinaire liberalism," while his paper retorted that the Slavic question could never be foreign to Russians, and anyway Proudhon, Zola, and so forth, were not exactly internal matters either.[71] It would be misleading to accept this accusation literally, however, just as it would be an oversimplification to assume that *New Times,* having praised the state power for so long in foreign wars, would then support it without reservation at home. In fact, as the possibility of war with England waned, the newspaper devoted much attention to defense of the Great Reforms, to pleas for freedom of the press, and to small suggestions for widening the practical competence of the zemstvo organizations. In his feuilletons Suvorin returned to the struggle against plutocracy, embezzlement, and greed, although with the new ingredient of Yid exploitation. In late 1878 the paper even revived the campaign against excessively classical education and for some months hit out regularly at the allegedly callous and reactionary pedagogical views of *Moscow Notices.* When a jury acquitted Vera Zasulich for shooting at the widely despised governor of Saint Petersburg in retaliation for the flogging of a political prisoner, *New Times* defended the verdict and the popular approval of the acquittal as acts of genuine patriotism, a rebuke to extraordinary and extralegal punishments. The decision was a "verdict of social conscience not against state and law, but in defense of lawfulness and consequently for state and law." The paper scornfully rejected the fears of *Moscow Notices* that the case and the sympathetic public response threatened the safety of the existing state order. It may be noted, however, that this was written early in 1878, in the first flush of San Stefano and before the great wave of successful assassinations that began soon after.[72]

The war of 1877 had revealed the weakness and incompetence of the imperial government in a manner reminiscent of the Crimean defeat, even though the Turks had been defeated. And as in 1905 and 1917, although on a lesser scale, the heightened political awareness and tremendous economic and social strains of the war led to widespread discontent and great expectations, further aroused and reinforced by the terrorist activities of small radical groups. In the lull of the late sixties a vigorous defense of the Great Reforms could mark a periodical as indisputably liberal. A decade later, in the midst of student disorders, constitutionalist rumblings, and underground revolutionary publications, a newspaper which contented itself with preserving past gains could not easily qualify as oppositional—especially when, like *New Times,* it coupled a defensist position with aggressive nationalism. When Suvorin's critics asked him what he had to say about the Kharkov zemstvo and about youth, they were demanding his opinions on constitutionalism and radicalism. In both cases his answers were ultimately unsatisfactory.

In August 1878, unnerved by mounting revolutionary terror, the government appealed for public support in its struggle against the "criminal propaganda" of a "band of evilly-disposed elements."[73] The emperor himself repeated the appeal a few months later. By that time the zemstvo organizations, or at least their liberal members, had already been caught up in the general social agitation. Numerous addresses to the emperor were drafted, although few were actually presented. Attempts were made to form a national union of zemstvo participants and to make contact with radical groups. From Geneva the émigré journal *Common Cause* (*Obshchee delo*) began to preach political emancipation. In response to the official appeal, several zemstvo leaders attempted to reply that effective public cooperation with the government remained impossible in the absence of educational reform, freedom of the press, and the strict rule of law. The Kharkov zemstvo humbly begged Alexander II to give his people what he had given the Bulgars—a constitution.

New Times responded at once to the government's appeal by affirming that in the recent war the "healthy forces" of society had already shown their ability and desire to work with the emperor in his great undertakings; however, for effective elimination of "destructive forces," society had to be able to express itself frankly through a press that could openly discuss the "inadequacies of social structure, inadequacies of education, inadequacies of our zemstvo self-government, inadequacies of the bureaucracy." In subsequent months the newspaper continued to express this essentially liberal view. It emphasized the valuable role the zemstvo ought to play and rejected the view of *Moscow Notices* that not publicity but police constituted the best means of struggle against secret societies. However, it also repudiated the circuitous hints of *Voice* that one could not sympathize with "very cruel, dictatorial means of preventing these crimes" any more than one could support the "wild elements" who perpetrated them. While significant sectors of educated society were indifferent or even sympathetic to those acts of terror which could be regarded as tyrannicide, *New Times* fulminated against internal apathy and the horror of hearing killers openly praised as "good people."[74]

As the number of attempts on the life of Alexander II mounted, Suvorin's horror evidently mounted too. He began to write long and emotional articles praising the person of the emperor in a manner entirely foreign to the customs of Russian oppositional journalism, no matter how moderate. He dwelt on the great heroic exploit of tsar and people, together side by side in the Balkans, when the Great Liberator had exposed himself to death many times; he assured his readers that Alexander had devoted his whole life to the well-being of the people, that he had not lost faith in his people, and so forth.[75]

At the same time Suvorin began to call for "self knowledge" of the Russian land, for thorough investigations into the condition of the peasantry. Since information coming into Saint Petersburg invariably adjusted itself to the bureaucratic demands of the moment, provincial committees like the pre-emancipation statistical committee should be established to study the life of the people. Exhortations to "know the life of the people" had filled the pages of radical periodicals for some years. In the late seventies, however, the spreading social breakdown and growing money economy evident in the countryside led some of their contributors to question the relevance of populist assumptions. Challenged by skeptics and by the rising political excitement of the time, intellectuals who remained true to the commune faith hastened to the villages to learn the facts. Both radicals and moderates, many employed by the zemstvos, poured out books, articles, and statistical tables on peasant life. As *New Times* noted, everyone was talking about the need to investigate village conditions and to publish the findings fully. But where the oppositional intelligentsia hungered to know the people so as to save them from bureaucrats and capitalists, *New Times* sought to aid the government in saving them from the oppositional intelligentsia. Precise knowledge, the newspaper explained, would make it possible to "eliminate all harmful influence over them by various evil-intentioned people, no matter in what form they should appear."[76]

To further the cause of knowledge Suvorin sent a special correspondent to travel through Russia and report his findings. The articles which resulted dwelt on news of the moment, especially measures against a plague epidemic then raging in some areas, and on commercial-industrial development in provincial cities. At the very end of the decade, when the government seemed on the verge of granting greater scope to the zemstvo movement, the struggles of the latter against local bureaucracies also received great attention. Both liberal and radical periodicals continually attacked *New Times'* wandering correspondent for his alleged false optimism and failure to know the *real* life of the people. Suvorin retorted angrily that the day of satirical descriptions had passed and that contemporary needs required objective truth.[77]

By the end of the decade *New Times* generally stood on the side of the government—or at least of the reform-minded wing of the higher bureaucracy—in any question that forced a contrast between official and liberal-constitutional views. Suvorin's attitude toward the newspaper *Order* illustrates his position in the period just before the assassination of Alexander II. In the midst of rumors that new reforms would issue forth shortly by the gracious favor of the Autocrat, the editors of *Herald of Europe* founded *Order* to further the cause of rule by law. The program statement explained that the rudeness of Russian life arose from ignorance. "There is no order without clear awareness on the part of each person of his rights and obligations."[78] The liberal newspaper's chief immediate targets were Aksakov's neo-Slavophile semi-monthly *Rus,* and the bureaucrats of the Ministry of

Internal Affairs who sought to bypass and limit the zemstvo organizations.

Suvorin and his colleagues attacked *Order* almost daily during its lone year of existence. Burenin undertook a campaign to ridicule it. The hostility of *New Times* became more marked after the fatal first day of March, when Suvorin's newspaper supported Aksakov's "Muscovite" reaction to the emperor's violent death. But even in January, when the future seemed bright and *New Times* stood for sweeping extensions of local self-government, Suvorin contrasted the boring doctrinaire liberalism and paper projects of *Order* to the dynamic activism of General Count M. T. Loris-Melikov, in 1880 "dictator of the heart" and in early 1881 minister of internal affairs. *Order* offered rules unrelated to the "original national character" of Russian life, according to Suvorin, while Loris-Melikov (who asked the moderate opposition to trust in him but made no concrete promises in return) was a "man of the present regime" who would realize the reform program of Alexander II, Great Liberator and Defender of the Russian land.[79]

In the days immediately following the death of Alexander II, *Order* urged that the sad event not hinder introduction of a constitutional regime with implementation of the rumored but now "postponed" reforms of the late ruler. *New Times* fumed with righteous indignation over the lightminded appeals of liberal organs which could thus overlook 1 March and could urge, like unfeeling automatons, the false idea that everything could proceed as before.[80]

While *New Times* turned against liberal constitutionalism only gradually, it rejected the "movement of youth" immediately and unequivocally. By opposing student demonstrations the paper made clear its hostility not only to hundreds of young men whose careers were cut short at their beginning by prison or exile (and who enjoyed great sympathy among much of the educated public) but also to the non-terrorist and comparatively moderate radicalism they symbolized. Moreover, at least since the early sixties youth (young *intelligenty*, especially students) had become a sacrosanct symbol of oppositional beliefs, a symbol to be criticized only by publicists of the reactionary camp. As Suvorin wrote bitterly in the late seventies, he found himself an object of hatred because he did not burn incense to youth.[81]

New Times' immediate reaction to the first important "student incident" of the period, the raising of the red flag before Kazan Cathedral in late 1876, typified its then overriding concern with the Eastern question. Such disorders, the paper wrote, aided enemies in Europe who looked for any excuse to claim that Russian society was not united. As student demonstrations multiplied in number and spread from city to city after the war, however, *New Times* became increasingly disturbed by the whole nightmare of "mindless disorders," including those of students, and by the "indifference, irony, or lyrical transports" with which too many publicists greeted them. Suvorin began to fill whole columns with ill-humored disquisitions on the theme that "students ought to study" and not imagine they could lead public opinion.[82]

But while the left attacked him for hatred of youth, Suvorin attacked the right for attempting to fight subversion by limiting educational opportunities and restricting curricula. Thus, he defended students of poorer origin from charges that they were responsible for the unrest; in fact, he urged that more young men from less wealthy strata of society be assisted to study. Confronted with an official decree that boys completing the seminary course might no longer enter a university without examination, *New Times* pointed out the importance of increasing—not decreasing—the number of young people who received higher education. When Katkov announced that more rigorous application of his classical principles constituted the true means of combating society's ills, Suvorin rushed to attack with accustomed vigor and argued as of old that Russia needed less narrow, less restricted, less oppressively difficult schooling. In fact, his new neo-Slavophile vocabulary gave him an additional anti-Katkovian argument. Russian pedagogues ought to develop a "national Russian" curriculum and cease to be slaves to Europe.[83]

It may be noted that Suvorin's vocabulary changed significantly during the course of the late seventies. In the first issue of *New Times,* as in previous years, he wrote of "shining personalities," "honest people," and similar terms from the customary language of the oppositional intelligentsia. By the end of 1876, however, such unaccustomed phrases as "organic idea" and "Slavic soul" appeared more and more frequently in his feuilletons. He discussed the "Russian spirit" and the "genius of the Russian people" and began to refer to the country by its pre-Petrine name, Rus. Although the heady winds of racial thought and biological metaphor blew everywhere through Europe in the last quarter of the century, Suvorin's linguistic transformation may be seen as a tribute to the influence of his new neo-Slavophile associates. His use of conventional ideological symbols demonstrates, however, that he did not fall completely under their sway. While he accepted "Moscow," he never fully rejected "Peter the Great."

For the earlier Suvorin and for other liberal journalists, Moscow was not only the special domain of the dreaded Katkov; it also symbolized (as in the epigraph to Chapter IV) all that was backward, slovenly, and submissive in the old Russia of pre-Reform days. In the disillusioned atmosphere of 1878 Suvorin discovered another Moscow, a "national Russian city" which "grew up around the Kremlin, the tsar, and the Russian saints, and has remained true to them to this day." When *Voice* accused him of wishing to return to pre-Petrine barbarism, Suvorin retorted that old Russia was not more barbarous than medieval Europe and had been characterized, moreover, by freedom and equality. Comparisons between the two capitals became commonplace in his writing from that time. Moscow preserved individuality while Saint Petersburg made everyone alike; Moscow grew out of the soil while Saint Petersburg was like a temporary encampment, and so forth. Hence it can have come as no surprise when, following the assassination of Alexander II, *New Times* seconded Aksakov's call to remove the center of government from Peter's city— "Home! Home! To Moscow!"[84]

At the same time Suvorin continued to praise Peter I as a great and necessary reformer. But his westernisms placed a heavy burden on the common people, who gained nothing until Alexander II "returned to the free foundations" of Rus when he emancipated the serfs. By 1881, however, Suvorin's enthusiasm for Peter was only slightly greater than his affection for the "Saint Petersburg liberals," who found somehow sympathetic the first emperor's "terribly cruel and despotic" struggle against old Rus. In reality, Suvorin explained, Peter had persecuted every manifestation of human freedom while achieving only very little in return.[85]

New Times' campaign for extension of zemstvo responsibilities

(1880–early 1881) reflected its owner's new "organic" orientation. For example, the paper agreed with various liberal periodicals that as many of the best people as possible must be attracted to zemstvo work; the wider the circle of participants, the greater the attention the government would give to zemstvo needs. But it also emphasized the undesirability of relying unduly upon the intelligentsia in local self-administration. The most talented *intelligent* was nevertheless foreign to the particular region, while true understanding of local conditions and problems required the historical bond with the land possessed by its "native, age-old representatives"—that is, the local gentry.[86]

Related to this strain of thought was Suvorin's rediscovery of the gentry as a class. The Russian gentry, he explained, had never been an aristocracy; rather, thanks to democracy of access, it consisted of the "educated democracy" and was characterized by a "fatherly relation to the younger brother" (the common people). *New Times* urged the supposedly vanishing gentry to reassume its corporate role and work together in the zemstvo and as a "cultural force." *Rumor* promptly accused the newspaper of supporting the views of General Fadeev and imitating the Polish or Baltic-German aristocracies. *New Times* retorted that the Russian gentry was not a closed caste and in fact formed a "middle estate, in the sense of the historical center of intellectual forces."[87] It may be noted, however, that access to the gentry estate lay only through state service. Hence Suvorin and his colleagues were offending against the anti-bureaucratic as well as the democratic strivings of the oppositional intelligentsia.

During the periods under consideration Suvorin analyzed the intellectual alignments of educated society as a return to the ideals of the forties and the opposition of Slavophiles to Westernizers. The neo-Westernizers of the late seventies were the liberals, who allegedly bowed before every western influence. Suvorin assured his readers and critics repeatedly that he valued European science and had no intention of building a wall between Russia and Europe; rather, he simply wished Russians to be Russians, not doctrinaire pseudo-liberal or pseudo-radical pseudo-Europeans. He himself, he wrote, had never been a liberal or an adherent of any party. Throughout his journalistic career his only aim had been to criticize the negative sides of Russian life. Nevertheless, he knew the liberals well: men who have convinced themselves that they represent the people and that what is good for them is good for the people. But in reality, Suvorin concluded, the liberals were like cats—quiet, mild, soft-pawed cats who pounce on the people and play with them as cats play with mice.[88]

While Suvorin rejected liberalism as hostile to the true interests of the *narod*, he refused to align himself decisively with the neo-Slavophile party. *New Times* affected an uncommitted aloofness from partisan allegiances. Even after March 1881 the paper continued to find both tendencies "too theoretical" (although the Slavophiles were "closer to the people") and went so far as to urge their reconciliation —despite the hostility of such papers as *Order* to the "national Russian party," which made the editors doubt the possibility of reconciliation.[89]

Although *New Times* cultivated the *juste-milieu* among the ideological tendencies of Russian educated society, it made no claim to neutrality on the question of nationality. Rather, it lost no opportunity to defend the preeminence of the Russian language, culture, and people in the Russian Empire. By the early eighties it had become noted for its hostility to Poles, German settlers, and other non-Russian groups who showed no eagerness to become culturally assimilated into the Russian population. As early as 1879 the paper boasted that it had been the first paper to ask if Finland really needed a separate national army. It urged that the Russian language be made mandatory for official transactions in the Baltic region, in order to eliminate German pretensions to privilege and to enable the small native peoples to ally themselves with the Russians more easily. In discussing Poland, where the Russian language was already mandatory in government, the paper somewhat contradictorily asserted that this in no way effaced Polish national culture and in fact enriched the Polish language with new words and turns of speech. It is interesting to note, however, that the paper continued to urge removal of the official prohibition on the printing of Ukrainian until such suggestions became imprudent after the accession of Alexander III.[90]

By 1881 *New Times* had identified the Jews as the chief internal threat to the happiness and well-being of the Russian people. As noted above in several contexts, Suvorin and his colleagues had found occasion to criticize Jewry as early as 1876. The Jews of

Odessa failed to show enthusiasm for the South Slavic insurgents, the "Yid-Viennese papers" (especially *Neue Freie Presse*) lied about Cherniaev and the Serbian army, Yid contractors sold sandy flour to the army, and so forth.[91] *New Times'* special interest in the Jewish question did not arise, however, until about the time of the famous ritual-murder trial in Kutais.

In March 1879, in the remote Caucasian town of Kutais, ten Jewish men from a mountain village were brought to trial for the alleged kidnapping and murder of a Georgian Christian girl. The chief evidence against the defendants lay in the state's suggestion that a mysterious death just before Passover might well be connected with the supposed use of Christian blood in Jewish ritual.

Reporters flocked to the Caucasus while the press debated the possibility of ritual murder. The spectacle of "rich Saint Petersburg Jews" raising money to send the best lawyers to Kutais infuriated Suvorin, evidently since he feared the trial would present an opportunity for many speeches on "brotherhood and the poor oppressed Jews." In addition, he noted, Russian society was already intensely irritated with "Yid tactlessness" of which their interference in the affairs of the Kutais district court represented only the most recent example. While periodicals as diverse in tendency as *Herald of Europe* and *Saint Petersburg Notices* expressed their amazement that medieval prejudice should have found a place in the modern judiciary of a civilized state, *New Times* hinted darkly of strange Jewish sects with unknown practices. When the trial ended in acquittal, Suvorin suggested that the judges must have been bribed. When the noted orientalist D. A. Khvolson published a refutation of the blood myth, *New Times* countered with an "impartial review" by the liberal historian Kostomarov, who suggested at length that where there is smoke there is bound to be fire.[92]

From this time *New Times* devoted great attention to the Jews. They were tactless people, trying to make a profit no matter what, displacing Russians at every opportunity, and thanks to their impudence and wealth, able to find protection where a Russian could not. Western countries might harbor a higher type of Jew, Suvorin and his colleagues admitted, but Russian Yids were only exploiters. Hence it was necessary to protect the Russian people from these human parasites, be they the great horde of small traders who monopolized manufacturing and ruined the Christian peasantry in the Pale, or the smaller number of great plutocrats who infested Saint Petersburg and Moscow. While *Herald of Europe* insisted that the Jewish problem could be solved only by granting Jews full religious and civil liberty, including the right to settle freely throughout the empire, *New Times* welcomed their exclusion from previously permitted territories and hoped for more such positive action.[93] Suvorin's newspaper also gave considerable publicity to German and Austrian legislation against usury, pointing out the desirability of stern measures in Russia as well. Other than occasional facetious suggestions that Jews be forced to intermarry with Russians or to colonize Kamchatka, for several years the paper was unable to find additional solutions to the Jewish question.

By the end of the decade the pages of *New Times* had acquired a distinctly Judeo-phobic character, to use a common term of the era. The Jews were subjected to continual attack and insult in areas unconnected with their alleged economic exploitation of the population of West Russia. *New Times* took every opportunity to condemn the "barbarism" and "anti-spiritual nature" of the Jewish religion. It conducted systematic press campaigns against the contents and editors of Russo-Jewish periodicals, especially *Russian Jew (Russkii Evrei)*, which *New Times* preferred to call *Russian Parasite (Russkii Lishei)*.[94] A publicist who defended the Jews—or indeed criticized any opinion in *New Times*—was promptly attacked as a Yid, a "Yidizing liberal," or at least in the pay of the Yids. Contrary to the suggestions of some scholars, however, Suvorin and his colleagues made no effort during the period under study to link Jewry with the revolutionary terrorist movement.[95]

The assassination of Alexander II was closely followed by a wave of anti-Jewish pogroms in southern and western Russia. *New Times* at first welcomed such incidents as manifestations of popular anger against Yid exploitation. The paper angrily rejected all "theories" that the entire blame for the "disorders" against them might not lie on the Jews themselves. As the pogroms spread, however, Suvorin and his colleagues expressed their concern that Russia might be "lowered to the level of an uncultured state in which every-

one acted on his own." While they understood the popular indignation, they also insisted that Jewish lives and property ought to be
protected by the appropriate authorities. Noting that repression alone
was not the answer, the editors proceeded to put forward their own
modest final solution to the Jewish question: promulgate great quantities of anti-Jewish legislation so restrictive that "at least half" the
Jews would forthwith resettle themselves in western Europe and
America. Brushing aside the horrified objections of Jews and "Yidizing liberals," and even of *Moscow Notices, New Times* continued to
support substantially the same position in the months and years to
come.[96]

Urgent irrational fear of the supposed economic power and
malign influence of Jews has been a striking characteristic of modern
European culture in general. *New Times'* discovery of the Jewish
threat in the late seventies, however, coincided with a similar awareness on the part of the heir to the throne, his tutor, and sectors of
officialdom. When Alexander III succeeded his father, the new administration not only inaugurated a policy of Great Russian nationalism and Russification of subject peoples, but also reversed an official
tendency of several decades by seeking to isolate and curb the empire's
Jews. Hence *New Times,* for "patriotic" reasons, found itself in full
support of the repressive measures of a reactionary government.[97]

Saltykov-Shchedrin invented an appropriate satirical label for
Suvorin's newspaper, *What Can I Do for You?* (*Chego izvolite?,*
signifying great servility before the powers that be). Figures as
diverse as Lenin and S. Iu. Witte referred to *New Times* as *What Can
I Do for You?*[98] Suvorin's political opponents on the left accused him
of having been "bought," but the state archives, opened in 1917,
revealed no evidence of payments or special arrangements: *New
Times* was chauvinist by conviction.[99] It must be admitted that the
paper stood in comparative favor with a government that clearly
would have preferred to rule a press-less society. Suvorin received
few censorship penalties and when in 1901 he published an article on
workers' disorders, a topic expressly forbidden by circular, his right to
publish was suspended for only one week rather than the six months
allowed by law. However, Suvorin was a very careful editor. His
private diary reveals how he hated the oppressive censorship (far

stricter after 1881 than before) and loathed his own bowing to it. "You begin to prevaricate," he noted in 1896, "and to be angry in your soul both at yourself and at your abasement, which there is no possibility of throwing off."[100]

If *New Times* was noted for its nationalism and loyalty to the government, it also continued to play the traditional "exposing" role of the oppositional press. If the emperor and ministers of state were beyond criticism, their underlings were not. Even his enemies admitted that Suvorin regularly destroyed all illusions about the energy and competence of the privileged estates. *New Times* unmasked aristocrats and plutocrats as of old; by no means was all the exploitation within the Pale of Jewish settlement. As late as 1892 the extreme right in the person of V. P. Meshcherskii and his followers continued to consider Suvorin a "socialist"—in other words, too frank about provincial corruption, bureaucratic parasitism, and other evils that could be criticized without intending any attack on the social and governmental system as a whole. The left despised what they saw as total eclecticism and lack of consistent direction: one ought to be servile or oppositional, but not mix the two indiscriminately. Suvorin preferred to say that he directed a literary parliament, a parliament that was, as his admiring employees told him on the twenty-fifth anniversary of *New Times,* "raising and strengthening national consciousness in the Russian people, faith in their own strength and in their great historical vocation." What this vocation might be, no one said.[101]

epilogue

*F*ollowing purchase of the newspaper *New Times* and aided by its success, Suvorin assembled under his personal ownership a remarkable array of enterprises and publications. After only a year, in March 1877 he acquired his own printing plant, for which he imported the first high speed rotary press employed in Russia. The rotary press was just then coming into demand in western Europe; by using cylindical stereotypes to print onto a continuous roll of paper, it made the large cheap editions of late nineteenth century daily papers technologically possible. Within a decade Suvorin had four such machines, as well as the latest equipment for photography, lithography, zincography, and electrotypography. In 1890 he rounded out his industrial acquisitions with a type foundry. Suvorin's appreciation of innovation remained confined to the mechanical side of the printer's art, however. His publications employed a small and unoriginal selection of type faces. Throughout its whole existence *New Times* continued to use the narrow, ordinary type face of the previous owners.[1]

Suvorin established his printing press mainly for the sake of *New Times*. But at the end of the same year, when he managed to move into a larger building, he divided the press into newspaper and book divisions and founded a publishing firm. In 1878, its first full year of existence, the A. S. Suvorin Publishing House issued nine books, most of them about the South Slavs or the Russo-Turkish war of that year. By 1900 Suvorin brought out more than 950 titles on widely varied subjects: belles lettres, popular science, history, social thought, even luxury editions of works of art reproduced in color. All the books, as well as those of his periodicals that came out in Saint Petersburg, were produced at his own press, which from 1884 also housed a school for apprentices—thus ensuring a future generation of printers raised in the heart of the Suvorin enterprises.[2]

With possession of a press and sufficient funds, Suvorin realized a long held dream, to "flood the book market" with cheap mass editions of the literary titans of the early nineteenth century. In 1879 he brought out the first volumes in his Inexpensive Library series, which eventually extended to almost 400 titles and included authors of antiquity and some cooperative living writers (Leskov, G. P. Danilevskii, and others). By the end of the century some four million pocket sized volumes had been produced; the price began at eight kopecks per volume, but rose with slow inflation over the decades. The appearance of the works of the great Russian poet A. S. Pushkin in ten little books, for only one and a half rubles, created a literary sensation long remembered. Thousands of sets were sold in a matter of hours to a huge and eager crowd that thronged the bookstore. Radical publicists sourly noted that even these prices were not low enough for the real people out in the villages, but there can be no doubt that Suvorin did much to place the classics of Russian and world literature in the hands of readers who could not otherwise have owned them.[3]

Suvorin's burgeoning enterprises were part of a general development. In 1861 there were only 164 printing establishments in the country, few of them private. By 1894 there were 1,315. The period of the seventies, especially, saw the widespread adoption of mechanized presses. Granted that many printers devoted themselves to producing labels and price lists rather than literature, which was thought not to pay as well, nonetheless book manufacturing grew many fold during the last third of the century. Suvorin was not alone as an industrialist of the Russian book. The two greatest literary entrepreneurs of the period, M. O. Volf and A. F. Marks, established their publishing houses some time before Suvorin. Like him, they controlled a variety of periodicals and special series. But all three owed part of their fame and success to the fact that, unlike most publishers of the period, they also formed vertical business combinations. Given the relatively underdeveloped condition of the Russian book market, it was necessary not only to write, edit, and print the book, but also to place it in the hands of the reader. The greatest names in Russian publishing were those most inventive in devising means for direct distribution of their wares.[4]

Suvorin opened his own bookstore in Saint Petersburg in 1878, in Moscow in 1879, and in subsequent years in Kharkov, Odessa, Saratov, and Rostov-on-Don. In 1889 he acquired the news and concession from the then largest Russian railroad line; his books and periodicals greeted the traveler in fifty railroad stations and a number of mineral spas. The bookstores did not stock only their owner's products, but they and their catalogs kept his name constantly before the public as well as aiding immediate distribution.[5]

The Suvorin enterprises devoted great attention to general self-advertisement. While his liberal former colleagues produced commemorative volumes reiterating past, present, and future support of civic ideals, Suvorin published tributes to the size and modernity of his plant and to his paternalistic care for his employees. The *New Times* family delighted in arranging exhibits at the great national and international expositions so characteristic of the era. A representation of the medal won at the All-Russian Trade Fair of 1882 appeared for decades thereafter on the title page of books issued by the firm. Any mention of principles was left to outsiders, whether friendly or hostile.[6]

In the early eighties Suvorin put up his own press building, a large stone structure on Ertelev Lane near the commercial center of Saint Petersburg. Eventually all his press and book publishing operations, as well as the editorial offices of *New Times* and its supplements and the private apartments of the owner, were located there or in nearby buildings on the same street. Thus Ertelev Lane, the seat of Suvorin's "empire," came to occupy much the same place in oppositional rhetoric toward the end of the century that Strastnoi Boulevard, headquarters of Katkov, had occupied for Suvorin and others several decades earlier.

As *New Times* gained readers, its circulation increased geographically also. From 1881 a second, noon edition appeared with news bulletins received since printing the regular morning edition; this was intended for mailing to the central provinces in the heavily inhabited region around Moscow. A telephoned version was published in Moscow during the Russo-Japanese War, but did not live through the 1905 Revolution. At one time Suvorin spoke of establishing a Paris *New Times,* but nothing came of that plan.[7]

Elaborate illustrations made their appearance in 1885, although simple outline maps and battle plans had been used in the paper from the beginning. Later the illustrations were transferred to the supplements, and sometimes even were in color. Western European and American newspapers add pages and whole sections to accommodate new features. Russian papers, then and now, have tended to stay slim by creating separate supplements of all sorts. Suvorin's first attempt to establish a literary supplement failed to survive the social and economic depression of the early eighties. A second attempt in the revitalized atmosphere of the nineties proved more successful; it brought to subscribers twice weekly an eclectic assortment of fiction and popularly written articles on history, literature, and natural sciences.

Suvorin was an ardent amateur of Russian history. When he became wealthy he collected a remarkable private library on the subject. The fruits of his study were disappointing: one five-act play on the first false tsar Dmitrii and a thin volume attempting to prove that Dmitrii was not false but Ivan the Terrible's true son, supposedly dead at Uglich years before. Earlier, however, Suvorin realized another long standing ambition when he became publisher of a historical journal, *Historical Herald (Istoricheskii vestnik).* Although this monthly sometimes attracted contributions from well-known scholars, it was clearly intended for the general reader and even included historical fiction in its pages (subscribers received a bonus of two historical novels each year also). The early financial success of *New Times* is nowhere more clearly shown than in the fact that Suvorin could support a monthly publication for five years at considerable loss, until in 1885 *Historical Herald* began to pay for itself.[8]

Despite business success, Suvorin clearly thought of himself as primarily a man of letters. He maintained wide contacts and correspondence with important literary and artistic figures on non-commercial matters. He took pride in publishing a newspaper that was literate as well as informative. For several decades he carefully corrected every-one's grammar and style each evening before the copy could be re-leased to the printers. His admirers claim that Suvorin actively sought new writing talent and by his nurturing care developed the abilities of his journalists. The only truly outstanding writer to emerge from the forcing bed of *New Times* was A. P. Chekhov who, however, had already shown considerable ability when he began to contribute to the paper in 1886. Suvorin's search for fresh talent must have been considerably hindered by the obligatory hostility that characterized most of the intelligentsia from the early eighties. Moreover, once a man had worked for Suvorin, he could look forward to great difficulty in finding a job elsewhere; even Chekhov, when known as a con-tributor to *New Times,* experienced problems in placing his work in *Herald of Europe.*[9]

Although Suvorin continued to take a lively interest in the literary side of *New Times* almost to the year of his death, he in-creasingly gave the day to day managerial tasks of the paper and related enterprises to his oldest sons Mikhail (1860–?) and Aleksei (1862–1937). New names began to appear over the famous Sunday feuilleton while he himself contributed only an irregular "Little Feuilleton." Instead he turned his attention to the Russian stage, writing perceptive theatrical criticism and a number of plays. The latter, while hardly among the classics of world drama, enjoyed a certain popularity in their time. Most successful were *Tatiana Repina,* a thinly disguised melodramatic account of the death of a famous actress, and *Medeia,* a sentimentalized reworking of the Greek tragedy. (Themes from classical antiquity were in vogue in the eighties.) His *False Tsar Dmitrii and Tsarevna Kseniia* was praised for the accuracy of its historical detail.[10]

In 1895 Suvorin established a theatrical company, the Literary-Artistic Society of Saint Petersburg (popularly known as Suvorin's Little Theater). Although he had no official position, he often took an active role in planning and offered advice at rehearsals. The society attracted attention from its first season by winning permission to per-form previously prohibited works: Lev Tolstoi's *Power of Darkness* (1895), Aleksei K. Tolstoi's *Tsar Fedor Ioannovich* (1898), and A. V. Sukhovo-Kobylin's *Death of Tarelkin* (1900). The group's later existence was marked by a series of mediocre works, rarely of socio-political meaning. Surovin's theater was always noted for the extreme realism of its sets and staging and—like *New Times*—for the eclecticism of its program. In the early twentieth century the theater published an illustrated magazine and ran a school of drama.[11]

As his enterprises multiplied, Suvorin retained individual private ownership. Like a Muscovite merchant of the traditional stamp, he appointed relatives and old friends to direct the separate divisions of his publishing empire while keeping its overall financial condition a closely guarded secret. Bookkeeping was long rudimentary, advance budgeting unknown, and the boundary between family and company funds insufficiently firm. After the turn of the century, as Suvorin grew older and less capable of dealing with his complex affairs, extravagant children and unlucky chance brought him into considerable debt.[12]

In 1901 his son Aleksei, who had long done much of the practical work of editing *New Times* and in 1896 had officially been named assistant responsible editor, quarreled with Suvorin and left the paper. Soon thereafter he established his own daily, *Rus,* and lured many of the younger writers from *New Times* to his staff. Aleksei as factual editor of *New Times* had been an arch-nationalist and even had become deputy chairman of the Russian Assembly, an organization formed in late 1900 to support unmodified autocratic principles in government. *Rus,* however, turned out to be a liberal publication; it greeted the 1905 Revolution with enthusiasm. Whether owing to lavish salaries or inability to adjust to post-revolutionary reaction, the new paper proved financially disastrous. It dragged out a feeble existence under constantly changing names, while the elder Suvorin assumed his son's personal debts and tried to save him from the bankruptcy that finally came in 1908.[13]

After Aleksei's revolt, the less literarily inclined Mikhail became factual editor and business manager of *New Times*. He was later joined by a younger brother Boris (?–1939). To the unavoidable loss of sales and advertising revenue during 1905 were now added general confusion of management and the failure of such ill-timed new ventures, undertaken by Mikhail, as *Telephone of New Times* and *Russian Land* (*Russkaia zemlia*), a conservative paper for workers, sponsored by an organization of Moscow industrialists. Although *New Times* was holding its own in circulation, it ceased to expand. Newer papers with greater mass appeal began to outstrip it, while yet larger and more efficient publishers appeared to challenge Suvorin's position in the book market. To pay existing obligations and satisfy the demands of a growing horde of Suvorin relatives, Mikhail enmeshed himself and the firm in a web of debt. Like the imperial Russian government, he soon was borrowing to pay the interest due on previous loans.

At long last the elder Suvorin, already dying of cancer of the throat, was persuaded by the director of the Volga-Kama Commercial Bank, a major creditor, to permit incorporation of his holdings and the sale of shares to outsiders. The charter of the A. S. Suvorin— *New Times* Corporation received official approval in late 1911. In two issues of stock, the company raised one million rubles; among the shareholders were the bank and members of the moderately conservative Octobrist Party, who presumably hoped to influence the editorial policies of the newspaper. However, controlling interest remained with Suvorin and thus, after his death, passed into the hands of his heirs.[14]

Suvorin died at his country home outside Saint Petersburg, on 11 August 1912, at the age of seventy-seven. His funeral was on a grandiose scale; a throng of admirers swelled the procession to the cemetery. But in 1912 and again the two following years, subscription to *New Times* declined.[15] However, *New Times* benefited, along with other newspapers, from the outbreak of war in the summer of 1914 and the subsequent creation of a great public hunger for information. Suvorin's sons expanded their operations and even founded a new daily in Moscow. The October Revolution brought an end to this last effervescence. The Military Revolutionary Committee of the Petrograd Soviet decreed the closing of *New Times* on 26 October/8 November 1917. Those of the other Suvorin publications that had not already perished through upheavals and scarcities ceased to exist by the end of the year.[16]

Today, the building that once housed Suvorin's drama company has become a theater named for Maksim Gorkii. Ertelev Lane is now Chekhov Street. Suvorin's sons continued their father's newspaper for a few more years in emigration, Mikhail in Belgrade and Boris in Shanghai, before *New Times* vanished entirely.

notes

The following special abbreviations are used in the notes:

ES   *Entsiklopedicheskii slovar* (*Encyclopedia*), St.P. 1890–1904 [pub. F. A. Brokhaus & I. A. Efron], 41 v.
L.   Leningrad
LN   *Literaturnoe nasledstvo* (Literary Heritage), M. 1931—
M.   Moscow
NV   *Novoe vremia* (*New Times*), St.P. 1868–1917, daily
OZ   *Otechestvennye zapiski* (*Notes of the Fatherland*), St.P. 1839–84, monthly
P.   Petrograd
S   Aleksei Sergeevich Suvorin
Sov.   *Sovremennik* (*Contemporary*), St.P. 1836–66, monthly
St.P.   Saint Petersburg
VE   *Vestnik Evropy* (*Herald of Europe*), St.P. 1866–1918, monthly

N.B. References to notes giving full titles of other works cited more than once are in brackets.

PREFACE

1. [V. G. Korolenko] *Russkoe bogatstvo* (Aug. 1913): 361.
2. M. Gorkii, *Sobranie sochinenii,* M. 1949–55, 28: 356.
3. V. I. Lenin, *Sochineniia,* 4th ed., M. 1941–50, 18: 250.
4. V. P. Meshcherskii, *Moi vospominaniia* 2, St.P. 1898: 158.
5. Lenin [n. 3] 18: 251.
6. *OZ* (Feb. 1878), rpt. N. K. Mikhailovskii, *Sochineniia,* St.P. 1896–97,

4: 493. Mikhailovskii meant also to condemn the fickle and nonprincipled attitudes of the reading public, whose tastes swung the weathervanes this way and that.

7. F. M. Dostoevskii, *Pisma*, M. 1928–59, 4: 166; D. I. Abramovich, ed., *Pisma russkikh pisatelei k A. S. Suvorina*, L. 1927: 12, 51.

8. Outlines of S's life are articles by the literary historian S. A. Vengerov, *ES* 31: 894–96, and by his admiring eulogist B. B. Glinskii, *Istoricheskii vestnik* (Sept. 1912): 1–60. N. M. Lisovskii wrote a fuller but unfortunately unfinished account: *Bibliograf* (Nov.-Dec. 1892): 353–59, 424–34. S published no memoirs; Glinskii's article includes extensive quotations from an unpublished superficial autobiography, as well as reminiscences by colleagues and friends. S's private diary for 1887, 1893, 1896–1904, 1907, with scattered references to earlier years, was discovered and published after the October Revolution.

INTRODUCTION

1. The word *zhurnalistika* has a far wider range of meaning than its English cognate *journalism*. N. A. Polevoi introduced it in 1825 as a collective noun for periodical publications. Since that time it has come to indicate all literary-publicistic activity in periodicals. *Publitsistika* pertains to contemporary socio-political questions. One of 19th century Russia's foremost publicists, N. G. Chernyshevskii, defined a journalist as one "who tries to keep abreast of the progress made in intellectual life in all questions of interest to educated people," "whose function is . . . to popularize the conclusions drawn by scientists, to ridicule crude prejudice and backwardness." *Sov.* (July 1861) ii: 169.

2. The first Russian journal for the general reader was the historical-literary *Ezhemesiachnye sochineniia, k polze i uveseleniiu sluzhashchie*, published by the Academy of Sciences (1755–64). The first privately published periodical was the monthly literary-satiric *Trudoliubivaia pchela* of the poet and critic A. P. Sumarokov (1759). The bibliographer Lisovskii managed to trace 119 periodicals of all kinds for the 18th century (most of them in its last third); the average life span was about 3½ years (*ES* 27: 416).

3. V. G. Berezina et al., *Istoriia russkoi zhurnalistiki XVIII–XIX vekov*, M. 1966: 43.

4. And even this is open to question; e.g., it is commonly asserted that *Sov.* could have continued to publish indefinitely if it had not been closed by the government in 1866. But by the end of 1865 its printing had already fallen by stages to only 4600, 65% of its all-time high 4 years earlier. *LN* 49/50 (1946): 101–2.

5. *ES* 7: 805; 27: 416–19. These figures do not include dozens of émigré and underground periodicals, most of them published during the second half of the century.

6. For figures on financial subsidies to official journals, see *Russkii kalendar Suvorina* (1875): 227, esp.

7. Provincial papers were introduced in 1838 in only 42 provinces of European Russia (plus similar bilingual papers in Warsaw and Tiflis) and were extended to other areas only gradually (to western Siberia in the late 1850s, to the Vistula region in the late 1860s, etc.) By the end of the century an official news-

paper was published in almost every *guberniia* or *oblast* of the Russian Empire, except Finland and the autonomous khanates of Central Asia.

8. The first *Diocesan Notices*, organized on the suggestion of a provincial bishop, appeared in Yaroslav in 1860. According to their program, they contained official diocesan news and unofficial articles of religious interest, sermons, etc. In the 18th century the old Russian word *vedomosti* was used for all newspapers. During the 19th century it became a characteristic title of official organs; almost all private newspapers adopted either *listok* (sheet, leaflet) or the Italian word *gazeta;* only *gazeta* is now current. See V. G. Berezina, "K istorii slova 'Gazeta' " in *Problemy gazetnykh zhanrov,* L. 1962: 155–65.

9. S. M. Propper, *Was nicht in die Zeitung kam; Erinnerungen des Chefredakteurs der "Birschewyja Wedomosti,"* Frankfurt/Main 1929: 37–8. *Sankt-Petersburger Zeitung* was at this time on lease by the Academy of Sciences to a private editor, a curious method of publication to which the academy often resorted for its Russian paper as well. When S worked on *Sankt-Peterburgskie vedomosti,* he was employed by a private lessee rather than the academy.

10. A. G. Dementev et al., *Russkaia periodicheskaia pechat (1702–1894),* M. 1959: 671–72.

11. See A. G. Rashin, "Gramotnost i narodnoe obrazovanie v Rossii v XIX i nachale XX v.," *Istoricheskie zapiski* 37 (1951): 28–80. Writing in 1859, Chernyshevskii estimated 4 million literates in a population of about 70 million (ibid.: 32). By 1897 the population had almost doubled and contained 25 million presumed literates. From fragmentary evidence, Rashin puts the number of literates 8 years of age and older at 38–39% in 1913 (the last educationally normal year of the Russian Empire's existence).

12. Dementev [n. 10]: 321, 343; *Sov.* (Jan. 1861) ii: 183–215; (Jan. 1862) ii: 167–98; V. I. Mezhov, *Povremennye izdaniia v Rossii v 1860-m i 1861-m godakh,* St.P. 1861: 116; G. A. Dzhanshiev, *Epokha velikikh reform,* 7th ed., M. 1898: 381–82. The newly important daily papers did a little better. Katkov's *Moskovskie vedomosti* had a circulation of 12,000 at the height of its anti-Polish outcry in 1863. Most successful in the early sixties were the private conservative papers *Russkie vedomosti* and *Syn otechestva,* with 20,000 subscribers each.

13. *NV* (15 Jan. 1878). In planning a bi-weekly publication in 1862, G. Z. Eliseev made no provision whatever for the possibility of advertising revenue. M. E. Saltykov-Shchedrin, *Polnoe sobranie sochinenii,* M. 1933–41, 18: 377–79.

14. On the history of Russian censorship, most valuable are the works of M. K. Lemke, who had access to the archives of the Third Section: *Ocherki po istorii russkoi tsenzury i zhurnalistiki XIX stoletiia,* St.P. 1904; *Nikolaevskie zhandarmy i literatura 1826–1855 gg.,* 2nd ed., St.P. 1909; *Epokha tsenzurnykh reform 1859–1865 gg.,* St.P. 1909. On the Great Reforms of Alexander II in relation to the press, see K. K. Arsenev, *Zakonodatelstvo o pechati,* St.P. 1903.

15. It might be argued that, since the notorious Bulgarin and Grech dealt mainly in trivia and chauvinism without actually presenting a reasoned defense of government policies, their publications were at best proto-*ofitsiozy.* A true type of *ofitsioz* in its purest form would be any of the newspapers initiated by P. A. Valuev, minister of internal affairs in the early sixties, to form public attitudes favorable to the government or at least to Valuev's plans for the government:

e.g., *Nedelia* (1866), *Otgoloski* (1879–80), *Bereg* (1880). See N. P. Emelianov, "Iz istorii russkikh ofitsiozov," *Voprosy zhurnalistiki,* L. 1960, 2: 72–80.

16. The size of a book freed from preliminary censorship had to be at least 10 printed sheets for an original work and 20 for a translation; the best American survey of Russian journalism incorrectly interprets printed sheet as the same as page. J. Jenson and R. Bayley, "Highlights of the Development of Russian Journalism, 1553–1917," *Journalism Quarterly* 41 (Summer 1964) : 411. A book of 10 sheets has 240 duodecimo pages. The point is of course that bulky books are expensive and repellent, while children and the masses prefer something less weighty. Following the same line of thought, the Temporary Regulations granted minor privileges to journals with an annual price of more than 7 rubles. For some salaries of the time, see below [Ch. 1 n. 22].

17. For a chronological list of the most important administrative prohibitions on press discussion, 1873–95, see S. A. Vengerov, *Samoderzhavie i pechat v Rossii,* 2d ed., St.P. 1906: 59–80. Careful collection and publication of facts about censorship was regarded in 19th century Russia as a means of struggle for freedom of the press. Formal announcement of warnings, suspensions, and other actions were printed in *Pravitelstvennyi vestnik* and the offending periodical. From 1872 to 1878 the Chief Administration of Press Affairs published a semi-monthly bulletin, *Ukazatel po delam pechati,* with all nonsecret official decisions and announcements on censorship, press trials, bookstores, photographic establishments, and other activities within its vast domain. Despite pious intentions, the partial reform of 1866 failed to introduce clarity, simplicity, or order into the administrative organization or into the censorship code itself, which grew by accretion in distinct geologic strata from the time of Catherine on. Nor did it eliminate the separate and overlapping jurisdictions of the ecclesiastical, imperial court, provincial-gubernatorial, medical, police (for posters), and other censors. Within the Chief Administration itself there were separate sections for review of domestic, foreign, and theatrical works, as well as for supervision of printing presses, libraries, and all other enterprises having to do with the printed word. No journal could change its editor or price, no lithographer could change the number of his machines, without official permission. The constituted authorities even concerned themselves with the size of playing cards and the design of tickets of admission.

18. Memoirists almost invariably describe editors of political publications as suffering from nerves. For example, V. F. Korsh (with whom S was associated during his liberal period) is reported to have been constantly in a state of nervous tension—both as a general trait of character and owing to "censorship ordeals." P. D. Boborykin, *Vospominaniia,* M. 1965, 2: 51, 140. S too, even as editor of a newspaper in the good graces of the government, complained continually about his nerves; see, e.g., numerous excerpts from his correspondence in *Istoricheskii vestnik* (June 1913) : 1–93.

19. *Vsiakie,* 2d ed.: xiii.

20. *Russkie vedomosti 1863–1913; sbornik statei,* M. 1913: 36–37.

21. Dementev [n. 10] : 530.

22. According to recent compilations, in 1913 2527 periodicals were appearing in the Russian Empire; about 80% were in Russian. *Pechat SSSR za sorok let 1917–1957,* M. 1957: 4, 32. France, with a much smaller population, published

2303 periodicals as early as 1870. *Russkii kalendar S* (1875): 228. For a more optimistic appraisal, see J. Walkin, "Government Controls over the Press in Russia, 1905–1914," *Russian Review* 13 (July 1954): 203–9.

23. E. S. Golomb and E. M. Fingerit, *Rasprostranenie pechati v dorevoliutsion-noi Rossii i v Sovetskom Soiuze*, M. 1967: 14–15. *Daily Mail* (London) passed the million mark in 1901, *Le Matin* (Paris) in 1913; in latter year, *Le Petit Parisien's* circulation was more that 1,500,000. G. J. Weill, *Le Journal*, Paris 1934: 252, 265.

24. This inability to compete successfully under conditions of preliminary censorship led Kraevskii, for example, to close his successful *Golos* after its sus-pension in 1883. The destructive potential of suspension even of street sales may be seen from circulation figures. As early as 1871 more than one-fifth of the circulation of *Sankt-Peterburgskie vedomosti* consisted of individual daily sales, though over half the subscribers also lived in the city. In the seventies *Golos* averaged one-fourth of its circulation in daily sales. *Russkii kalendar S* (1872): 135; V. O. Mikhnevich, *Piatnadtsatiletie gazeti Golos 1863–1877*, St.P. 1878.

25. Dzhanshiev [n. 12]: 385–98; *Sbornik svedenii po knizhno-literaturnomu delu za 1866 god*, M. 1867, ii: 137–44. Although the Temporary Regulations were confirmed by the emperor 6 April 1865, they did not take effect until September. Associated trial regulations went into effect only in 1866.

26. The fact that no newspaper (with the possible exception of *Russkie vedomosti* in its later, liberal days) managed to reflect in its pages a single strictly held world-view led to unfavorable comparisons with the thick journals. In addition, oppositional publicists suspected some entered the field for profit rather than propaganda; especially in the seventies they continually denounced the appearance in journalism of bankers, industrialists, merchants, etc.; see, e.g., *Delo* (Mar. 1876): 451–79. For a physical description of a "large newspaper" (*NV*) in the late seventies, see below (Ch. 5).

27. Evidently the boulevard press has never been studied; samples examined for this study emphasized light entertainment more than calamity and scandal. Compared to their American sisters of the tabloid type, the boulevard press seems very tame. Absence of display headlines (and of course, photographs) together with a predilection, perhaps imposed by the constant threat of censorship, for reproducing in small type complete transcripts of criminal trials created an unexciting visual effect. Generally speaking, all types of 19th century Russian newspapers devoted an extraordinary amount of space to literary features. It has been suggested that they printed such items, especially serialized fiction, to gain subscribers who otherwise would not have been interested. B. P. Kozmin, *Russkaia zhurnalistika 70-kh i 80-kh godov XIX veka*, M. 1948: 30–31. But this argument presupposes an educated society more interested in literature than news, especially since serious papers published much more criticism than fiction.

28. Ostentatious silence had its dangers; e.g., in 1865 the biweekly *Narodnaia letopis* was suspended when it failed to note the death of the heir to the throne— although it had published a full report with black border on the death of Abraham Lincoln. V. V. Chubinskii, "K voprosu o sudbe gazety *Narodnaia letopis*," in *Voprosy teorii i istorii zhurnalistiki*, L. 1960: 133–34.

29. To take one of innumerable examples, in 1875 S wrote that "conservative parties are stronger here than in any other land, since we have four: *Moskovskie*

vedomosti, Sankt-Peterburgskie vedomosti, Grazhdanin, and *Russkii mir,* while in Germany there is one, *Kreuz-Zeitung."* *Ocherki* 2, iii; 127. A typical remark by K. K. Arsenev, liberal of liberals and longtime contributor to *VE,* may serve as another example of this rhetoric. In 1871, in the course of an attack against restrictions on freedom of the press, he wrote that the influence of literature on society could "reach great intensity only upon a wide development of political life, with the existence of parties whose representatives serve journals and newspapers." Otherwise, he explained, literature could be important only at certain moments, as with Belinskii in the forties, and its influence would die with the individual. Arsenev [n. 14]: 81.

30. *Pravitelstvennyi vestnik* was supposed to replace the separate newspapers of a number of ministries, a move partly connected with attempts of the then minister of internal affairs to gain ascendency in the government. E. M. Feoktistov, *Vospominaniia,* L. 1929: 349–51.

31. *NV* (10 Sept. 1877). On another occasion *NV* (8 Feb. 1879) complained that although its subscription cost 200 rubles a year, for which it expected diplomatic news, half the bulletin for that day was devoted to a benefit performance for a prima donna.

32. *NV* (19, 25 Oct. 1876).

33. This was the Russian Telegraph Agency of publisher and entrepreneur K. V. Trubnikov. B. I. Esin, "K istorii telegrafnykh agenstv v Rossii XIX veka," *Vestnik Moskovskogo universiteta: filologiia, zhurnalistika* (Jan. 1960): 61–67. Early private agencies were connected with their owners' newspaper enterprises and were purely commercial undertakings; several times a day they distributed bulletins of late dispatches to their customers.

34. For a description of Bismarck's attempts to gain control of dispatches to Russia, see Propper [n. 9]: 28–35.

35. See *NV* (11 June 1879) for a catalog of ITA's sins. ITA's successor, Northern Telegraph Agency (1882–94), came into existence only after the last suspension of *Golos* by the censors, a punitive measure which led Kraevskii to close down both paper and agency. Despite all difficulties and complaints, ITA had increased its subscribers from 50 in 1872 to 100 in 1880. B. I. Esin, "Materialy k istorii gazetnogo dela v Rossii," *Vestnik Moskovskogo universiteta: zhurnalistika* (July 1967): 85.

36. A weekly paper such as the populist *Nedelia* (1866–1901) could, thanks to its clearly defined world-view and less frequent appearance, cultivate a "principled" and meaningful survey of provincial news. However, this type of weekly paper resembled thick journals more closely than newspapers even of the Russian type.

37. See, e.g., a complaint by that grand old guardian of zemstvo liberalism, *Vestnik Evropy,* which regarded pointlessness in news as clearly reprehensible and would have preferred that daily papers act in the provinces as combination muckraker and Action-Line. *VE* (Feb. 1868): 851–58.

38. ITA's domestic telegrams did not always provide full coverage of the domestic scene. When half the city of Uralsk burned to the ground, *NV* (3 May 1879) first learned of it from the pages of *Pravitelstvennyi vestnik.*

39. [n. 20]: 65.

40. Of the remaining papers, 3 appeared in Moscow and one (short-lived) in

Saratov. See N. M. Lisovskii, *Russkaia periodicheskaia pechat 1703–1900,* St.P. 1915.

41. This is not to say that other dailies lacked a following. Colorlessly conservative *Syn otechestva* (1862–1901) had more subscribers in more places (11,000 outside St.P. in 1869) than any of the papers noted in the text. The St.P. police daily (1839–1917) had a smaller but faithful public. In 1863 *Moskovskie vedomosti* had a circulation of 12,000; *Sankt-Peterburgskie vedomosti* had 8000 (11,000 by 1874). *Golos* had 2000 in 1863 and almost 23,000 at its height in 1877. *Russkii kalendar* S (1872): 135–36; Dzhanshiev [n. 12]; S, *Ocherki* 1, iii: 4; Mikhnevich [n. 24]: 1 (50).

42. Other papers and journals could reprint Russian war news from *Russkii invalid,* just as until 1855 they reprinted general news and announcements from the other monopolists (*Sankt-Peterburgskie vedomosti, Moskovskie vedomosti, Severnaia pchela*). From 1855 to 1866 dispatches from abroad continued to be censored, so in effect papers got them from the Ministry of Foreign Affairs or waited to copy from official organs.

43. *VE* (Dec. 1868): 867; Feoktistov [n. 30]: 335–38; Dementev [n. 10]: 147, 431.

44. *Ocherki po istorii russkoi zhurnalistiki i kritiki,* L. 1965, 2: 448.

45. A. F. Koni, *Sobranie sochinenii,* M. 1966, 1: 15.

46. [n. 44]

CHAPTER ONE

1. Voronezh *guberniia* straddles the middle reaches of the Don River in south-central European Russia. In the mid-19th century the province displayed a low degree of urbanization even for Russia. Well over half the peasants were "state settlers" rather than serfs strictly speaking. More than a third of the inhabitants were Ukrainians, concentrated on the right bank of the Don (S came from the left, Great Russian bank). The number of non-East Slavs in the province— German colonists, Polish conscripts, gypsies—was negligible. See G. M. Veselovskii, *Voronezh v istoricheskom i sovremenno-statisticheskom otnosheniiakh,* Voronezh 1866.

2. N. I. Vtorov, *Pamiatnaia knizhka dlia zhitelei voronezhskoi gubernii na 1856 god,* Voronezh 1856, ii: 8–10. Under Alexander I there were only 3 genuine academies for future line officers in the entire empire (which unduly limited the availability of trained officers while limiting the opportunities of the provincial gentry to advance in state service). Hence the provincial gentry welcomed Nicholas' decree of 1830 on cadet corps. Nonetheless, the Voronezh Corps was delayed for 15 years, since the local nobility had to raise most of the money. The school owed its opening in 1845 to an especially large single donation of 1,500,000 paper rubles and 1,000 "souls" (taxable male serfs).

3. *Istoricheskii vestnik* (Sept. 1912): 11.

4. Lisovskii [Pref. n. 8]: 354–55.

5. To his scholastic misfortune, S was about 3 years too early for higher education on an empty purse. After the Crimean defeat and the loosening of regulations, penniless students flocked to the universities and lived in groups, surviving on tutoring and enthusiasm. Some young men of the activist generation of the

sixties took up schoolteaching for "principled" reasons, as part of the awakening interest in the education of the masses (e.g., N. V. Uspenskii, later also a teacher at Tolstoi's Iasnaia Poliana school in the same year that S was briefly involved with Tolstoi's educational experiments). See I. G. Vasilev, *Proza pisatelei-demokratov shestidesiatykh godov 19 veka,* M. 1962. Whether S had any reasons, other than the necessity to support himself, must remain unknown.

6. Veselovskii [n. 1]: 96, 101. Voronezh city, on a tributary of the Don, was founded in 1586 as one of a series of forts on the southeastern steppe border of the Muscovite state. Its finest hour came in 1695 when Peter the Great arrived to construct the first (unsuccessful) Russian Black Sea fleet. In the early 19th century Voronezh had been a center of woolen manufacture in serf-labor factories, but the importance of this industry decreased greatly even before the emancipation of the serfs in 1861.

7. A. P. Serebrianskii (1808–38) and A. V. Koltsov (1809–42). The latter, the better known of the two, was called by his admirers the Robert Burns of Russia. The province produced many other chroniclers of the *narod,* including the ethnographer A. N. Afanasev (1826–71), the historian N. I. Kostomarov (1817–85), and the writer A. I. Ertel (1855–1908). M. E. Piatnitskii, another native, here organized his famous folk chorus, which first appeared in M. in 1911.

8. Veselovskii [n. 1]: 251, 255. Actually, a public library was first founded in 1832, during a brief earlier flurry of intellectual activity, but it had very few readers and only about 600 titles; eventually the key was lost.

9. Prior to 1856 a single periodical, the official *Voronezhskie gubernskie vedomosti,* appeared in the province. During the 1860s 4 private newspapers, an ecclesiastical journal, and a scholarly philological journal were successfully established. [Glavnoe upravlenie po delam pechati] *Sbornik svedenii o povremennykh izdaniiakh,* St.P. 1870.

10. The number of participants in intellectual society in Voronezh cannot have been very great. In the peak year of 1861, Nikitin's lending library had only 192 subscribers. To judge from the large number of items borrowed, however, each subscriber could have kept several others supplied with reading matter. S reported that the majority of the poet's customers were army officers and cadets; the merchant class did not read at all. In 1860, 400 people paid a silver ruble apiece to attend a public reading for the benefit of the Society for Assistance to Needy Writers and Scholars. *Russkoe slovo* (Mar. 1860) iii: 24–44; (May 1860) iii: 122–29.

11. *VE* (July 1869): 897.

12. M. De-Pule and P. Glotov, eds., *Voronezhskaia beseda na 1861 god,* St.P. 1861 [Nikitin circle] vs. P. Malykhin, ed., *Voronezhskii literaturnyi sbornik,* Voronezh 1861 [Vtorov circle].

13. *Sov.* (Oct. 1861) ii: 322–23; (Dec. 1861) ii: 195–210. The most interesting of Nikitin's contributions, "Diary of a Seminarian," is a horrendous description of life in the *bursa,* the scholarship dormitory of an elementary school for future priests; the "truthful sixties" saw a wave of such denunciations by former *bursaky.*

14. See below for a bibliographic list of S's major published works. In fairness to S and the taste of the period, I should point out that authors and

readers of mid-19th century America (cf. Edward Eggleston) also combined a desire to know the life of the common people with a conviction that mispronounced words can be supremely amusing.

15. *Dnevnik S:* 208. Sadovskii (pseud. of P. M. Ermilov, 1818–72) specialized in slice-of-Russian-life theater such as that of Ostrovskii and A. V. Sukhovo-Kobylin.

16. Arsenev [Intro. n. 14]: 5–6. Such figures vary somewhat with different sources, depending upon the number of irregular miscellanies and literary annuals included as periodicals. Even genuinely periodic publications often failed to last beyond a few issues. *Sov.* mournfully reported that in 1858–59, 46 ceased to appear; in 1860, 30 more vanished: *Sov.* (Jan. 1861) ii: 142–52. Some publications were harassed to failure by the government, or after 1862 more often simply forbidden. Nonetheless, far more collapsed on their own than through official hostility. The life expectancy of a periodical in the Russian Empire was always low. Lisovskii found an average length of existence of almost 9 years for the entire 18th and 19th centuries—but for political and literary titles, less than 6 years. Even official publications enjoyed an average life of only 19 years. *ES* 27: 419.

17. E.g., for years *Sov.* carried an illustration of fashionable Parisian dresses in every issue. N. A. Nekrasov, ed., insisted that without fashions he would lose half the subscribers. Kozmin [Intro. n. 27]: 8–9.

18. As Dobroliubov caustically expressed it, "at one time the epidemic of laughter was so strong they were stopping serious people on the street and putting a knife to their throats: laugh, or else!" *Sobranie sochinenii,* M. 1962, 3: 244. Radical publicists intensely disliked this flurry of comedy, chiefly because it dealt only with unimportant matters like drunken shop clerks and strove to amuse readers rather than educating them to political awareness and radical convictions. *Veselchak* admitted openly that its purpose was to provide pleasant after dinner laughter "for the sake of the stomach," and was the target of special ire because its editor dared to satirize the civic poet Nekrasov and I. I. Panaev, then editors of *Sov.* See *Sov.* (Sept. 1858) ii: 85–93; M. A. Antonovich, "Vospominaniia," in *Shestidesiatye gody,* ed. V. Evgenev-Maksimov and G. F. Tizengauzen, M. 1933: 134–36; I. G. Iampolskii, "Iz istorii russkoi satiricheskoi zhurnalistiki," *Doklady i soobshcheniia Filologicheskogo instituta LGU* 2 (1950): 117–46. One must bear in mind that most present day studies of the mid-19th century press commence from a conceptual framework derived from the views of the radical publicists of the time (and especially the views of Chernyshevskii). Thus the opinions of these men are possibly of greater importance today than during their own lifetimes.

19. S insisted it could have continued with its 1000 subscribers of 1859, but closed simply because the publisher wished to pocket the money. This was a common complaint, whether justified or not. *Russkoe slovo* (Mar. 1860) iii: 27. Concrete questions of the financial problems and economic viability of the press have been treated only in the cases of certain radical journals, and then incidentally. *Sov.,* which in the sixties charged 12 rubles plus postage for an annual subscription of 12 issues, usually spent about 5 rubles of this on author's fees and a similar sum on paper, printing, binding, and other expenses. Hence almost 3 rubles per subscriber represented income for the editorial staff and publisher.

But expenses fluctuated and inflation took a toll, since roughly the same number of subscribers in 1860 and 1864 brought a 12,000 ruble income in the first year and an even greater loss in the second. "Gonorarnye vedomosti *Sovremennika,*" *LN* 53/54 (1949): 229–88. These subscription figures do not correspond to those publicly announced by *Sov.* (Jan. 1862) ii: 195. To take another example, the semi-monthly *Knizhnyi vestnik* ceased to run a deficit when it reached 1000 subscribers (1862). E. N. Viner, *Bibliograficheskii zhurnal Knizhnyi vestnik 1860–1867,* L. 1950: 101.

    20. "Stsena v uezdnom gorodke Bubnove," *Veselchak* (18 Sept. 1858): 279–83; (25 Sept. 1858): 287–90. S also contributed to *Veselchak* in 1859 (not available). I. F. Masanov, *Slovar psevdonimov russkikh pisatelei, uchenykh i obshchestvennykh deiatelei,* M. 1956, 3: 145. The editor and major writer of *Veselchak,* until his death after 4 issues, was O. I. Senkovskii (1800–58), founder and long-time editor of the first thick journal in Russia, the monthly literary and scientific *Biblioteka dlia chteniia.* His witty and entertaining feuilletons, under the pseudonym of Baron Brambeus, enjoyed great popularity among the general reading public during the thirties and forties despite the hatred of progressive elements.

    21. "Voronezhskie pisma 1," *Russkoe slovo* (Mar. 1860) iii: 24–44; "Pismo iz Voronezha," *Russkaia rech* (no. 5, 1861) described in *Russkoe slovo* (Apr. 1861) iii: 49–50. *Russkaia rech* not available; for references to many of S's contributions, see Masanov [n. 20] 1: 59. Several standard bibliographies list an early book by S: A. Bobrovskii [pseud.], *Drama konkurentsiia,* St.P. 1860; e.g., see *Istoriia russkoi literatury XIX veka: Bibliograficheskii ukazatel,* M. 1962, no. 15,195. I have found no trace of this work.

    22. For a young provincial of no means, journalistic activity could be financially as well as intellectually rewarding (although in view of the low circulation and short life of most periodicals, it probably rarely was in fact). As a teacher in an *yezd* school in the late fifties, S received slightly less than 15 rubles a month, but he probably got living quarters or other benefits as well; for a single story printed in *Sov.* he was paid 60 r. (Throughout the late fifties and early sixties, *Sov.* generally paid 50 r. per printed sheet—16 pages in octavo format of thick journals.) Despite some periods of impoverishment, S managed to live from journalism. As a secretary on *Russkaia rech* his salary was 75 r. a month. He started on *Sankt-Peterburgskie vedomosti* in 1863 at 2000 r. a year, increased to 4500 by the time he left in 1874. *Dnevnik S:* 83, 85, 87, 162; N. A. Nekrasov, *Polnoe sobranie sochinenii i pisem,* M. 1948–52, 10: 471; *LN* 53/54 (1949): 229–88.

CHAPTER TWO

    1. At the time, in the very early sixties, many Russian intellectuals who lay between the two poles called themselves liberals; this was especially true of those who consciously identified their aspirations with the supposed ideals of English Liberalism. The radicals, from the example of both western and Russian liberalism, equated the term with bourgeois class interest, hypocrisy, impotence, uselessness, and/or disguised conservatism. No doubt in response, the liberal-

minded came to avoid the term except with visible or understood quotation marks. Conservatives, reactionaries, and government censors used liberal (or ultraliberal) for the whole oppositional intelligentsia. See G. Fischer, *Russian Liberalism from Gentry to Intelligentsia,* Cambridge, Mass., 1958: 71n. Even while writing for periodicals known by all to be liberal, S rarely used the term and then usually in ironic context; e.g., in a satiric description of a visit to a medium he wrote that "as a moderate liberal" he had been very much touched by the orderly, mild, and modest habits of the spirits in attendance there. *Ocherki* 2, ii: 246. After he acquired *NV* and became involved in polemics against newspapers regarded as liberal, S began to employ the term (often with the adjective doctrinaire) very frequently—as an insult. See below.

2. Chernyshevskii, by Jan. 1862 thoroughly disillusioned by the sheeplike meekness of just about every element of Russian society, disgustedly explained *glasnost* as a "bureaucratic expression devised as a substitute for the expression 'freedom of speech' . . . on the conjecture that the expression 'freedom of speech' might seem unpleasant or harsh to someone." *Polnoe sobranie sochinenii,* M. 1939–53, 10: 107.

3. *Moskovskie vedomosti* (30 Oct. 1860).

4. *Sov.* (Mar. 1861) ii: 195–226. This article was long prized by radicals as an outstanding example of anti-liberal, anti-parliamentary writing. For an account of the defense called forth from the Russian liberal press, including *Russkaia rech,* see Dobroliubov, *Pervoe polnoe sobranie sochinenii,* St.P. 1911, 4: 629–36.

5. *Russkoe slovo* (Jan. 1861) iii: 25; (Apr. 1861) iii: 19–24. The radicals were using Russell to illuminate a favorite theme: despite professions to the contrary, liberals in fact have no attachment to the people and give to them only as much as necessary in order to maintain their own position.

6. N. K. Piksanov and O. V. Tsekhnovitser, eds., *Shestidesiatye gody,* M. 1940: 453–68. *Moskovskii vestnik* was published from Feb. 1859 to May 1861 in M. Like so many other ventures, it started well, gained 2000 subscribers, and then gradually declined into oblivion.

7. Pleshcheev (1825–93) was, like Dostoevskii, condemned and deceitfully led out to be shot; he was sent instead to serve as a common soldier. During the sixties he produced short stories of a sort typical of the period, exposing the passivity of well-intentioned liberal gentry and the dismal tedium of provincial towns. In the seventies and eighties he worked on the leading radical journals of those decades. His most beloved poem, "Po chuvstvam bratia my s toboi" (1846), passed into the oral tradition of generations of Russian students (including the Ulianovy). "When the wished-for hour strikes / And the sleeping peoples rise / The holy army of liberty / Will see us in its ranks" (etc.). *Polnoe sobranie stikhotvorenii,* M. 1964: 90.

8. Piksanov [n. 6]: 454. Pleshcheev had hoped to attract Chernyshevskii to participation in *Moskovskii vestnik* and to guide its policies in a more leftward direction; he was disappointed in both these hopes.

9. S, *Vsiakie,* 2d ed.: x; *Dnevnik S:* 84–86. Despite considerable later divergence of views, S and Pleshcheev remained friendly. See the latter's letters, 1860–92, in Abramovich [Pref. n. 7]: 105–37.

10. Evgeniia Tur was the pen name of Countess E. V. Salias de-Turnemir, b.

Sukhovo-Kobylina (1815–92). Her first published fiction, on the idle and futile life of the higher aristocracy, gained her in 1849–50 an immediate great success (which she was never able to duplicate, however). In the late fifties she wrote critico-bibliographical articles for *Russkii vestnik* until, after an obscure but very public quarrel with Katkov, she left to found her own short-lived paper. In 1862, infatuated with the Polish cause, she went to Paris where she associated with Polish émigré circles. After the events of the following year she turned against Poland, abandoned liberalism, and became religious. In later years her critical articles appeared in *NV*. Her son Count E. A. Salias de-Turnemir entered government service after a brief fling with radicalism. A prolific and widely read author, he was best known for his historical novels (despised by radicals for their antipopular and reactionary historical conception).

11. E. M. Feoktistov, *Vospominaniia,* L. 1929: 368. Feoktistov was tutor to Tur's son and in 1861 chief editor of *Russkaia rech.* In the seventies he was editor of *Zhurnal Ministerstva narodnogo prosveshcheniia* and in 1883 he was appointed director of the Chief Administration of Press Affairs, where he was noted for his severity.

12. *LN* 67 (1959): 463.

13. S, *Vsiakie,* 2d ed.: ix. This was a bold era; Leskov invited S to study Fourier and Proudhon with him, or so S claimed. *Ocherki* 2, ii: 209.

14. *LN* 67 (1959): 463.

15. S, *Ocherki* 2, ii: 213–14. Over a decade later S still admired Bazarov's independence and strength of will, although he thought that "contemporary reality demands other people, with other much more peaceful convictions." Of the radical publicists of the early sixties only Pisarev accepted Bazarov as a positive model; non-radicals of all views condemned him as a sort of monster. See P. G. Pustovoit, *Roman I. S. Turgeneva "Ottsy i deti" i ideinaia borba 60-kh godov XIX veka,* 2d ed., M. 1964.

16. "Literatura 60-kh godov po orchetam III Ordeleniia," *Krasnyi arkhiv* 8 (1925): 211. See also S. M. Petrov, *Russkii istoricheskii roman XIX veka,* M. 1964: 315–16.

17. *Iasnaia Poliana: Shkola, zhurnal pedagogicheskii* and *Iasnaia Poliana: Knizhki dlia detei.* Both were published monthly at Tolstoi's country estate during 1862, and had no more than 400 subscribers; Tolstoi wrote much of the material.

18. "Nikon," *Iasnaia Poliana: Knizhka* (Aug. 1862).

19. For the society's program, see *Sov.* (June 1861) ii: 412–14; A. F. Cherenin, pub., *Sbornik svedenii po knizhno-literaturnomu delu za 1866 god,* M. 1867, 1: 136.

20. *Russkii kalendar S* (1875) ii: 155.

21. These included an especially fatuous and effusive biography of an English nurse by Evgeniia Tur, a founding member of the society.

22. *Sov.* (Aug. 1861) ii: 317–24.

23. *Sov* (May 1861) ii: 76–77; (June 1861) ii: 412–20.

24. *Boiarin Matveev,* M. 1864: 24–25. S must have been fond of his 3 historical booklets, since he reprinted them in a single volume several years later and separately several times, 1887–1904, as volumes in his own "Inexpensive Library" series. For the second and subsequent editions of *Boiarin Matveev* he moderated and partially eliminated his earlier assertions that extortion had caused

uprisings and that decent men look with horror on informers and authors of denunciations; otherwise the texts remained unchanged.

25. *Kolokol* (1 Oct. 1866) : 1868.

26. The historical booklets and ethnographic tales discussed above, although published 1862–64, were written in 1862. The fiction from this period was collected posthumously: *Rasskazy*, St.P. 1913. S seems never to have returned to peasant themes; all his subsequent fiction concerns the life of educated urban classes.

27. Pleshscheev, e.g., became a regular contributor to Dostoevskii's next journal, *Epokha*, which radicals considered even worse than *Vremia*.

28. As Chernyshevskii said of the philanthropists: "They write about the people exactly as Gogol wrote about Akakii Akakievich [protagonist of *Shinel* (Overcoat), the archetype of the genre—although not in its rural variation]. Not a single cruel or reproachful word. They hide all inadequacies, they conceal them, they slur over them. . . . Wonderful and noble. . . . Only, what good is it to the people?" [n. 2] 7: 859. *Sov.* especially liked fiction that depicted an innately rich, strong human nature destroyed by repaeted collisions with hostile conditions.

29. The paper's peculiar position as a state-owned organ with an independent editor gave rise to an anomalous censorship history; e.g., on one occasion when the censors suspended publication for 3 months after the third warning (Sept. 1866), Korsh was permitted to continue issuing government announcements and other items that the contract with the Academy of Sciences obligated him to print. Upon petition by the academy, moreover, a temporary substitute editor was allowed to resume full publication after only 8 days. Cherenin [n. 18] 2: 143.

30. Korsh (1828–83), a relative and student of K. D. Kavelin, was a member of the circle of Granovskii. In later years he published in *VE* and other liberal journals on questions of European social development. His necrologist summarized his lifelong views as "service to the principles that lay at the base of the Great Reforms [i.e., that Russian liberals wistfully hoped lay at their base], to their logical and full realization, their unceasing wide development." He added that thanks to the reaction that set in from the sixties, such views took on almost an oppositional character. K. K. Arsenev, *Za chetvert veka*, P. 1915: 132–42.

31. *ES* 31: 895. In 1865 S wrote the feuilleton, "Vsiakie; nechto v rode povesti" (All Sorts; Something in the Nature of a Tale), under the pseudonym A. Bobrovskii, and from mid-sixties the Sunday feuilleton "Nedelnye ocherki i kartinki" (Weekly Sketches and Pictures) as Neznakomets (Unknown). Having gained fame with the latter heading and sobriquet, he carried them with him in 1875 to *Birzhevye vedomosti* and in 1876 to *NV*.

32. *Polnoe sobranie sochinenii*, M. 1933–41, 20: 106. Cf. E. Zhurbina, *Iskusstvo feletona*, M. 1965: 8–11. On the development of the Russian genre, see also *Feleton: sbornik statei*, L. 1927; P. Ia. Khavin, *Ocherki russkoi stilistiki*, L. 1964: 56–62. A. V. Zapadov and E. P. Prokhovov, eds., *Russkii feleton*, M. 1958, presents a selection of progressive feuilletons from 1759 to 1917 (18th century examples defined retroactively). None of these modern works on the Russian feuilleton mentions S, despite his renown in his own time. For a concise description of the Soviet feuilleton as it should be, see N. K. Vogdanov and B. A. Viazemskii, *Spravochnik zhurnalista*, L. 1961: 260–61.

33. S, *Ocherki* 2, ii: 307.

34. Istoricheskii vestnik (Sept. 1912) : 21; Nikitenko, *Dnevnik,* L. 1955–56, 3 : 257.

CHAPTER THREE

1. S's apartment was searched at the classical hour of 3 A.M. His account of the event illustrates the importance of the old school tie: the young Guards officer in charge, learning that S had been a cadet of the Regiment of Nobility, dropped all his former severity of manner, chatted amiably, and omitted to search where the children were sleeping. (He still impounded all S's papers.) *Vsiakie,* 2d ed.: xvi–xviii.

2. *Russkii kalendar S* (1872) : 133–34.

3. *LN* 25/26 (1936) : 680–82; *Vysshie zhenskie (Bestuzhevskie) kursy,* M. 1966: 136. Anna Ivanovna Suvorina (b. Baranova) died young in 1874. S's second wife, Anna Ivanovna Orfanova, outlived him.

4. *Russkii biograficheskii slovar* 19, M. 1909: 608. S later claimed to have written the essay himself. *Dnevnik:* 208. As N. K. Mikhailovskii pointed out, in Russia for some reason people pinned labels on themselves, doubtless without ever examining the matter: "Into the program of the people with the label *con-servative* enters, among other things, hatred for democratic ideas and apprehensions regarding the pernicious influence of natural sciences. In the program of people with the *liberal* label, on the contrary, is esteem both for the natural sciences and for democratic ideas." *Sochineniia,* St.P. 1896–97, 1: 908. Whatever the real significance of the vogue for popular scientific readings, many activists of the sixties held high expectations for it; e.g., I. A. Khudiakov, author of a self-teaching primer which minister of internal affairs Valuev listed with the more dangerous productions of Likhacheva-Suvorina, explained that his book was designed to arouse the interest of the masses in the natural sciences and thus "change the whole structure of the world-consciousness of the reader." *Zapiski karakazovtsa,* M. 1930: 93. The dissection of frogs leads to philosophical ma-terialism, and materialism to revolution.

5. *Dlia chteniia; sbornik povestei, rasskazov, stikhotvorenii i populiarnykh statei dlia detei vsekh vozrastov* [pub. Likhacheva & Suvorina], St.P. 1866; Viner [Ch. 1 n. 19]: 191; L. A. Vezirova, ed., *Khrestomatiia po istorii russkoi knigi 1564–1917,* M. 1965: 211–12; L. M. Dobrovolskii, *Zapreshchennaia kniga v Rossii 1825–1904,* M. 1962: 10.

6. *LN* 25/26 (1936): 681. F.-A. Mignet, *Istoriia frantsuzskoi revoliutsii,* ed. K. K. Arsenev [pub. Likhacheva & Suvorina], St.P. 1866–67, 2 v. (suppl. bound in of several chs. from Edgar Quinet, *Revoliutsiia*). A second edition appeared in 1895 without incident.

7. I. Kalnev, ed., *Sistematicheskii katalog knigam, rassmotrennym uchenym komitetom Ministerstva narodnogo proveshcheniia i uchebnym komitetom pri Sv. sinode* . . . Odessa 1876, no. 992.

8. "A. Bobrovskii," *Vsiakie; ocherki sovremennoi zhizni* [pub. S], St.P. 1866. Like the 1865–66 publications of Likhacheva-Suvorina, it was printed by N. Tiblen & Co. (N. Nekliudov), a leading "idea" printing establishment of the sixties. In 1907, in a period when many curious relics of the past appeared again

in bookstores, S reissued *Vsiakie* (with luxury binding). (Hereafter this edition is cited in the text in parentheses.) S explained in a new introduction that the situation in the sixties was similar to that of the era just lived through, in that "the ideals of the majority of society were the same"—evidently ideals of a *zemskii sobor* and a constitution. Had the Polish uprising not exploded and Karakozov not fired his shot, the reforms of 1905 would have been completed by Alexander II (xxiii). Whether S was so optimistic in 1866, it is impossible to say.

9. Piksanov [Ch. 2 n. 6]: 409. Chernyshevskii was a native of Saratov, like Samara a chief center of the lower Volga; in an autobiographical novel written in Siberia, Chernyshevskii called himself Volgin.

10. Ibid.: 406, 409.

11. The first and second episodes (and several minor scenes omitted here) took place in Moscow. Ilmenev ought to have been studying in St.P. in 1861–62, but S was in M. Is this simply poor literary craftsmanship, or is Ilmenev more of an alter ego to his creator than his lurid life at first suggests?

12. [n. 9]: 408.

13. In ref. to *Vsiakie,* modern annotators often state that the book was on sale for about a week before its seizure; e.g., Saltykov-Shchedrin [Intro. n. 13] 8: 537n. Dobrovolskii [n. 5] traces this common error to a bibliography published in 1904. Eventually, more than a year later, the police destroyed 1462 copies; 20[!] were preserved for the library of the Chief Administration of Press Affairs. The book did not pass altogether out of the ken of mortal man. S himself managed to buy a copy at a bookstore soon after—marked in blue and red pencil with censorial notations; presumably an employee of the Chief Administration had sold it to supplement his income (xxii). The Library of Congress has one copy.

14. For a collection of relevant documents from police and censorship archives, see Piksanov [Ch. 2 n. 6]: 406–12.

15. The first courts of the new type, serving 10 provinces in the judicial districts of St.P. and M., did not come into being until April 1866. Certain courts of the old system were opened to the public 6 months before. Dzhanshiev [Intro. n. 12]: 436–52.

16. *Sadebnyi vestnik* (1866–77), *Glasnyi sud* (1866–67), *Iuridicheskaia gazeta Moskovskogo iuridicheskogo obshchestva* (1866–92). Transcripts also appeared in various collections of "press data" or "outstanding legal cases" of which so many were compiled at that time; the most accessible is Cherenin [Ch. 2 n. 18] 2: 78–136. S included a verbatim account in *Vsiakie,* 2d ed.

17. Nekrasov [Ch. 1 n. 22] 2: 242; 11: 79–80.

18. Young and still unknown in the mid-sixties, Arsenev worked with S on *Sankt-Peterburgskie vedomosti* for several years. He contributed at least two forewords to publications of Likhacheva-Suvorina. He continued to argue this typically liberal point in articles on press laws for *VE;* e.g. (June 1869): 774–75.

19. V. E. Evgenev-Maksimov, ed., *N. A. Nekrasov 1878–1938,* L. 1938: 240–41; Dzhanshiev [Intro. n. 12]: 383.

20. *What is to be Done?,* which passed the censor by error, was published in *Sov.* (Mar.–May 1863). Of the considerable exegetical literature which has grown up around this work, two recent and informative studies are by G. P. Verkhov-

skii, *O romane N. G. Chernyshevskogo "Chto delat?"* Iaroslavl 1959, and M. T. Pinaev, *Kommentarii k romanu N. G. Chernyshevskogo "Chto delat?"* M. 1963.

21. *Delo* (Dec. 1868) ii: 18–23.

22. Organized in 1859 by the indefatigable enthusiast M. V. Trubnikova and her circle. At its height of activity the circle had its own dwelling-house, a school, and a sewing workshop. *What is to be Done?,* mirroring its own times as well as preparing its readers for better, probably took this establishment as a basis for its model seamstresses' artel. Pinaev [n. 20] : 68–69.

23. Young women sold their valuables to buy copies of *Sov.* with the description of the wonderful sewing workshop, so as to follow the directions completely. E. M. Vodovozova, *Na zare zhizni i drugie vospominaniia,* M. 1934, 2: 228–29.

24. Vasilev [Ch. 1 n. 5] : 172–76; *400 let russkogo knigopechataniia 1564–1964,* M. 1964, 1: 389–91.

25. Piksanov [Ch. 2 n. 6] : 407. S wanted to salvage the first part of the book, which he promised was "entirely free of political character," but the censor noted that although those chapters had already been published with approval, various additions and changes had given them an entirely different, undesirable meaning (409). It is hard to believe that a journalist raised under Russian censorship conditions could be as innocent and ingenuous as S tried to be in this letter. But the weeks following Karakozov's shot were full of remarkable displays. The leading literary figures of the capital signed an address humbly protesting loyalty to the tsar. Nekrasov composed and read in public a hymn of praise to Gen. M. N. Muravev, the "hangman of Poland," appointed to investigate the attempted regicide (but he no more saved *Sov.* than S saved his book).

26. I. S. Turgenev, *Polnoe sobranie sochinenii,* M. 1949, 11: 215.

27. *Evgenii Onegin* viii. 51.3

28. Chernyshevskii's seminal novel of course provided the example for this type of literature. But *What is to be Done?* is concerned with many other matters as well, and in the end makes clear that "service to the people" is secondary to immediate revolution.

29. This was a real debate which displeased the authorities as much in the original as in the pages of *All Sorts.* Piksanov [Ch. 2 n. 6] : 409.

30. Ibid.: 407.

31. *Sankt-Peterburgskie vedomosti,* no. 152 (1867), in *Delo* (Dec. 1868) ii: 19.

CHAPTER FOUR

1. On the importance of S's contributions to the eventual reputation of *Sankt-Peterburgskie vedomosti* see, e.g., S. A. Vengerov, *Russkaia literatura v ee sovremennykh predstaviteliakh,* St.P. 1875.

2. *VE* (Dec. 1872): 890; *LN* 49/50 (1946): 107. See K. K. Arsenev, "Vzgliad na proshloe *VE* 1866–1908," *VE* (Jan. 1909): 216–32. K. Sanine has pointed out how much greater was the objectivity and subtlety of understanding of *VE* in the analysis of contemporary French literary currents than was that of its much more fiery rival *OZ*. *"Annales de la patrie" et la diffusion de la pensée française en Russie (1868–1884),* Paris 1955: 100–1.

3. *VE* (Mar. 1866) in M. K. Lemke, ed., *M. M. Stasiulevich i ego sovremenniki v ikh perepiske*, St.P. 1911–13, 1: 556.

4. *VE* (Jan. 1909): 225. Arsenev, who practised law as well as writing about it, regarded the courtroom as a more satisfactory arena for struggle than even journalism or zemstvo assemblies; the independent bar afforded "even something similar to political work." "Iz vospominanii," *Golos minuvshego* (Feb. 1915): 117. It is therefore understandable that he felt justified in giving so much space in *VE* to journalistic reinforcements of recent courtroom struggles.

5. N. I. Kostomarov, *Avtobiografiia*, M. 1922: 396. A. F. Koni, *Na zhiznennom puti*, St.P. 1912, 2: 248.

6. S, *Ocherki* 1, iii: 4. Another developmental factor, contributing especially to early rise in significance of *Sankt-Peterburgskie vedomosti*, may have been the dearth for almost 2 years of important journals of oppositional character. Only one number of *Russkoe slovo* and 4 of *Sov.* appeared in 1866, before they were both closed forever by government order. Nekrasov and his associates did not take over *OZ* until Jan. 1868 (although *Delo* replaced *Russkoe slovo* in 1866). The weekly *Nedelia* did not acquire a populist character until 1868. *VE* adopted a general political rather than a historical program only in 1868. Thus, a number of writers and readers were left at loose ends precisely when daily newspapers were beginning to attract wide attention.

7. Vengerov [n. 1]: 18. *Delo* (Mar. 1876): 455. *Russkii vestnik* (Sept. 1875): 476–83. Shchedrin employed the same caricaturing titles and names over many years and a number of them passed into journalism's common stock of polemical invective. See M. S. Altman, "Parodiinye i polemicheskie naimenovaniia russkikh gazet i zhurnalov," *Uchenye zapiski Gorkovskogo gos. universiteta* 58 (1963): 390–421. S in *Vsiakie* satirized *Golos* as "Chicken Echo," a title employed by Shchedrin and Nekrasov; in later years S rarely used such mock names.

8. *Sankt-Peterburgskie vedomosti* (31 Dec. 1874), repeated in V. F. Korsh, *Etiudy*, St.P. 1885, 1: xi–iii.

9. Ibid. (12 Apr. 1866). ES 38: 2. The zemstvos were elected all-class assemblies on *uezd* and *guberniia* levels, charged with certain local governmental functions formerly carried out by estate owners and their serfs (e.g., maintenance of bridges and roads). As a sop to the constitutional yearnings of the gentry, who dominated the assemblies, they were also permitted to advance education, public health, agricultural technique, and poor relief on the local level. During 1865–66 zemstvos were established in 27 provinces of European Russia and by 1914 had been gradually extended to 43, but were never introduced in ethnically non-Russian areas. The government began to chip away at the scope and independence of the zemstvos from their very first year of operation.

10. *VE* (Jan. 1871): 459. To be fair, this was several months before the Paris Commune, the trial of the Nechaevites, or any of the other events for which radicals remembered 1871.

11. In the hands of Count Salias, an inexperienced and uninterestingly conservative editor, and without the assistance of its former staff, the paper experienced a very rapid fall in both circulation and importance. A. I. Delvig, *Moi vospominaniia*, M. 1912–13, 4: 479–80. E. V. Korsh, "Materialy po istorii russkoi literatury i kultury," *Russkaia mysl* (Oct. 1913) ii: 90–95.

12. Lemke [n. 3] 3: 48, 51. Unfortunately it has not been possible to discover

the circumstances of S's connection with the liberal journal or the reasons for his departure and the editor's coolness toward him when he was left unemployed. Of 11 projected volumes of correspondence and papers of Stasiulevich and his circle, only 5 were published; the promised letters of S from his liberal period remain unpublished. In the comparatively abundant reminiscences on the early days of *VE* by other contributors, references to S are almost nonexistent—so much so that one may suspect deliberate neglect.

13. S, *Ocherki* 1, iii: 6; 2, ii: 319–20.

14. A. A. Pleshcheev, *Moe vremia,* Paris 1939: 95. A. M. Skabichevskii, *Literaturnye vospominaniia,* M. 1928: 266–67. The initial printing order for *Ocherki i kartinki* (S's wondrously successful 2-volume collection) called for 1500 copies, an edition of normal size for belles lettres and nontechnical works at that time. Dostoevskii's novels were appearing in about 1200 copies, while the more popular works of the Ukrainian story teller Marko-Vovchok went out in double that number. Volumes by Turgenev, one of the bestselling novelists of the period, appeared in editions of 5000–6000. V. I. Mezhov, *Russkaia istoricheskaia bibliografiia za 1865–1876 gg. vkliuchitelno,* St.P. 1882–90. *400 let russkogo knigopechataniia 1564–1964,* M. 1964, 2: 377. As an example of S's prestige and of the company he was keeping, in April 1875 he took part in a public reading for the benefit of the Literary Fund, along with Nekrasov, Pleshcheev, and A. N. Maikov. Shchedrin would have taken part but for illness. Nekrasov [Ch. 1 n. 22] 11: 354.

15. *Delo* (Oct. 1875) ii: 74. Shelgunov (who spent most of his life in mourning for the lost fervor of the early sixties) linked the popularity of S with the growth of a new, non-idea intelligentsia—readers of feuilletons and investors in railroad bonds. He went so far as to compare S, as a chronicler of his times, to Gogol and Turgenev. By this he meant not so much to praise S as to condemn the times.

16. In analyzing S's writing for *Sankt-Peterburgskie vedomosti,* I have had to rely principally upon S's own selection of his feuilletons, as made for *Ocherki i kartinki.* According to S, he chose those of greatest current interest at the time of collection (late 1874–early 1875), about one-seventh of a total output of some 400 to that date.

17. Compare the famous final advice of Turgenev's spokesman in *Dym* (1867), a novel S considered a most valuable guide to the realities of the era: "Every time you enter upon an undertaking, ask yourself: are you serving civilization, in the precise and strict sense of the word . . . has your work that pedagogical and European character which alone is useful and fruitful in our times, in our country? If so—go forward boldly . . . You are not alone now. Hard workers are already appearing, pioneers . . ." *Polnoe sobranie sochinenii i pisem,* M. 1960, 9: 313. Needless to say, the radical journals mercilessly jeered S's "civilization"; e.g., *Delo* called it an "empty and capricious phrase" (Dec. 1868) iii: 19.

18. *VE* (Feb. 1869): 986; (Apr. 1869): 980–81; (Aug. 1869): 922. *Ocherki* 2, ii: 277.

19. As S exclaimed in the midst of reviewing a play by Ostrovskii: "Oh, if the conservatives were so open and stupid, then there would be nothing to fight against, nothing to fear. [In fact they are capable of] energetic intrigue, which on all fours, by dark paths, under guise of loyalty and patriotism . . . winds a

web so thick that it shuts off the light of the sun and threatens darkness." *Sankt-Peterburgskie vedomosti* (1868), rpt. in V. Zelinskii, ed., *Kriticheskie kommentarii k sochineniiam A. N. Ostrovskogo*, M. 1894–97, 3: 111.

20. S, *Ocherki* 1, iii: 38. Fadeev, author of several militaristic-nationalistic works, including the notorious *Chem nam byt?* (1874), was a common object of liberal attack. The editor of *VE* scorned his neo-Slavophile and anti-European ideas; (Apr. 1870): 824–29, e.g. During the seventies Fadeev was an editor of *Russkii mir,* a small pan-Slavic newspaper; on his "revolutionary conservative" views, see E. C. Thaden, *Conservative Nationalism in Nineteenth-Century Russia,* Seattle 1964: 146–163.

21. The picnic is in *Dym* [n. 17]: 198–208. Turgenev's jolly generals not only wished to undo the emancipation of the serfs, but even were not loath to return to the pro-Polish oligarchy of 1610–12.

22. *VE* (Mar. 1871): 468.

23. See, e.g., *VE* (June 1869): 924–25, where traces of "more rational measures" taken by other European governments are said to be visible in Russian life, for instance in 1766–67 (when delegates convened to discuss Catherine II's proposals for an enlightened law code).

24. S managed to discover this basic conflict between the selfish and truly patriotic factions even in pre-Petrine days; e.g., "the greatest act of selflessness in our history was accomplished by the Nizhnii Novgorod zemstvo, at the time when certain aristocrats were putting together the government of the seven boyars and from narrow egoism, for the sake of profit, were handing over our much suffering motherland to Poland" (*Ocherki* 2, iii: 77).

25. S to Korf, 2 May 1868, in M. L. Peskovskii, ed., *Baron Nikolai Aleksandrovich Korf v pismakh k nemu raznykh lits,* St.P. 1895: 36–37. Korf was an active participant and publicist of zemstvo activity.

26. *Russkii kalendar S* (1872): 137–44.

27. *VE* (Apr. 1869): 981.

28. By this I do not mean to say that S never criticized the radicals as a group; on the contrary, he regarded their ideas as "senseless dreams." But such remarks were made only in passing, while attacks on reactionaries formed one of his chief literary occupations.

29. *VE* (Apr. 1869): 978–87; cf. *Sankt-Peterburgskie vedomosti* (2 Apr. 1872).

30. *Russkov slovo* (Feb. 1864) in D. I. Pisarev, *Sochineniia,* M. 1955–56, 2: 331–65. Saltykov-Shchedrin [Intro. n. 13] 18: 234.

31. K. Sanine, *Saltykov-Chtchédrine; sa vie et ses oeuvres,* Paris 1955: 163, 191, esp.

32. Assessment of his position in the *Chetyi-Minei* of "revolutionary democrats" has undergone some variation. The historian of Russian journalism B. P. Kozmin thought the Pisarev line had some reason in the sixties "when the world view of Saltykov-Shchedrin was not entirely defined, but became an anachronism in the second half of the seventies, when Saltykov came out as a convinced opponent of the autocratic state structure and triumphant capitalist class." P. N. Tkachev, *Izbrannye sochineniia na sotsialno-politicheskie temy,* ed. Kozmin, M. 1932–37, 4: 434n. Typical of more recent views is that of M. S. Goriachkina, who found

that "the whole artistic creative work of Shchedrin served the aim of propagandizing revolutionary ideas" (in *Istoriia russkoi kritiki,* M. 1958, 2: 146).

33. *VE* (Apr. 1869): 984.

34. *VE* (Apr. 1871): 718–41.

35. Saltykov-Shchedrin [Intro. n. 13] 18: 237–41.

36. *OZ* (May 1871) in ibid. 8: 446–50.

37. *VE* (July 1871): 462–64. The antihistorical claims made for *History of a Certain Town* are puzzling. Since the book version includes obvious parodies of the earliest Russian chronicle and the *Tale of Igor's Campaign,* as well as numerous clear hints about particular events and personages from the time of Catherine II to the accession of Nicholas I, it is not startling that S could take it for a satire of history, historiography, and historical methods. On the other hand, there is much to be said for the radicals' insistence on the essential contemporaneity of all satire. As *Iskra* put it (still attacking S's review 2 years later in 1873): "Historical satire! What sort of historical satire can this be? With what aim would a satirist ridicule the past, long ago lived through and buried? . . . Historical satire never was and never will be" (in M. S. Goriachkina, *M. E. Saltykov-Shchedrin v russkoi kritike,* M. 1959: 226). In other words, a satire of the past would be idle unless it exposed general peculiarities of Russian life and mentality, in which case it would have a current significance and cease to be historical satire. (At any rate, S would not have accepted the implication that Russia had not essentially changed.)

38. *VE* (July 1871): 463.

39. Saltykov-Shchedrin [Intro. n. 13] 18: 439n. Presumably the safest and most acceptable progressive review of *History of a Certain Town* would follow the model of *Nedelia,* which managed to strike a nice balance between praise for the brilliance of Shchedrin's historical perception and praise for the brilliance of his work in arousing present-day readers to do something about it (1871). N. Denisiuk, *Kriticheskaia literatura o proizvedeniiakh M. E. Saltykova-Shchedrina,* M. 1905, 2: 64–67. Some journals may in fact have been skeptical, but thought it best to follow the directive that Dostoevskii once sarcastically put into the mouths of the editors of *Sov.:* "You must respect, screen and protect all those who declare themselves to be progressives. Even if they are not worth it . . . even if they are obviously behaving improperly." *Epokha* (1864), in *Notes from the Underground and the Grand Inquisitor,* ed. R. E. Matlaw, N.Y. 1960: 217.

40. *VE* (Nov. 1869): 467–76 (review of *Polozhenie rabochego klassa v Rossii*). This fat and depressing book aimed, according to S, to destroy all the reader's illusions about Russian life—e.g., the superior health and consumption of the Siberian peasant—by demonstrating that the working class was everywhere cold and hungry, conditions incomparably worse than anywhere abroad. S questioned at length the author's scientific objectivity, consistency, and statistical methods, urged him to correct certain mistaken ideas about England by reading *Lettres sur l'Angleterre* of Louis Blanc, but ended by wishing the book all possible success. "It is one thing when people of a certain party talk about the poverty of the Russian people, and another thing when a person with the views of Mr. Flerovskii talks about it. He does not seek this poverty in laziness and drunkenness . . . but in the poverty of the soil, the poor allotments of land, the huge taxes." Bervi-Flerovskii responded with an article asserting that the deficiencies

of the review in *VE* were characteristic of that journal and its whole circle of readers. "Literaturnye liberaly," *LN* 2 (1932): 61–74. This dishonest liberal party, he wrote, refused to share in the general tasks of society yet wished power and influence over society; the author could only warn the *narod* not to heed the deceitful promises (freedom of speech, new land for settlement) made by those who would become the new masters. The article was to have been published in *Delo* but was forbidden by the censor.

41. *VE* (Mar. 1869): 513–17. Becher's book had been translated into Russian by Tkachev, who added the statutes of several European workmen's associations. F. Venturi terms this book a "small work of moderate views" but adds that in his notes Tkachev tried to indicate the extremist logical consequences of Becher's principles. *Roots of Revolution*, N.Y. 1960: 400–1. Tkachev and Venturi both thought the former's commentary a triumph of revolutionary exposition in the face of censorship; S pronounced it obscure and useless. The censorship authorities concluded the editor was maintaining communist ideas and withdrew the book from circulation (although one censor noted that the "problem of the proletariat and the means to solve it is in no way a Russian problem").

42. *VE* (Nov. 1869): 476–77.

43. *VE* (Aug. 1869): 914–19. The supposed fatal fruits of censorship were the military defeats of Austria in 1859 and 1866 and the military defeat and fall of the French Second Empire in 1870.

44. *Ocherki* 1, ii: 45–52. The celebration featured public remarks ("military-patriotic transports") by numerous gorgeously uniformed naval officers; convinced civilians think of armaments only as defensive, S expressed his shame that none of the civilians present rose and "pointed out that in addition to battleships armed with cannon there are battleships, so to speak, of enlightenment and liberty, behind which peoples live so much better."

45. "America is the freest country in the world, America is the most religious country in the world." *VE* (Apr. 1870): 903. Cf. *VE* (Oct. 1870): 810 (on German piety strengthened rather than weakened by the higher criticism).

46. *Ocherki* 2, ii: 224–27, 291–301. *VE* (Oct. 1869): 948–60. In 1868 S came under especially heavy verbal barrage from *Delo* and *Iskra* for his "bushman" attitude to the female question. *Delo* (Dec. 1868) ii: 18–23, 132–41; I. F. Iampolskii, *Satiricheskaia zhurnalistika 1860-kh godov: zhurnal revoliutsionnoi satiry Iskra 1859–1873*, M. 1964: 387.

47. In a famous phrase Katkov's *Moskovskie vedomosti* called itself the "organ of a party which may be called Russian, ultra-Russian, exclusively Russian." *VE*'s own editorial pages left no doubt as to its views on such "pseudo-patriots"; e.g., on the 500th anniversary of Jan Hus *VE* clearly denounced the inconsistency of those who bewailed so loudly the lack of liberty of the Czechs in the Austrian Empire. "If we find that liberty is necessary in one land, then we should find that it is necessary also in another; if we affirm that a certain nationality in one state should exercise autonomy, then there is no reason to make an exception for another state." *VE* was perhaps not quite as generous as one might at first suppose, however, since it added that the "Russification of the borderlands will be accomplished much more firmly by the successful development of the Russian people." *VE* (Oct. 1869): 892–93.

48. *VE* (Jan. 1870): 500; (Sept. 1870): 434–37.

49. *VE* (Aug. 1869): 895.

50. *VE* (Mar. 1869): 491–501. *Ocherki* 2, iii: 93–106. The Slavophile Iu. F. Samarin published abroad his denunciatory study of the German ruling classes in the Baltic provinces, *Okrainy Rossii* (1867–76).

51. *Ocherki* 2, ii: 291.

52. M. P. Dragomanov, "Avtobiografiia (1841–1889 gg.)," *Byloe* (June 1906): 189; he attempted, from a "democratic-federal point of view," to dispel the fog created about the Ukraine by the "aristocratic-Polish and bureaucratic-Muscovite tendencies." In 1873 restrictions on printing in Ukrainian (forbidden after the Polish revolt a decade earlier) were considerably relaxed and Kievan ethnographers were permitted to organize a Southern Section of the Geographical Society. The Southern Section, in which Dragomanov took an active part, became the center of an upsurge in Ukrainian literary—and therefore political—activity. In 1876 the section was dissolved and the use of Ukrainian in publications and on the stage once again prohibited. Dragomanov, forbidden to reside in Kiev or continue teaching at the university, chose to go abroad.

53. *VE* (Jan. 1870): 493–96; (Aug. 1871): 898–99; *Sankt-Peterburgskie vedomosti* (30 July 1867), cited in *LN* 67 (1959): 730n.

54. S's version was a condensation to about one-fifth the original length, but it carefully retained the long digressions on the power and idiocy of the House of Lords, the sadistic Fun Club of young London bluebloods, etc. *VE* (June 1869): 819–70; (July 1869): 297–353. *L'Homme qui rit* was published in Paris that same year. From its first appearance to the present day it seems to have been more appreciated in Russia than in the West. As a recent commentator neatly put it, the central scenes constitute a "magnificent exposure of the hypocrisy and lie of bourgeois parliamentarianism." *Victor Hugo 1802–1885*, M. 1952: 21–22. It is true that, although the action is laid in the reign of Queen Anne, criticism of such English customs as the Established Church and the antiquated judicial system are clearly tied to the 19th century situation—thus inviting the reader to conclude nothing has really changed.

55. *VE* (June 1869): 819–20. Two recent studies have demonstrated at length that the view of Katkov's ideas, held by his contemporary journalistic opponents and by almost all subsequent writers, is essentially mythic: Katkov was never truly "liberal" and never thought in constitutionalist molds, he did *not* "turn" from liberal to reactionary in 1863 or at any other time, he shunned religious prejudices and extreme national exclusiveness, he never became a blind servant of the bureaucracy, etc. See J. Backor, "M. N. Katkov; Introduction to His Life and His Russian National Policy Program, 1818–1870" (Ph.D. diss., Indiana Univ. 1966); M. Katz, *Mikhail N. Katkov; a Political Biography 1818–1887*, The Hague 1966. Certainly past scholars may justly be criticized for their failure to uncover the genuine Katkov behind the myth. But for the purposes of political polemic as practised by S and his colleagues, Katkov as symbol of aristocratic and bureaucratic reaction clearly was more important than Katkov as Hegelian and (in Katz's terminology) Conservative Westerner.

56. *Ocherki* 1, iii: 26. S at least got the point, a considerable achievement in view of the fact that he could not yet have read more than one-sixth of the entire novel (which appeared serially 1875–77). S perceptively identified Levin as chief sympathetic character and as mouthpiece for those "hermitic" ideals of

natural peasant life and happiness among the cows, of which Tolstoi had been speaking privately for some time. *Russkii mir* and other conservative organs were then praising the novel as a beautiful representation of the highest levels of society, such as had not been seen for many years in Russian literature. Turgenev claimed to feel the "influence of Moscow, of the Slavophile gentry, of Orthodox old maids." Boborykin [Intro. n. 18] 2: 577n.

57. *VE* (May 1871): 465–78.

58. *VE* (Feb. 1870): 822. Such a comparison would seem to the uninitiated to place S outside the pale of progressive forces forever. But in fact, quite inexplicably, the leading radical journal regarded Flaubert with sympathy and respect. See Sanine [n. 2]: 97.

59. *VE* (Aug. 1871): 897–902. *Ocherki* 2, ii: 21.

60. *VE* (May 1869): 467. *Ocherki* 2, ii: 313.

61. *VE* (Nov. 1871): 283–320. Arsenev demonstrated his liberalism further by stating that repressive governmental measures led youth to form such secret societies (for which the censor gave the journal an official warning).

62. Kraevskii had hoped to gain control of *Sankt-Peterburgskie vedomosti* in 1862; when the Academy of Sciences rented its paper to Korsh instead, Kraevskii established *Golos* (1863–83). During its first years *Golos* received a subsidy from the anti-obscurantist minister of education A. V. Golovnin (dismissed 1866), and printed articles prepared under the direction of the anti-Katkovian minister of internal affairs P. A. Valuev (forced to resign 1867). At the end of the decade *Golos* veered toward the camp of Katkov, but regained the middle of the channel after the liberal historian V. A. Bilbasov became co-editor in 1871. See Kozmin [Intro. n. 27]: 32–34. While in the first half of the seventies S complained of the inconstancy of *Golos'* direction, during the second half he accused it of doctrinaire and slavish liberalism.

63. *VE* (Sept. 1870): 307. *Ocherki* 2, iii: 93–106.

64. *Ocherki* 2, ii: 232.

65. *VE* (Jan. 1870): 488–500; (Mar. 1870): 465–77. *Ocherki* 1, iii: 29–33.

66. *Moskovskie vedomosti* (8 Jan. 1870), cited in Saltykov-Shchedrin [Intro. n. 13] 8: 536–37. The Greco-Roman bondage commenced with the approval of the Gymnasium Statute at that time. However the complete system, as envisioned by Katkov, was erected only gradually and was not crowned until 1887 (with the infamous circular closing the gymnasia to "cooks' children" and others of low origin).

67. *Ocherki* 2, ii: 268; 1, ii: 47.

68. The anonymous editorialist of *VE* took a more definite position against the extreme left than S was taking at this time: the former spoke of the "pyromania of the composers of proclamations"—which, like the "hydrophobia of the lead articles of *Moskovskie vedomosti*," exercised influence only thanks to the immaturity of public opinion and if heeded would lead only to the eternal night of reaction. *VE* (Feb. 1870): 840–60.

69. *VE* (Jan. 1870): 497–500. *Ocherki* 1, iii: 30.

70. *Ocherki* 1, iii: 29–33. It is of course possible Katkov really was accepting gifts for his lyceum in return for favorable publicity to certain railway projects, as S alleged. However, everything known of Katkov's character indicates this is unlikely. Moreover, he was at this time actively urging railway construction (if

undertaken by Russian subjects) for principled reasons connected with his entire world view. See Katz [n. 55]: 115–16.

71. E.g., *Sankt-Peterburgskie vedomosti* (16 May 1871), cited in Saltykov-Shchedrin [Intro. n. 13] 8: 539n. According to *OZ*, its lack of interest in the burning question of the day arose from the fact that most people did not have access to education at all—and it was this majority that concerned *OZ*. The indifference was not complete; the journal received its first warning (July 1872) for an article by a regular staff member criticizing the new school regulations.

72. *Ocherki* 2, iii: 49–65. *VE* (July 1870): 391–407.

73. *VE* (Sept. 1870): 305. As so often, S was unfortunate in his timing. The article on Germany was written sometime after the declaration of war by France in July, but before the capture of Napoleon III at Sedan, 2 Sept. (Gregorian), and proclamation of the Republic 2 days later. By the time the second installment appeared (Oct.) Paris was under siege and the tide of Russian public opinion was running high in sympathy for France.

74. *VE* (Sept. 1870): 300.

75. Ibid.: 309, 308.

76. *VE* (Oct. 1870): 809, 829. On court and public opinion, see W. E. Mosse, *The European Powers and the German Question 1848–1871,* Cambridge 1958: 393–94; L. I. Narochnitskaia, *Rossiia i voiny Prussii v 60-kh godakh XIX v. za obedinenie Germanii "sverkhu,"* M. 1960; Z. S. Efimova, "Parizhskaia kommuna i organ russkoi revoliutsionnoi demokratii *Iskra,*" *Istoricheskie zapiski* 59 (1957): 310–27.

77. *OZ* (Oct. 1870), in *Saltykov-Shchedrin* [Intro. n. 13] 7: 194.

78. E.g., P. D. Boborykin, who began to sympathize with the French predicament only when he realized the Germans intended to defeat France completely and to detach Alsace and Lorraine against the will of the inhabitants. [Intro. n. 18] 2: 116–17. Boborykin was at this time engaged by *Sankt-Peterburgskie vedomosti* as a correspondent from the war area; by his account he began to lose sympathy for that paper when Korsh detailed S to cast doubts on the accuracy of some dispatches in which Boborykin described destruction effected by German shellfire.

79. *VE* (Nov. 1870): 424–34, quoting with continued confidence from the Aug. issue. As late as Oct. a lead article in *Sankt-Peterburgskie vedomosti* stated that Berlin stood at the head of civilization while France was decaying and demoralized. Efimova [n. 76]: 316. Several months earlier, however, Utin (a member of the inner circle of *VE*) had already published an article describing the victory of Prussia as a triumph of militarism and reaction. *VE* (Aug. 1870): 810–43.

80. *Ocherki* 1, ii: 27–48.

81. *Iskra* (1871), cited in Iampolskii [n. 46]: 489. V. P. Burenin, later chief literary critic of S's *NV,* at that time wrote regularly for *Iskra* and contributed at least one "sonnet" to the anti-S campaign of the moment: "I dreamt that from end to end / In all Europe the Prussians ruled. / And from the people they formed regiments / Introducing peaceful order everywhere [etc.]." *Poety Iskry,* ed. I. Iampolskii, L. 1955, 2: 750. Burenin's technique of attack on "Visiting and at Home" was typical in that it chiefly consisted of deriding S's minor (and easily ridiculed) enthusiasms for foreign ways while neglecting to mention the

major points of criticism that S had hoped thereby to score. Shchedrin, for example, held up to repeated scorn the twin inanities of return railway tickets and gummed postage stamps. From the opposite direction, *Moskovskie vedomosti* sneered at "postal liberalism." *VE* (Nov. 1870): 386–93. In fact S described the postal system in order to praise the inviolability of sealed letters and packages— for him another example of that high degree of trust between the public and the administration which he found in Germany and missed in Russia. Or again, when he described the convenience and efficiency of public transportation, it was to emphasize the ease and freedom with which Germans of all ages traveled through their fatherland—while no one asked to see their internal passports or accused them of constituting a secret society with revolutionary aims; Russia, in contrast, remained unknown to her inhabitants, a fact with obvious if unspoken implications for the quality and maturity of the patriotism that Russia might inspire. The main point of Saltykov-Shchedrin's rebuttal, other than to reaffirm the primacy of universal (i.e., radical) ideals over "bourgeois" small-deedism, seems to be the assertion that a people kept in ignorance and permanent state of infantilism with regard to internal affairs cannot be expected to show enthusiasm and initiative in defending the state from outside forces. *OZ* (Oct. 1870) in [Intro. n. 13] 7: 174–94. By reading the famous satirist alone, one would gain the impression that S argued just the opposite—which was not at all the case.

82. *VE* (Sept. 1870): 317.

83. Cf. *VE* (Apr. 1871): 897–907; (July 1871): 459–62.

84. E.g., *NV* (21 Dec. 1876).

85. *Ocherki* 1, ii: 1–144; 2, ii: 145–207. The populist Mikailovskii even welcomed S's exposé of plutocracy, although regretting that S concerned himself only with educated society and not with the "politically, economically, and morally despoiled peasant." *OZ* (May 1875) in Mikhailovskii [Ch. 3 n. 4] 3: 466.

86. Cf. J. N. Westwood, *A History of Russian Railways,* London 1964.

87. *Ocherki* 1, ii: 5.

88. *VE* (Oct. 1870): 818. *Ocherki* 2, ii: 171–73, 199–200, 205–6. In view of S's later nationalism and anti-semitism, it should be noted that at this time he did not draw attention to non-Russian plutocrats as more exploitative in any way than were pure Russian plutocrats (although he did upon occasion ridicule the German and Jewish accents heard on the stock exchange and over banking counters).

CHAPTER FIVE

1. Although this sum was thrice as much as the previous publisher had paid 2 years earlier, it was considerably less than the 125,000 rubles paid by Baimakov for the already much more successful *Sankt-Peterburgskie vedomosti* in Dec. 1874. For comparison, in that same year, his last with Korsh, S received an annual salary of 4500 rubles. Likhachev was the husband of E. O. Likhacheva, publishing partner of S's late wife. *Drevnik S:* 85, 328; *NV* (29 Feb., 31 May, 12 Dec. 1876).

2. Although the paper was printed by an independent firm until S and Likha-

chev acquired their own building in 1877, advertisements offering old printing machinery for sale appeared in *NV* simultaneously with announcements that new highspeed equipment had been purchased from abroad (late 1876).

3. S (who was in a position to know) thought that if Baimakov had been able to keep all the former subscribers to *Sankt-Peterburgskie vedomosti,* he would have made up to 35,000 rubles profit in the first year. *NV* (12 Dec. 1876). A fire destroyed all statistical information for the first 3 years of S's *NV.* Some partial figures for expenses in later years have been published: Lisovskii [Pref. n. 8]: 429. The files of the business manager were probably lost in a second fire which swept the *NV* building in late 1917.

4. *NV* (29 Feb. 1876); *ES* 33: 926–7; "Kak voznikla gazeta *NV,*" *Vestnik vsemirnoi istorii* (Dec. 1899): 156–76. As an example of inadequate sales volume, the experience of Ustrialov may be cited. Despite his paper's oppositional leanings, the number of subscribers never exceeded 1500 and he lost large sums of money on the venture. A. G. Stepanova-Borodina, "Vospominaniia," *LN* 49/50 (1946): 582–4.

5. *ES* 21: 278.

6. Police document in *LN* 49/50 (1946): 523. Korsh's *Sankt-Peterburgskie vedomosti* had wide ties with zemstvo participants, no doubt the origin of the "vast contacts with the provinces" predicted by the police. Nekrasov [Ch. 1 n. 22] 12: 39.

7. *LN* 49/50 (1946); 584–6; Skabichevskii [Ch. 4 n. 14]: 315–20; Nekrasov [Ch. 1 n. 22] 12: 355, 361–62; Saltykov-Shchedrin [Intro. n. 13] 18: 250, *LN* 51/52 (1949): 487; Abramovich [Pref. n. 7]: 114. The government of course allowed several radical monthly journals, evidently fearing total repression would increase radicalism and force it wholly underground. But as B. I. Esin has demonstrated in the example of Karl Marx's work, the censorship authorities considered "negative" material in newspapers to be more dangerous than similar material in either fat journals or books. "Politseiskaia kara za statiu o I tome *Kapitala,*" *Vestnik Moskovskogo universiteta: zhurnalistika* (Mar.–Apr. 1967): 86–87.

8. B. I. Esin, *Russkaia zhurnalistika 70–80kh godov XIX veka,* M. 1963: 162; *Kratkii ocherk izdatelskoi deiatelnosti Alekseia Sergeevicha Suvorina i razvitiia prinadlezhashchei emu tipografii NV,* St.P. 1900: 3; *NV* (23 Feb. 1909).

9. Saltykov-Shchedrin provided, with appropriate changes, an article on graft during the Crimean War that had been destroyed by the censor along with the contributions of 6 other writers in a particularly offensive issue of *OZ* 2 years earlier. Hence his offering to *NV* was in no sense new work undertaken for that paper. One often encounters the statement in works on journalism and in the notes to standard editions of Russian authors that both Nekrasov and Shchedrin agreed to collaborate in *NV* but had cut short all connection with S by the end of 1876. This misapprehension would be too insignificant to note, were it not so widespread. As shown above, Nekrasov declined to participate; by Feb. 1876 he had already entered upon his long final illness and was able to contribute little new work even to his own journal. As his letters show, however, the poet remained friendly to S until his death in Dec. 1877. During his last 2 years he gave S about a dozen short poems of civic content (all eventually appeared in *NV*). See his last known letter to S (6 Dec. 1877), Nekrasov [Ch. 1 n. 22] 11: 416. Saltykov-Shchedrin, on the other hand, did in fact react favorably to

the first number of *NV* and offered to help with a projected "cooperative feuilleton-novel." As he had already quite correctly pointed out, however, he was severely limited by his contract to devote all his energies to *OZ*. His sole collaboration, described above, was slight. By May he was arguing that even that one article had been sent only as a personal favor to Likhachev (a friend since childhood) and Nekrasov ([Intro. n. 13] 18: 346–49, 363). Hence it is misleading to say that Saltykov "severed ties" with *NV* in 1876—since he never had significant ties—and absolutely false to say it of Nekrasov.

10. M. Gershenzon, ed., *Russkie propilei*, M. 1916, 3: 247–52, 331–39.

11. Abramovich [Pref. n. 7]: 55.

12. Burenin (1841–1926), grandson of a serf and trained as an architect, began to publish in *Kolokol* and legal radical periodicals in 1861. A clever versifier and parodist, he became one of the leading satirists of *Iskra*. Although he wrote literary feuilletons regularly for *Sankt-Peterburgskie vedomosti* from 1865, he also continued to attack liberals (including S) in *Iskra* until a quarrel with the editors of *OZ* led to a break with the entire radical camp in the early seventies. In contrast, Skalkovskii (1843–1906) seems to have passed through no radical phase. Trained as a mining engineer, he conducted numerous investigations of commercial and industrial problems for the Ministry of Finance; even while working on *NV* he continued to serve in the Mining Department and became its director in 1891. Throughout his career he urged industrial development, tariff protectionism, and facilitation by the state of mineral exploitation by private interests. Although he wrote a great variety of material for *NV*, he specialized in short but serious articles on financial conditions and economic problems of the day. Since his signed economic articles for *NV* reflect his general views, it is reasonable to assume the numerous unsigned lead articles that urged free trade, direct taxation, economic protection of peasants, etc., during the early years of publication came from the hand of S. See V. Evgenev-Maksimov, *Nekrasov i ego sovremenniki*, M. 1930: 320–26; *ES* 30: 172; B. B. Glinskii, *Sredi literatorov i uchenykh*, St.P. 1914: 56–101, 430–31; A. I. Pashkov and N. A. Tsagolov, eds., *Istoriia russkoi ekonomicheskoi mysli: epokha domonopolisticheskogo kapitalizma*, M. 1959, 1: 54–55.

13. Korsh [Ch. 4 n. 11].

14. E.g., M. M. Ivanov, who became regular music critic of *NV* in 1876, had come to admire S for his feuilletons in *Sankt-Peterburgskie vedomosti;* in the early 20th century Ivanov was still his employee and admirer. *NV* (23 Feb. 1909).

15. The only significant exception was S. A. Vengerov who, although of Jewish origin, devoted his life to Russian letters; he severed all ties with *NV* by the end of 1876. Some sources cite the Jewish writers N. M. Vilenkin-Minskii and L. O. Levanda as *NV* contributors during 1876; in fact the first named published short verses on the South Slavic uprisings in *NV*, but I have found nothing signed by Levanda. See *Kniga o russkom evreistve*, N.Y. 1960: 557. On the identity of contributors to *NV*, see *Na pamiat o desiatiletii NV*, St.P. 1886; "Sorokaletie gazety *NV*, 1876–1916 gg.," *Istoricheskii vestnik* (Apr. 1916): 166–93; *ES* 21:278–79; Glinskii [n. 12].

16. G. A. deVollan, "Ocherki proshlogo; 1883 god," *Golos minuvshego* (Aug. 1914): 158. Vollan contributed to *NV* in 1876 and 1881–83.

17. A statistical study made in 1900 shows the Russian daily newspaper then was little different from that of the seventies. Advertising had increased to occupy an average third of all space, while editorial articles and feuilletons lost ground slightly to news and other features. Size, format, and content, as well as the high proportion of foreign to domestic news, remained the same. A. Peshekhonov. "Russkaia politicheskaia gazeta (statisticheskii ocherk)," *Russkoe bogatstvo* (Mar. 1901) ii: 1–21.

18. See, e.g., *NV* (21 Mar. 1876). Unlike other newspapers, *Moskovskie vedomosti* placed the usually very uninteresting "Governmental Orders" at the top of the first page. Both *Moskovskie vedomosti* and Katkov's journal, *Russkii vestnik*, used 18th century type faces and followed a format which seemed old-fashioned.

19. Although the idea for such a newspaper column hardly seems remarkable or startling, the official historiography of *NV* emphasized its innovative character; e.g., Glinskii [n. 12]: 82, 430. Skalkovskii himself greeted each new "imitation" by another paper with withering scorn in *NV*.

20. Mikhnevich [Intro. n. 24]: ii; N. A. Engelgardt, *Ocherk istorii russkoi tsenzury v sviazi s razvitiem pechati*, St.P. 1904: 377–81; Berezina [Intro. n. 3]: 517; *NV* (4 July 1880).

21. *NV* (29 Feb. 1876). For identification of S as author, see *Istoricheskii vestnik* (Apr. 1916): 167.

22. Quoted in *NV* (17 Apr. 1876).

23. *OZ* (Mar. 1877) in Mikhailovskii [Ch. 3 n. 4] 2: 880. In fact, descriptions of demimonde boudoirs were far from prominent in *NV*. Mikhailovskii often used such phrases to stand for all the trivial, corrupt, and non-idea interests of philistines and bourgeois. As far as S's newspaper is concerned, Mikhailovskii may also have been referring to the serialized fiction which appeared there. The first important work to be published in *NV*, Zola's *L'Assommoir*, was followed within 5 years by 2 other novels by Zola. In the late seventies *OZ*—and especially Mikhailovskii—conducted a campaign against Zola and naturalism; this hostility was not diminished by the fact that he was contributing letters from Paris on events of the day and on his philosophy of writing to the liberal *VE*. Sanine [Ch. 4 n. 2]: 82–89. *Delo*, on the other hand, published one of Zola's novels in 1878. Contemporary fiction by such authors as Bret Harte, Wilkie Collins, Alphonse Daudet (who from 1879 wrote a regular column on French literary and intellectual events), and a host of secondary Russian writers also appeared in serial form in *NV*.

24. Kozmin [Intro. n. 27]: 35.

25. Mikhnevich [Intro. n. 24]: iii; Backor [Ch. 4 n. 55]: 156–64; Dzhanshiev [Intro. n. 12]: 634.

26. E.g., *NV* (16 Apr., 29 May, 1876).

27. *NV* (12, 18 May 1876).

28. *NV* (20 Apr., 30 May, 4, 17 July 1876).

29. *NV* (13, 14 Mar., 27, 30 Apr., 17 June 1876).

30. *NV* (21 Mar. 1876).

31. Following the unsuccessful uprising of 1863, the area of the former Congress Kingdom of Poland received the new official designation of Vistula Region (*privislinskii krai*) and lost its separate Polish administration. At the

time that S wrote, aggressive Russification of the civil service, courts, schools, and university had been underway in the area for a decade.

32. *NV* (24 Mar., 17 Apr. 1876). While European Christendom, especially its Iberian and Slavic extremities, regarded Islam historically as a principal enemy, the special virulence of this attack must be seen rather as part of the nationalist and pan-Slavic upsurge of anti-Turkish feeling during that period. Not only did the fanatics of the Ottoman Empire threaten to destroy the in-surgent South Slavs, but also the fanatics of small Turkish states in Central Asia impeded the triumphal advance of Russian conquest in that area. In the latter area and in the Caucasus a whole generation of Russian army officers spent their lives fighting Moslems, which cannot have been without effect on the outlook of large segments of educated society even before the plight of the Orthodox Slavs began to arouse widespread sympathy. The "revolutionary con-servative" Gen. Fadeev (see above) initially formed his views on the stagnation of Islamic society and the conquering mission of Russia in Asia while he was serving in the Caucasus. Thaden [Ch. 4 n. 20]: 147–48.

The opinions of *Golos,* in 1876 the leading liberal newspaper, were only slightly less virulently anti-Moslem than those of *NV. Golos* called attention to the fanatical hatred of Moslems for Christians and the rising tide of fanaticism which (with assistance from the Ottoman sultan) threatened the peace in areas from Turkestan to North Africa, and noted with pride it had been the first to draw attention to this dangerous Moslem movement which, it asserted, had since been noted by almost all Russian periodicals of importance. *Golos* (23 Jan., 18 Aug. 1876).

33. *NV* (9, 16 May 1876).

34. The indictment, published as a special supplement to *NV* (3 Oct. 1876), occupied 12 pages of fine print in quarto.

35. *NV* (23, 30 May, 28 Oct. 1876). If by the public S meant the press, his accusation was certainly not true. *Golos, NV*'s arch-rival, devoted at least as much space to Strousberg and associates. *VE* gave considerably more attention to the case than it was accustomed to give to such fleeting "evils of the day." In June it printed a résumé of a pamphlet on Strousberg (a leading figure of the *Gründerzeit* in Berlin in the sixties) by the German anti-semitic publicist Otto Glagau; in Nov. and Dec. it printed articles on the revelations of the trial. *Delo* gave 59 pages of its Nov. issue to financial scandals. None of this agitation seems to have had a definite anti-Jewish intent; rather it was aimed against financial speculation and fraudulent paper schemes, wherever they might arise. Nor did entrepreneurial St.P. neglect Strousberg. By late Oct. *NV* carried large advertisements for a popular pamphlet on his life ("from the cradle to the defendant's dock") and an exhibition of his life-size likeness at a wax museum.

36. *NV* (1 May 1876).

37. *NV* (30 May, 10 Dec. 1876). Every rail scandal or fatal accident brought the proposal that the government put an end to the present system "whereby profits go into the pockets of private persons, while deficits are met by the state." *NV* (22 May 1876). As the war clouds gathered at the end of the year, *NV* became ever more concerned about the low quality and unstrategic placement of new railway construction. Yet it seemed unable to explain if the state should take

over all construction, or withdraw its profit guarantees to private builders, or what.

38. *NV* (16 Mar. 1876).

39. Kozmin [Intro. n. 27]: 16–19; *NV* (17 May 1876). *Nedelia* was founded in 1866 as a covert organ of P. A. Valuev, then minister of internal affairs; in 1868 it passed into private hands and at once became a legal-radical organ. G. S. Lapshina, "Gazeta *Nedelia* v 1868–1869 gg. i tsenzura," *Vestnik Moskovskogo universiteta: zhurnalistika* (Jan.–Feb. 1968): 46–56. In 1873 *Nedelia* had about 2500 subscribers; by 1878 they had tripled and by the nineties reached 15,000. It ceased publication by government order in 1901. Dementev [Intro. n. 10]: 484–86. Other periodicals, especially *OZ*, contained quantities of writings in the commune-idealizing vein. But *Nedelia* represented the purest deposit, the mother-lode so to speak, excluding all more skeptical strains of thought.

40. *Delo* (Feb. 1876) ii: 176–86. The term *pochvenniki* (from *pochva*, soil) refers to the adherents of the theory of literary criticism, developed by A. A. Grigorev (1822–64), which held that Russian literature must have an organic link with the Russian soil. Since Grigorev's views were esthetic and nationalistic, his associates Slavophiles, and his publicistic career bound up with such journals as *Moskvitianin* and *Vremia*, radical publicists such as Tkachev regarded him as a reactionary of the murkiest hue.

41. *NV* (18 Mar., 22 Apr. 1876).

42. *OZ* (Apr. 1876) in Mikhailovskii [Ch. 3 n. 4] 3: 730–32.

43. *NV* (29 Apr. 1876). Vengerov claimed that *VE*, despite its cloak of objectivity, in fact also rejected the notion that the laws of general human development did not apply to Russia. *VE*, he announced triumphantly, "stands for 'Europe' *à outrance*."

44. *NV* (21 Mar., 23 May 1876).

45. *NV* (16 May 1876). One of *NV's* most concrete suggestions for the liberation of the peasantry—removal or easing of regulations on internal passports—was intended to aid not agriculture but industry in labor-short South Russia (12 June 1876).

46. E.g., *NV* (11, 29 May 1876).

47. *NV* (3, 4 June 1876). The similarity of some aspects of neo-Slavophile and populist rhetoric was indeed confusing, as was the whole realignment of the various intellectual camps of the sixties on the basis of the new nationalism of the seventies. *Delo* complained that strange bedfellows were appearing everywhere; no press organ knew *what* it stood for and such words as Europe and village had lost their former significance (July 1876, ii: 41–61).

48. *NV* (2, 3 Mar. 1876).

49. *NV* (9, 11, 29 Apr., 7 May, 1876).

50. *NV* (24 Aug. 1876).

CHAPTER SIX

1. B. H. Sumner, *Russia and the Balkans 1870–1880*, Oxford 1937: 158–60; D. MacKenzie, *The Serbs and Russian Pan-Slavism 1875–1878*, Ithaca 1967; S. A. Nikitin, *Slavianskie Komitety v Rossii v 1858–1876 godakh*, M. 1960: 269–91.

2. *NV* (1, 12 Mar. 1876).

3. *NV* (19 Mar. 1876).

4. *NV* (31 Mar. 1876).

5. *NV* (7 Apr. 1876).

6. Lamanskii had won a certain secular fame at the M. Slavic Congress of 1867 when he proposed that Russian become the common Slavic language. On the group of ideas and emotions known as pan-Slavism or neo-Slavophilism, the militant and stridently nationalistic child of the more philosophical and religious Slavophilism of the forties, see M. B. Petrovich,, *The Emergence of Russian Panslavism 1856–1870*, N.Y. 1956; S. Lukashevich, *Ivan Aksakov 1823–1886*, Cambridge, Mass., 1965.

7. *NV* (25 Apr. 1876).

8. *NV* (2 May 1876). *NV* referred to the capital of the Ottoman Empire by its Greek name Constantinople or by its old Russian name Tsargrad, but almost never by its Turkish name Istanbul (well known at this time to the liberal and radical Russian press).

9. *NV* (5 June 1876).

10. *NV* (18 May 1876).

11. *NV* (13 May 1876).

12. *NV* (14 June 1876). The London *Daily News* began to report on the massacres only from 11 June, O.S.; other investigations by westerners followed. Sumner [n. 1]: 171.

13. *NV* (16 June 1876).

14. E.g., *NV* (15 May, 6 June 1876). Veselitskii-Bozhidarovich evidently harbored no ill feelings; in the late seventies, after the Balkan crisis ended, he served as London correspondent for *NV*.

15. *NV* (19 June 1876).

16. *NV* (22 June 1876).

17. *NV* (30 May 1876). See D. MacKenzie, "Panslavism in Practice: Cherniaev in Serbia (1876)," *Journal of Modern History* 36 (Sep. 1964): 279–97. Saltykov-Shchedrin's satires on various types of "Tashkenters," published in *OZ* in the early seventies, made that word almost a synonym for rapacious, corrupt officialdom.

18. *NV* (29 May, 1, 20 June 1876). In fact *Golos* (30 May 1876) also extended to Cherniaev somewhat tepid wishes for success, but *NV* chose to ignore this.

19. MacKenzie [n. 17]: 279, 295.

20. For an especially clear call to armed intervention, see lead article, *NV* (2 Sept. 1876). In July the St.P. Slavic Benevolent Committee transferred publication of names of contributors and other announcements from *Golos* to *NV* (although in fact the committee's announcements continued to appear in *Golos* as well). In Dec. an unsuccessful attempt was made to expel Kraevskii from the committee, of which he had been a nominal member for some time. *NV* (4, 7 July, 7 Dec. 1876).

21. In a rare public address on policy Alexander II assured the nobility of M. that if deliberations between the great powers failed to improve the condition of the Balkan Christians, he was prepared to act independently. *NV* acclaimed the emperor's words with transports of joy (2 Nov. 1876).

22. *NV* (25 Dec. 1876).

23. *NV* (6, 20 June 1876). Between 1873 and 1876, thanks to lightened censorship and the existence of the Southern Section of the Geographical Society as a center, Ukrainophile literary agitation flourished in Kiev. S complained that the Ukrainian linguistic cause had become a "sore point for many persons sincerely devoted to the people." "If you just don't have enough sham and sentimentality to place Shevchenko above Pushkin and Lermontov and give him political significance, right away they assign you to the camp of Katkov." In 1876 the government dissolved the Southern Section and on 5 June prohibited almost all types of publication in Ukrainian; but since the prohibition was not made public for several months, it is doubtful S knew of it.

24. *NV* (27 June, 4, 6, 11, 14 July 1876). Ignatev, chief Russian representative in Constantinople for over a decade, was the Ministry of Foreign Affairs' chief exponent of and eager plotter for pan-Slavic ideas. Based as they were on the concept of Russian hegemony over all the Slavs, one might more precisely term his ideals pan-Russian.

25. *NV* (18, 22 July 1876).

26. *NV* (25 July 1876).

27. *NV* (6, 8, 10, 11, 13 Aug. 1876).

28. *NV* (15, 22 Aug. 1876). S continued to defend Cherniaev long after, admitting only that the general did not know how to choose able associates. *Dnevnik S:* 81; deVollan [Ch. 5 n. 16]: 157.

29. Glinskii [Ch. 5 n. 12]: 81.

30. *NV* (1, 3, 6, 10, 30 Aug. 1876). *Golos* (or rather its affiliate International Telegraphic Agency) at first had managed to receive almost no news from the Serbian front. Its reporters, as personae non gratae to the Correspondence Bureau, finally had to go to Austrian territory to send their dispatches. Since ITA was the only such organization in Russia at that time, small papers without their own correspondents were left during the first weeks of the Serbo-Turkish War to rely entirely on Cherniaev's bureau or on stale news copied from foreign papers. Despite its flock of correspondents and its contempt for *Golos, NV* subscribed to ITA and used its service from everywhere other than Serbia.

31. Lisovskii [Pref. n. 8]: 428; *Dnevnik S:* 328–29.

32. *Golos* (7 Nov. 1876); *NV* (8 Nov. 1876).

33. *NV* (1, 19, 22 Dec. 1876). Unfortunately for S's theory on the value of war, Russian society was far from healthy. Moreover, the financial situation of the state was extremely precarious.

34. *OZ* (Oct. 1876) in Mikhailovskii [Ch. 3 n. 4] 3: 815–54.

35. *Delo* (Oct. 1876): 402, 404.

36. "Istoricheskii fatalizm," *Vpered!* in *Osvobozhdenie Bolgarii ot turetskogo iga; dokumenty* 1, M. 1961: 72–76.

37. *Delo* (Jan. 1876) iii: 105. The Turkish state system, as described by *Delo,* bore a close resemblance to that of the Russian Empire; e.g., this article emphasized not only the absence of rule of law, but also how the sultan squeezed the last drop from the peasantry in taxes to pay his foreign loan obligations.

38. *Delo* (June 1876) ii: 152–92; *OZ* (Nov. 1875): 110; *VE* (Sept. 1875): 399–400.

39. *Delo* (Aug. 1876) ii: 96–102; iii: 97–121; *OZ* (July 1876): 140;

(Sept. 1876): 67–97; *NV* (8 June 1876); *Vpered!* (1 Oct. 1876) in *Osvobozhdenie* [n. 36] 1: 434–36.

40. Eliseev to Nekrasov (27 Sept. 1876) in *LN* 51/52: 257; *OZ* (Oct. 1876) ii: 190–214; *VE* (Aug. 1876): 781–803; *Molva* (10 Oct. 1876); *Delo* (Oct. 1876): 490–92. S replied to *VE* with accusations of cosmopolitanism, defeatism, and doctrinaire liberalism. *NV* (3 Oct. 1876).

41. *Molva* (10 Oct. 1876); M. P. Dragomanov, *Turki vnutrennie i vneshnie,* Geneva 1876: 24.

42. *VE* (Nov. 1876): 385–413; (Feb. 1877): 807–17; (Mar. 1877): 357–87; *OZ* (Dec. 1876) ii: 171–85; *Delo* (Oct. 1876): 411–12; *NV* (1 Jan. 1878). J. H. Billington, *Mikhailovsky and Russian Populism,* Oxford 1958: 100.

43. *NV* (11 Mar., 19, 20, 22, June 1876); MacKenzie [n. 1]: 42, 57, 110–11.

44. Cherniaev himself had even opposed the emancipation of the serfs. In 1876, when given the rare opportunity to move pan-Slavism from the realm of theory into that of practice, he attempted to subvert and destroy parliamentary government in Serbia and to establish a military dictatorship. MacKenzie [n. 17]: 280–87. S, professionally attuned to political currents and in Serbia during part of Cherniaev's campaign, must have been aware of at least some of the general's less generous ideas and activities.

45. *Golos* (6, 28 Jan., 4, 19 Sept. 1876); Mikhnevich [Intro. n. 24]: xi–xviii; MacKenzie [n. 1]: 115, 192.

46. *NV* (7, 20 June 1876).

47. *NV* (12, 29 Sept. 1877); Arsenev [Intro. n. 14]: 100.

48. Nikitin [n. 1]: 327–28; Saltykov-Shchedrin [Intro. n. 13] 19: 78; deVollan [Ch. 5 n. 16]: 157–58; I. N. Kramskoi, *Pisma,* L. 1937, 2: 374–77; *Dnevnik S:* 82–83; Esin [Ch. 5 n. 8]: 162; A. V. Bogdanovich, *Tri poslednikh samoderzhtsa; dnevnik,* M. 1924: 53. Bogdanovich, who held a salon patronized by the higher spheres of officialdom in St.P., was the wife of the general sent to persuade S (who agreed to write against clemency). It is clear from her diary that she was personally acquainted with S at least from Jan. 1880.

49. The only less dangerous "Tashkenters of practice" attempted to take over Serbia. *Delo* (Oct. 1876): 489. For Tashkenter, see above (n. 17).

50. *Delo* (Oct. 1876): 404–7; *NV* (3 Sept. 1876); Eliseev to Nekrasov (27 Sept. 1876) in *LN* 51/52 (1949): 257. Two decades later S recalled that circulation in 1876 reached only 15,000. *Dnevnik S:* 25. By 1880 *NV* was indeed printing 20,000. Esin [Intro. n. 35]: 85.

51. *Golos* claimed only 6 subscribers cancelled. Mikhnevich [Intro. n. 24]: 1 (50). Propper, on the other hand, wrote that people cancelled by the hundreds and copies were even snatched from newsboys and burned in the street. [Intro. n. 9]: 28. For statistics from official records, see Esin [Intro. n. 35]: 85–86. For police reports on the popular mood, see *Osvobozhdenie* [n. 36]. Cf. V. M. Khevrolina, "Ob otnoshenii russkogo obshchestva k voine i osvobozhdeniiu Bolgarii ot turetskogo iga," *Kratkie soobshcheniia Instituta slavianovedeniia AN SSSR* 40 (1964): 41–44.

52. The phrase—which summarizes all the rhetoric of *NV* at this time—is taken from *Voennaia khronika russko-turetskoi voiny,* a pamphlet of 8 pages, which S wrote in May to explain to the masses that the tsar had taken up the sword against Moslem fanaticism (incited by perfidious Albion) to free Christian

peoples, give triumph to the cross, and lead the western Slavs to a new and better life. Brightly colored illustrations showed Turkish soldiers exploding in mid-air or fleeing before Russian bayonets.

53. Marx to Sorge (27 Sept. 1877), cited in Sumner [n. 1]: 337n.

54. *NV* (6, 8, 23 Sept. 1877).

55. *NV* (25 Sept. 1877).

56. *NV* (13, 15 Sept. 1877). Throughout this book the Russian word *evrei* has been translated as Jew and the opprobrious term *zhid* as Yid. Vengerov, in reviewing a play on the struggles of young Jews in the sixties to gain secular education and become Russian in culture, drew a linguistic distinction between the emancipated *evrei* and the narrow, superstituous, profiteering village *zhid* (like other liberals of the time, he expressed confidence that Jews, given modern education, would eventually blend with the Russian population). *NV* (22 Apr. 1876). S and the other editors of *NV* seem to have been innocent of such linguistic subtleties.

57. *NV* (18, 20, 28 Sept. 1877).

58. Tkachev [Ch. 4 n. 32] 4: 435n; *Delo* (Jan. 1878): 10. In the spring of 1878 *NV* opened a campaign in its pages on behalf of Russian drovers "deceived and exploited" by the food contractors (14 Apr.). Strangely enough, not until 26 Aug. (after months of agitation) did it announce it at last had evidence to prove its allegations.

59. *NV* (1, 10, 22 Jan. 1878); *Delo* (Feb. 1878): 431.

60. *NV* (11, 14, 15 Apr. 1878).

61. *Moskovskie vedomosti* claimed to have originated the scheme 2 years earlier, but *NV* thought the idea arose of itself at the same time in both capitals (20 Apr. 1878).

62. *NV* (2, 7 Aug. 1878). News of India came to St.P. via London rather than directly. At one point *NV* openly stated that Russia would have lost "everything" by the Berlin treaty, if Austria had not been busy in the Balkans and England occupied in India—"diversion in Central Asia is our salvation." After the initial shock, the paper did not find the division of Bulgaria so distressing; "living popular force" would soon restore the San Stefano boundaries (9 Sept. 1878).

63. V. I. Ado, "Vystuplenie I. S. Aksakova protiv Berlinskogo kongressa 1878 g. i otkliki na nego v Rossii i Bolgarii," *Istoriia SSSR* (Nov.–Dec. 1962): 132–35.

64. *NV* avoided censure until it received a warning for an excessively gloomy New Year's Day survey terming 1878 "a year of deceived hopes . . . of unbelievable confusion" (1 Jan. 1879).

65. *VE* (Aug. 1878): 740–51; *NV* (2, 11 Aug. 1878).

66. *NV* (4 Aug., 1 Sept. 1878, 1 Jan. 1879).

67. *NV* (12 Sept. 1878). In fact here Bismarck was praised as a genius who was willing to tread new paths to improve the life of the people, even while sternly suppressing socialist subversion. Such unlikely comrades-in-arms as *Nedelia, Golos,* and *Sankt-Peterburgskie vedomosti* indulged themselves in this campaign, which reached its height in the spring of 1879 and was answered in full force by the German press. *NV* did oppose the German tariff war against Russia, a concrete aspect of Russo-German hostility of the time, but it avoided personal attacks on Bismarck even then (30 Apr. 1879).

68. *NV* (9 Aug., 11 Sept. 1878, 22 Feb. 1879).

69. *NV* (29 Jan. 1878). The Magyars, according to *NV*, had contributed nothing to European culture; their capital city was barren of art and science— even Odessa was better (9 Sept. 1877).

70. *NV* (8 Aug. 1878).

71. *NV* (9–11, 14, 21 Jan. 1879). As the editors of *OZ* once pointed out in an era of relaxed censorship, foreign problems occupied such an important place in that journal "not at all because we find nothing more interesting to improve at home, but rather because it is impossible to write about what is at home" (Oct. 1880). Cited by V. G. Serebrennikova, "Demokraticheskaia zhurnalistika perioda vtoroi revoliutsionnoi situatsii," *Obshchestvennoe dvizhenie v poreform-ennoi Rossii,* ed. L. M. Ivanov, M. 1965: 357. During the entire war period *NV* gave sustained attention to only one foreign news story not connected with the Eastern question: the French election campaign of late 1877. It firmly supported the Republicans and opposed MacMahon, pointing out for example that his election manifesto contained all the usual reactionary terminology of so-called saviors of society, "including threats against all who opposed the policy of the 'honest' warrior" (11 Sept. 1877).

72. *NV* (3, 8 Apr. 1878). On 1 Jan. 1879 *NV* announced that "no one seriously believed in war with England"!

73. *NV* (21 Aug. 1878).

74. *NV* (22–23 Aug. 1878, 20 Mar., 13 May 1879). A special commission of ministers appointed to study the problem of combating subversion reported in June 1879 the "almost complete failure of the educated classes to support the government in its fight . . . Though taking no part in the struggle and though not acting on behalf of the government, they are to some extent waiting for the result of the battle." Cited in Venturi [Ch. 4 n. 41]: 633.

75. E.g., *NV* (8, 11 Apr. 1879). Eliseev, writing in the eighties, saw the glorification of the emperor as the pivotal point of S's apostasy from liberalism. "This shy sparrow modestly chirped his feuilletons with Korsh, envying the glory and splendor of such a falcon as Katkov. But suddenly he decided to direct his chirps to the praise of Alexander. He tried it and money and fame were showered upon him. Now he is recognized as a political sage, and is . . . already on familiar terms with ministers of state." Evgenev-Maksimov [Ch. 1 n. 18]: 464.

76. *NV* (22 Apr., 13 May, 26 June 1879). On the industrious accumulation of information on peasant life in the late seventies, see R. Wortman, *Crisis of Russian Populism,* Cambridge 1967: 26–32. *NV* also wished to save the peasants from so-called kulaks and exploiters, especially if Jewish.

77. *NV* (18 Mar. 1879).

78. *NV* (2 Jan. 1881). On *Poriadok* (*Order*), which the founder wanted to call *Legal Order,* see Lemke [Ch. 4 n. 3] 1: 16–18.

79. *NV* (4 Jan. 1881); Glinskii [Ch. 5 n. 12].

80. *NV* (25 Mar., 1, 2 Apr. 1881); Koni [Intro. n. 45] 1: 15.

81. *NV* (14 Jan. 1879).

82. *NV* (8 Dec. 1876, 8 Aug. 1878).

83. *NV* (21 Jan., 26 Mar., 3, 17 June 1879).

84. *NV* (16, 30 Apr. 1878, 22 Apr., 17 June 1879, 10, 11 Mar. 1881).

85. *NV* (8 Mar. 1881).

86. *NV* (17 July, 23 Dec. 1880, 11 Jan. 1881).

87. *NV* (10, 11, 13 Jan., 15 Feb. 1881).

88. *NV* (14 Jan., 18 Mar. 1879).

89. *NV* (1, 2, 5, 7 Apr. 1881).

90. *NV* (27 Mar., 10 June, 2 Oct. 1879, 9 Jan. 1881).

91. The Viennese liberal daily *Neue Freie Presse* was an important source of information on Balkan events for Russian periodicals that lacked their own foreign reporters. As early as June 1876 *NV* regarded any paper that quoted *Neue Freie Presse* as thereby automatically discredited.

92. *NV* (11, 16, 17, 28 Mar., 1 Apr., 5 June 1879); *VE* (Nov. 1880): 313–17. It must be noted that *NV* allowed Khvolson (a Jewish convert to Christianity) to publish a point by point refutation of Kostomarov (25 June 1879).

93. *NV* (11 Mar., 3 May 1879, 27 July 1880). Throughout the period under study *VE* consistently defended full and equal rights for Jews, as well as for all other categories of the population; see (May 1871): 411–15; (Mar. 1878): 352–81; (June 1881): 805–7. It must be admitted, however, that Russian liberal journalism gave comparatively little attention to the Jewish question. Radical journalism gave even less.

94. Entirely typical was an attack on *Russkii Evrei* for daring to defend the *kheder* (elementary religious school) as a teacher of loyalty to the Jewish faith and deep love of the Jewish people. According to *NV*, "reconciliation of Europeans and Jews" would become possible only after the full elimination of the Jewish faith and group identity. Moreover, the *kheder* produced only men "in the line of Kogan, Gorvits, Strousberg, Poliakov, and the heroes of Kutais" (14 Oct. 1879).

95. See, e.g., Billington [Ch. 6 n. 42]: 142 ("Katkov and the chauvinistic press").

96. *NV* (26 Apr., 1, 5 May, 5 June 1881). *Poriadok* and a few other papers put the greatest share of the blame for pogroms on the anti-Jewish agitation of papers of "national direction"—with *NV* in the lead.

97. See R. F. Byrnes, *Pobedonostsev*, Bloomington, Ind., 1968: 202–9, on the discovery of Jewish malevolence by K. P. Pobedonostsev, tutor and adviser to Alexander III and long-time procurator of the Holy Synod. Observers agree that educated society grew more generally nationalistic in the eighties. Even such old-line western liberals as Turgenev wept when Dostoevskii told a cheering audience in 1880 that the "all-embracing humanitarian Russian soul" would somehow, thanks to its universality, bring all nations to harmony and brotherhood. Thousands of people followed the funeral cortège of Ivan Aksakov in 1886, while the deaths of earlier Slavophiles aroused no such public demonstration. F. M. Dostoevskii, *Sobranie sochinenii*, M. 1958, 10: 458; Lukashevich [n. 6]: 162.

98. S. Iu. Vitte, *Vospominaniia*, M. 1960, 3: 66; Lenin [Pref. n. 3] 18: 250–51. Saltykov-Shchedrin introduced *Chego izvolite?* into his work in late 1876 as a title for servile, idea-less newspapers that fed on the Balkan crisis. Contemporary critics did not identify it immediately with *NV*. Denisiuk [Ch. 4 n. 39] 3: 8–157.

99. S's heirs did not avoid corruption. His son Mikhail allowed the govern-

ment to buy stock in *NV* in 1916 (to encourage support of the government viewpoint) and before the war Mikhail and Boris became involved in a scheme to agitate for a government concession to a telegraphic company in return for a share in the firm. V. P. Alekseev, "Podkup *Novogo vremeni* tsarskim pravitel-stvom,' *Krasnyi arkhiv* 21 (1927): 223–26.

100. *Dnevnik S:* 82–83. See also *Pisma A. S. Suvorina k. V. V. Rozanovu* [1893-1912], St.P. 1913. In his diary S wrote of the courtiers as rabble and the high bureaucrats as abortions and degenerates.

101. "Iubilei *NV* 1876–1901 g.," *Istoricheskii vestnik* (Apr. 1901): 287. Bogdanovich [Ch. 6 n. 48]: 155; V. S. Solovev, *Pisma*, St.P. 1908-23, 2: 170.

EPILOGUE

1. On S's type fonts, see A. Shitsgal, *Russkii grazhdanskii shrift 1708–1958*, M. 1959: 213–15.

2. *Na pamiat o desiatiletii izdatelskoi deiatelnosti A. S. Suvorina*, St.P. 1887; *Kratkii ocherk* [Ch. 5 n. 8]: 4; S, *Shkola pri tipografii gazety NV 1884–1911 gg.*, St.P. 1911.

3. S. F. Librovich, *Na knizhnom postu*, P. 1916; *Katalog izdanii A. S. Suvorina*, 3d ed., St.P. 1902; V. Ia. Adariukov and A. A. Sidorov, eds., *Kniga v Rossii* 2, M. 1925: 464–66. For radical reaction, see, e.g., *Russkaia mysl* (Mar. 1888) iii: 118.

4. *400 let* [Ch. 3 n. 24]: 366–94. M. O. Volf (1825–83) began his publishing activity in 1853, A. F. Marks (1838–1904) more than a decade later. Marks's greatest success came in the nineties when he gave away "free" every month to all who subscribed to his magazine *Niva* an especially printed volume from the world's great literature. The outstanding Russian book entrepreneur of all time, I. D. Sytin (1851–1934) reached his peak in the early 20th century. In 1914 his corporation was responsible for a fourth of the country's book production. Sytin, *Zhizn dlia knigi*, M. 1962: 12n.

5. One catalog ran to 1012 pp.: *Katalog knizhnogo magazina Novogo vremeni A. S. S 1878–1901*, St.P. 1902. For periodicals published by the bookstores, see list below.

6. Even in the midst of the Balkan crisis, Likhachev displayed the paper and pictures of the machinery at a Paris fair. *NV* (23 Aug. 1878). Employee bene-fits in 1900 included a medical dispensary, credit union, free library, and in some instances inexpensive housing, but no provision for pensions (other than lump sum settlements from the burial society). In slack periods the press prepared materials for free distribution to the blind. By the end of the century S had well over 500 employees.

7. On talk of a Paris *NV*, see A. P. Chekhov, *Polnoe sobranie sochinenii i pisem*, M. 1944–51, 15: 430.

8. *Istoricheskii vestnik* began to pay for itself when the number of subscribers reached 4000. By 1900 it had 10,000, twice as many as the most popular of the 3 other, far more solid, private historical journals. Lisovskii [Pref. n. 8]: 433; *Ocherki istorii istoricheskoi nauki v SSSR* 2, M. 1960: 611–13; B. B. Glinskii, "Sergei Nikolaevich Shubinskii 1834–1913 gg.," *Istoricheskii vestnik* (June 1913): 1–93. Shubinskii edited *Istoricheskii vestnik* for many years. On S's

library, see *Catalogue de la section des Rossica de la bibliothèque de A. S. Souvorine*, P. 1914.

9. After years of urging by friends, S wrote a single novel, *V kontse veka; liubov*, on the then timely subjects of spiritualism and the occult; although he enlarged and reworked it many times, it never found critical success. Chekhov's 1st contribution to *NV* was "Panikhida" (15 Feb. 1886); he was closely associated with *NV* for only 2 years, although he continued to publish there occasionally until the early nineties. Chekhov remained a close personal friend of S until *NV* conducted a virulent anti-Dreyfus campaign in 1898–99, and even then they did not break completely. R. Hingley, *Chekhov*, N.Y. 1950. For a typical example of obligatory hostility to S, consider the distress experienced by the civic poet S. Ia. Nadson upon learning that S had published his hitherto uncollected verses and that *NV* had reviewed them favorably. I. I. Iasinskii, *Roman moei zhizni*, M. 1926: 186–87.

10. S gradually abandoned the rubric "Nedelnye ocherki i kartinki," with which he won fame in earlier years, and contributed an irregular "Malenkii feleton." Out of this grew the "Malenkie pisma," so loathed by the left around the turn of the century. For 3 years before his death S published almost nothing. *Medeia* and *Tatiana Repina* were first performed by the state-owned Little Theater in St.P. N. G. Zograf, *Malyi teatr vtoroi poloviny XIX veka*, M. 1960: 607, 613. S's greatest coup as drama critic was his recognition of the merits of Chekhov's *Seagull* after its first disastrous performance, condemned by all other reviewers. V. I. Nemirovich-Danchenko, *Literaturnoe nasledie* 1, M. 1952: 87.

11. E. Lo Gatto, *Storia del teatro russo*, Florence 1952; B. Varneke, *History of the Russian Theater*, N.Y. 1950: 399–428; A. A. Pleshcheev, *Moe vremia*, Paris 1939: 152–57; E. P. Karpov, "A. S. Suvorin i osnovanie Teatra Literaturno-artisticheskogo kruzhka," *Istoricheskii vestnik* (Aug.-Sept. 1914): 449–70, 873–902. Karpov (1857–1926), sometime radical populist, was long director of S's theater. The establishment of privately owned theaters became possible only in the eighties; before that time legal restrictions and prohibitive taxation ensured state monopoly of Russian drama in the 2 capitals. S took active part in the publicistic struggle for "freedom of theaters"; his most noted contribution pointed out that St.P., under conditions of govt. monopoly, had 2 Russian and 5 foreign language theaters. *VE* (Jan. 1871): 382–403.

12. Unfortunately the major source on S's growing financial tangle is a disgruntled oldtimer of the *NV* editorial staff who admired S extravagantly and blamed his sons Mikhail and Boris for all misfortunes. N. Snessarev, *Mirazh Novogo vremeni*, St.P. 1914.

13. On the younger Aleksei S, see biographical sketch by A. M. Aseev in A. A. S, *Ozdorovlenie pishcheiu*, 3d ed., Buenos Aires 1960: 9–27. In 1913 Aleksei opened a bookstore and publishing house specializing in occultism, health foods, and yoga, subjects on which he himself began to write. During the war and revolution he published various short-lived papers. He left Russia with the Volunteer Army in 1920 and settled in Belgrade, where he achieved some success in the late twenties as an apostle of the benefits to health of fasting. His younger brother Boris, son of the second marriage, for a time edited *Telefon NV* and *Vechernee vremia*. He was also editor-publisher of a variety of short-lived periodicals on tennis, aviation, and horse racing; 2 other sons, Valerian and

Vladimir, died young, Vladimir by suicide. S had 2 daughters, A. A. Kolomnina and Nataliia A. Miasoedovaia-Ivanovna.

14. At S's death, his widow, children, and grandchildren divided 560 of a total of 800 shares outstanding—but many of these were soon mortgaged or sold. Snessarev [n. 12]: 112; *LN* 2 (1932): 165–68.

15. According to Snessarev [n. 12]: 124–26, who attributes part of decline to public disgust with *NV*'s sharp campaign against M. Beiliss, acquitted of a ritual murder charge in a famous trial in Kiev in 1913.

16. Mikhail and Boris published *Vremia* (M. 21 Aug. 1914–11 Dec. 1917, daily); Mikhail alone published 2 weeklies and a monthly of Anglo-Russian friendship and trade during the war. Mikhail published *NV* in Belgrade daily, 1921–29; Boris published *Vremia*, later *Vechernee vremia*, in Shanghai in the early thirties. See K. Maichel, *Soviet and Russian Newspapers at the Hoover Institution*, Stanford 1966: 203, 222.

appendix

Writing and Publications of A. S. Suvorin

I

At various periods of his life, as noted in the text, Suvorin was employed as a regular contributor and staff member of the following:

Russkaia rech, later *Russkaia rech i Moskovskii vestnik* (Russian Speech & M. Herald). M. 1861–62, twice weekly.

Sankt-Peterburgskie vedomosti (St.P. Notices). St.P. 1728–1917, daily (from 1800).

Vestnik Evropy (Herald of Europe) St.P. 1866–1918, monthly.

Birzhevye vedomosti (Stock Market Notices). St.P. 1861–79, daily.

Novoe vremia (New Times). St.P. 1868–1917, daily.

II

The following works by Suvorin have been published in other periodicals or separately:

"Stsena v uezdnom gorodke Bubnove" (A Scene in the County Town Bubnov), *Veselchak* (18, 25 Sept. 1858): 279–83, 287–90.

"Voronezhskie pisma, 1" (Voronezh Letters, 1), *Russkoe slovo* (Mar. 1860) iii: 24–44.

"Chernichka," *Voronezhskaia beseda,* ed. M. De-Pule & P. Glotov, St.P. 1861, i: 20–62.

"Garibaldi," ibid., ii: 213–28.

"Soldat da soldatka" (The Soldier and the Soldier's Wife), *Sov.* (Feb. 1862) i: 663–80.

"Nikon," *Iasnaia Poliana knizhka* (Aug. 1862).

"Otverzhennyi" (The Outcast), *OZ* (Jan. 1863) i: 20–69.

"Alenka; kartiny narodnoi zhizni" (Alenka; Pictures from the Life of the People), *OZ* (July–Aug. 1863) i: 1–59, 353–408.

Ermak Timofeevich pokoritel Sibiri (Ermak Timofeevich, Subjugator of Siberia). M. 1863. 6th ed., St.P. 1904.

Boiarin Matveev. M. 1864. 4th ed., St.P. 1900.

Vsiakie; ocherki sovremennoi zhizni (All Sorts; Sketches of Contemporary Life). St.P. 1866. 2d ed. (suppl.) 1907.

Russkie zamechatelnye liudi (Remarkable Russian Men). St.P. 1866. 3d ed. 1874.

Ocherki i kartinki; sobranie rasskazov, feletonov i zametok (Sketches and Pictures; a Collection of Stories, Feuilletons, and Notes). 2 v. St.P. 1875. 2d ed. 1875.

"A. S. Pushkin v sele Mikhailovskom (Po povodu kartiny Ge)" (A. S. Pushkin in Mikhailovskoe Village [With Regard to the Picture by Ge]), *Drevniaia i novaia Rossiia* (Apr. 1875): 363–71.

Voennaia khronika russko-turetskoi voiny (Military Chronicle of the Russo-Turkish War). [M. 1877].

[and V. P. Burenin] *Medeia* (Medea). St.P. 1883. 3d ed. 1892. Play; 1st performed 15 Nov. 1883, StP.

"*Gore ot uma* i ego kritiki" (*Woe from Wit* and its Critics), in A. S. Griboedov, *Gore ot uma,* St.P. 1886: 1–22.

Zhenshchiny i muzhchiny (Women and Men). St.P. 1887. 2d ed. (under title *Tatiana Repina*) 1889. 4th ed. 1911. Play; 1st performed 16 Jan. 1889, St.P.

V kontse veka; liubov (At the End of the Century; Love). St.P. 1893. 6th ed., enl., 1904. Novel.

On v otstavke (He is in Retirement). St.P. 1894. Comic 1-act play.

Ne poiman—ne vor (If You Don't Catch Him, He's Not a Thief). M. 1894. 2d ed. St.P. 1899. Comic 1-act play.

(Ed.) *Poddelka "Rusalki" Pushkina* (Falsification of Pushkin's "Rusalka"). St.P. 1900. Collection of articles by literary critics.

Potemkinskii prazdnik (A Deceptive Holiday). St.P. 1902. 2d ed. 1903. Opera libretto; music by M. M. Ivanov.

Vopros (The Question). St.P. 1903. 2d ed. 1904. Comic play.

Tsar Dmitrii Samozvanets i tsarevna Kseniia (The False Tsar Dmitrii and Tsarevna Kseniia). St.P. 1904. 2d ed., rev., 1905. Play; 1st performed 24 Oct. 1902, St.P.

Staroe ukhodit (The Old Passes Away). St.P. 1905. Play.

O Dimitrii Samozvantse; kriticheskie ocherki (About the False Tsar Dimitrii; Critical Sketches). St.P. 1906. Historical study.

Khokhly i khokhlushki (Little Russians). St.P. 1907. Articles on theater.

Shkola pri tipografii gazety Novoe vremia 1884–1911 gg. (The School

at the Press of the Newspaper *New Times* 1884–1911). St.P. 1911.
Rasskazy (Stories). St.P. 1913. Posthumous reprinting of S's early fiction.
Pisma A. S. Suvorina k V. V. Rozanovu (Letters of S to V. V. Rozanov).
V. V. Rozanov, ed. St.P. 1913.
Teatralnye ocherki 1866–1876 gg. (Theatrical Sketches 1866–76). N.
Iurin, ed. St.P. 1914.
Dnennik A. S. Suvorina (Diary of S). M. Krichevskii, ed. M. 1923.
Das Geheimtagebuch von A. S. Ssuworin. O. Buek & K. Kersten, trans.
Berlin 1925.
Journal intime de Alexis Souvorine, directeur du Novoïe Vremia. M.
Lichnevsky, trans. Paris 1927.

III

Periodical publications under the ownership of A. S. Suvorin ("A. S.
Suvorin—*New Times* Corporation" after Aug. 1911):

Russkii kalendar A. S. Suvorina (Russian Calendar of A. S. S). St.P.
1872–1914(?), annually.
Novoe vremia (New Times). St.P. 1868 (1st issue by S, 29 Feb. 1876)–
26 Oct. 1917, daily. 1881–1905, 2 daily eds.
Ezhenedelnoe Novoe vremia (Weekly New Times). St.P. 1 Mar. 1879–
31 Jan. 1881, weekly. Reorganized as *Literaturnyi zhurnal* (Literary
Magazine). Feb.–Dec. 1881, monthly.
Russkoe delo (Russian Cause). M. 23 Jan. 1883 (not examined; ref.: *ES*
27: 336)
Istoricheskii vestnik (Historical Herald). St.P. Jan. 1880–Dec. 1917,
monthly.
Illiustrirovannoe prilozhenie k Novomu vremeni (Illustrated Supplement
to New Times). St.P. 1891–1917, weekly (1896–1908, twice weekly).
Ves Peterburg; adresnaia i spravochnaia kniga (All Saint Petersburg;
Address and Reference Book). St.P. 1894–1923(?), annual. From
1915, called *Ves Petrograd.*
Vsia Moskva; adresnaia i spravochnaia kniga (All Moscow; Address and
Reference Book). M. 1894–1917, annual.
Vsia Rossiia (All Russia). St.P. 1895–1903, annual.
Knizhnye novosti magazinov Novogo vremeni A. S. Suvorina (Book News
of the New Times Stores of A. S. S.). St.P. 1897–1917, monthly.
Telefon Novogo vremeni (Telephone of New Times). M. 22 July 1904–
28 Nov. 1905, daily.
Russkaia zemlia (Russian Land). M. 1906–15, daily (1911–13, weekly).
S was pub. 1906–early 1909.
Teatr Literaturno-khudozhestvennogo obshchestva (Theater of the Literary-

Artistic Society). St.P. 1906–10, weekly or thrice monthly in theatrical season. From 1907/8 season, called *Zhurnal teatra Literaturno-khudozhestvennogo obshchestva* (Magazine of the Theater . . .).

Vestnik knizhnykh magazinov Novogo vremeni A. S. Suvorina (Herald of the New Times Book Stores of A. S. S). St.P. 3 Mar. 1907–29 Sept. 1913, weekly.

Vechernee vremia (Evening News). St.P. 26 Nov. 1911–Sept.(?) 1917, daily.

Index

Note: all periodicals listed were published in Saint Petersburg unless otherwise noted.

Effie Ambler is assistant professor of history, Wayne State University. She did her undergraduate work at Bryn Mawr College, and earned her M.A. and Ph.D. (1968) degrees at Indiana University.

Charles H. Elam edited the manuscript. The book was designed by Donald Ross. The typeface for the text is Garamond Olde Style, designed by Claude Garamond about 1540, and the display is Mistral, designed by Roger Excoffon in 1955.

The text is printed on Glatfelter's Antique paper and bound in Elephant Hide and Bayside Chambray cloth over binders' boards. Manufactured in the United States of America.